To Dan,

Love

Em

Sydney and Violet

Sydney and Violet

THEIR LIFE WITH T. S. ELIOT, PROUST,
JOYCE, AND THE EXCRUCIATINGLY
IRASCIBLE WYNDHAM LEWIS

STEPHEN KLAIDMAN

NAN A. TALESE | DOUBLEDAY
NEW YORK LONDON TORONTO
SYDNEY AUCKLAND

All rights reserved. Published in the United States by Nan A.
Talese / Doubleday, a division of Random House, LLC.,
New York, a Penguin Random House Company, and in
Canada by Random House of Canada, Toronto.

www.nanatalese.com

DOUBLEDAY is a registered trademark of Random House, Inc.
Nan A. Talese and the colophon are trademarks of
Random House, LLC.

Pages 253–54 constitute an extension of this copyright page.

Book design Pei Loi Koay
Jacket photographs: T. S. Eliot and Aldous Huxley © Everett
Collection Inc./Alamy; Ezra Pound © Pictorial Press Ltd./Alamy;
James Joyce, Marcel Proust, and Dame Edith Sitwell © Hulton
Archive/Getty Images; Katherine Mansfield © Keystone-France/Getty
Images; Lady Ottoline Morrell © National Portrait Gallery, London.
Jacket designed by Emily Mahon

LIBRARY OF CONGRESS CATALOGING-IN-PUBLICATION DATA
Klaidman, Stephen.
Sydney and Violet : their life with T. S. Eliot, Proust, Joyce,
and the excruciatingly irascible Wyndham Lewis /
Stephen Klaidman. — First edition.
pages   cm
Includes bibliographical references and index.
1. Hudson, Stephen, 1868–1944—Friends and associates.
2. Modernism (Literature).   I. Title.
PR6037.C37Z73 2013
823'.912—dc23   2013006199

ISBN 978-0-385-53409-3

MANUFACTURED IN THE UNITED STATES OF AMERICA

1 3 5 7 9 10 8 6 4 2

First Edition

This book is for Kitty, my love, my joy, my inspiration.

May truth, unpolluted by prejudice, vanity or selfishness,
be granted daily more and more as the due of inheritance,
and only valuable conquest for us all!

—Margaret Fuller, from the preface to *Woman in the Nineteenth Century,* November 1844

CONTENTS

*I*n an age of literary license in which memoirs and autobiographies are often imaginatively embroidered, I prefer to begin with full disclosure. This book portrays the title characters and the glittery modernist milieu they inhabited. But there are many gaps in the record of Sydney's and Violet's lives, especially before they met. A thorough account would have been futile without conjecture. Documentation of their life together is better because they and their contemporaries were avid correspondents. More than twelve hundred letters survive, which is why we know as much as we do about them. Regrettably, though, most were written to them, not by them. Of the ones they did write, Violet's were in an often unreadable, self-acknowledged chicken scrawl, and not one was from Sydney to Violet or from Violet to Sydney. The cause, as in the similar cases of Joan Didion and her husband, John Gregory Dunne, and Joyce Carol Oates and her husband, Raymond Smith, was that they were almost never apart. Sydney wrote to his friend Max Beerbohm that "except for two or three times we've not been separated for more than a few hours." Evocative scraps of information from family members and friends remain along with marriage and divorce records, birth and death certificates, and a will. But beyond these meager remnants the biographical background would fade to black if not for one crucial exception: Their lives were tightly entwined with many of the defining figures of literary modernism. Because of close relationships and extensive correspondence with Marcel Proust, T. S. Eliot, Wyndham Lewis, Aldous

Huxley, and Katherine Mansfield, among others, far more is known about them than would otherwise be the case.

The biggest challenge in writing this book was deciding how to overcome the lack of information about Sydney's life before he married Violet. Apart from the sketchy documentation noted above, the only significant source material is the provocatively titled *A True Story*, a sprawling fictionalized autobiography influenced by Proust, written by Sydney using the pseudonym Stephen Hudson, and edited, perhaps heavily, by Violet, in which Sydney is portrayed as a character called Richard Kurt. It is tantalizing because it is rich in insight, feeling, and detail, but frustrating because there is no way to verify much of it. The Schiffs' nephew, Edward Beddington-Behrens, wrote in his own autobiography that with the exception of what he called "external details" everything was true. But there is no way of knowing exactly what he thought was true.

Faced with these uncertainties, I have drawn on *A True Story* in recounting Sydney's life before Violet and aspects of their life together. The novel offers insights into what Sydney thought about himself, or perhaps what he would have liked to think about himself. There are lacunae in Violet's early personal and family history as well, but her background is better documented than Sydney's. She had distinguished ancestors whose lives have been recorded, family memoirs survive, and there are several living descendants who have preserved fragments of oral history, papers, and photographs.

Caveat lector.

—SDK

Sydney and Violet

*L*ondon, where Sydney and Violet Schiff were born and where they were based between 1911, the year they were wed, and 1944, the year Sydney died, was the undisputed capital of the English-language literary world. It was also the baptismal font of modernism. There were important outposts, most notably in Paris, but also in Rome, Berlin, New York, and even Chicago. But the seminal modernist creed was composed in and disseminated from London. The most influential "little magazines" were published in London and the poets and novelists with whom modernism is most closely identified lived and worked either there or in Paris. These were Sydney and Violet's colleagues and friends. They included T. S. Eliot and Marcel Proust, Aldous Huxley and Katherine Mansfield, and the now mostly forgotten writer, painter, polymath, and insufferable curmudgeon Percy Wyndham Lewis. Eliot, Mansfield, and Lewis read, reviewed, praised, and criticized Sydney's novels and published his stories and translations in their journals. And Sydney and Violet reciprocated, critiquing and publishing their articles, stories, and poems and soliciting contributions from Proust for Eliot's *Criterion*.

The Schiffs were accomplished hosts, and invitations to their homes in the city and country were avidly sought. Evenings consisted of small dinners with sparkling conversation and vintage champagne followed by wicked games usually involving role playing. They were respectful of their guests without being deferential, intellectually curious without being intellectually arrogant, and physically attractive. Violet, whose Semitic background was evident, was in her mid-thirties when they were married. She wore her dark hair piled atop her head in the style of the time, her eyes were brown with long lashes, and she had the slim, graceful fingers of a musician. Her gaze was unself-conscious, reflecting her confidence and interest in others. Sydney, who was in his mid-forties, wore a sandy-colored toothbrush mustache and carried himself with what looked to some like military bearing and to others like pretentious posturing. In either case the image was undercut by his sad brown eyes, a side effect of twenty years of heartache produced by his first wife's relentlessly demeaning treatment.

Although the modernist world Sydney and Violet inhabited was internally disorganized, modernism had no organized competition. If you were a writer, painter, or composer during those years there was no escaping its influence. None of this, however, presupposed tranquil acceptance of a single view of modernism. To the contrary, divisions about the meaning of modernism, both as an aesthetic idea and as a way of life, although sometimes intellectually trivial, were often socially divisive. As a result, factions were formed, fences were built, and vituperation emerged as the extreme sport of the day. The two principal factions were deliciously contrasted by the acid-tongued poet Edith Sitwell.

"On the one side," she wrote, "was the bottle-wielding school of thought to which I could not, owing to my sex, upbringing, tastes, and lack of muscle, belong." With this taut description, as with a wave of the hand, she dismissed Ezra Pound, Eliot, Lewis, and their cohorts, most of whom lived in the London district known as Bayswater. She saved her undiluted invective, however, for the relatively effete intellectual alternative whose members resided in the neighborhood known as Bloomsbury. The "society of Bloomsbury," according to Sitwell, was "the home of an echoing silence." She said it was described by Gertrude Stein as " 'the Young Men's Christian Association—with Christ left out, of course.' Some of the more silent intellectuals, crouching under the umbrella-like deceptive weight of their foreheads, lived their toadstool lives sheltered by these. The appearance of others raised the conjecture that they were trying to be fetuses."

A less colorful but more devastating critique of the moral world inhabited by the Woolfs, the Bells, and their circle came from one of their own, John Maynard Keynes. The Bloomsburys' ostensible ethical touchstone was G. E. Moore's *Principia Ethica*, a moral treatise whose pleasure-laden values of love, aesthetic experience, and the pursuit of knowledge they subscribed to religiously while regularly ignoring its guiding principle of benevolence. Many years after the heyday of Bloomsbury, in an essay called *My Early Beliefs*, Keynes wrote, "We were . . . in the strict sense of the term immoralists. . . . we recognized no moral obligation on us, no inner sanction to conform or obey." Citing this confession, if that's what it was, by a leading Bloomsbury figure is not, however, meant to suggest that Bayswater was morally superior—different, perhaps, but not holier.

The Schiffs, who were not especially ideological, were attracted to the conservative Bayswater element among the modernists more likely because of their aesthetic rather than their social or political preferences. They had almost no contact with the Stephen sisters, better known as Virginia Woolf and Vanessa Bell, or their husbands, Leonard and Clive, respectively, or with the art critic Roger Fry or Keynes. To be fair, there is no evidence they were eager to socialize with them. In one rare instance the Schiffs did attend a tea at Clive and Vanessa Bell's, which prompted Violet to write archly to Wyndham Lewis—who had his own self-interested flirtation with the Woolfs and their crowd—"We have just penetrated to the heart of Bloomsbury." It was, as things turned out, a rare if not singular penetration.

But there is a view of Sydney and Violet—Sydney especially—that was too widely held at the time to be ignored and that if correct, which I don't think it was, would suggest they did want to be admitted into Bloomsbury society. It is that they were irrepressible social climbers and could not possibly have resisted courting that intellectually prominent congregation. But even if they had sought entreé, their close association with Bayswater probably would have kept them out. Although they occasionally met, and sometimes showed respect for each other's work, by and large Bloomsbury and Bayswater lived in mutual contempt. In the Schiffs' case, Bloomsbury's bountiful snobbery, intellectual and otherwise, might also have played a role. Who were these Schiffs, after all? What had they done? Weren't they just a couple of rich poseurs, pseudo-intellectuals, sycophants? Only Eliot, whose ability to suck up rivaled his (not unjustified) lofty opinion of his intellectual stature, moved easily between the two factions.

Another world from which Sydney and Violet were excluded, or at least which they never entered, was known as Garsington. Although many who were or would become their friends, such as Huxley and the painter Mark Gertler, were habitués. Eliot and his wife, Vivienne, were frequent guests, and even Lewis turned up occasionally, but there is no record of Sydney and Violet ever having been invited. Garsington was the name of the country house of Lady Ottoline Morrell, the horse-faced yet oddly attractive keeper of a hedonistic salon for, among others, sophisticated pacifists of the Bloomsbury persuasion who wished to rusticate in luxury in the years leading up to and during World War I. Despite her hospitality, she was devilishly satirized in many novels written by her guests, including ones by D. H. Lawrence (Hermione Roddice in *Women in Love*) and Huxley (Priscilla Wimbush in *Crome Yellow*),

and in a novella by Walter Turner (Lady Caraway in *The Aesthetes*).
Osbert Sitwell also caricatured her as Lady Septugesima Goodley in
a story called *Triple Fugue*. His description of her seemingly endless
nose, isosceles chin, shocking red hair, and extraordinary height
was glaringly obvious.

This kind of satire of persons who were meant to be your friends
and were often your hosts and benefactors, and which might more
precisely be called character assassination, was endemic among the
modernists. In due time, Sydney and Violet would become the victims of a lengthy, unusually mean-spirited caricature in this vein
created by their frequent guest and beneficiary of their patronage,
Wyndham Lewis. Writers typically and shamelessly denied that
their "creations" had anything to do with the victims even when
it was self-evident. Huxley parodied Gertler and Bertrand Russell,
among others who frequented Garsington, and vehemently denied
his characters were based on them. Turner created characters based
on Bloomsbury luminaries including Lytton Strachey and Virginia
Woolf, and used them to pummel Lady Ottoline: One character
described her as a woman from whom "normal males have invari-
ably fled before her eagerly offered embraces." Another wondered
if there was a human face "underneath the chalky mask, with its
withered, lip-salved gash."

Other long-forgotten novels of this genre include *Diary of a
Nobody* by George and Weedon Grossmith and *The Green Carnation*
by Robert Hichens. And Ada Leverson, Violet Schiff's eldest sister, was a notable satirist of a slightly earlier generation. All of her
books, however, as well as those by Hichens and the Grossmiths,
were written with a gentler touch than those of Lawrence, Huxley, Turner and especially Lewis. Remarkably though, despite the
poisonous quality of their satire, even the most vindictive authors
were often forgiven, although it sometimes took a while. In her
memoir, Lady Ottoline wrote about Lawrence: "After twelve years
the wound had healed and I was very glad to hear again from some-

one who obviously was fond of me, and in one letter at least he has spoken of me in a way that shows that his real feeling for me was good and appreciative, while now and always I feel he was a very lovable man."

There is something touching about this in its neediness, and forgiveness is said to be a virtue. I would leave it at that except in the same memoir Lady Ottoline said she showed the passages in *Women in Love* to Huxley, who said he was horrified. *Women in Love* was published in 1920 and *Crome Yellow*, which similarly skewered the mistress of Garsington, in 1921. Horror among at least some of the modernists, it turns out, was a relatively short-lived feeling. But according to Miranda Seymour, who wrote an adoring biography of Lady Ottoline, the way her friends characterized her had no malicious intent. It had to do with "a love of language and gossip." As Seymour put it rather generously, "sincerity was sacrificed to a lively turn of phrase." There may be something to this, but assuming there is I'm not sure whether we should like Bloomsbury more or less.

In any event, Sydney, a conspicuous victim of this particular species of nastiness, who could be unsparing in his verbal candor, never sacrificed sincerity to a lively turn of phrase in *his* books. His reaction to Lewis's searing satire of him and Violet in a novel called *The Apes of God*, the publication of which put an end to their somewhat tortured relationship, was more sorrow than anger. Violet, who was more philosophical and less easily wounded, kept up a sporadic correspondence with Lewis even after Sydney died.

CHAPTER I

SYDNEY'S TRAVELS

*In the year of Queen Victoria's Golden Jubilee, 1887, a rather effete-looking, pink-cheeked, eighteen-year-old Londoner named Sydney Schiff set sail from England. His destination was an immense cattle ranch in the Canadian west where he was being sent by his father to work and ponder his future. It was a compromise of sorts worked out after Sydney had rejected a position at A. G. Schiff & Co., his family's merchant banking firm, and refused to attend Oxford on his father's terms. Alfred Schiff had been willing to send his son to the university, but only as a prelude to working at the firm, and only if he prepared for a learned profession such as the law, which would be useful in banking. It was not the first time Sydney had displeased his father, about his future among other things. And it would not be the last. Alfred, like most Victorian males of his class and generation, believed his son owed him absolute obedience and he found Sydney's disregard of his wishes deeply disrespectful.

He was not a patient man, so having been turned down twice one has to wonder what possessed him to offer Sydney a way out. Perhaps he believed the experience would be unpleasant enough to make banking look more attractive. But if that's what he thought, he badly misjudged his son. Another possibility is that he thought exposure to North America's aggressive commercial culture would be good for Sydney. He might even have offered to arrange a job on the ranch, thinking Sydney would turn it down. After all, why would he expect that someone who was no one's idea of a rugged outdoorsman—whose tastes ran to books and pictures, and who was brought up with every comfort wealth could buy—would want to leave London, the world's most vibrant city, for the vacuous grasslands of Alberta? He knew his son loved horses, but that would hardly have been sufficient, all of which raises another obvious question: Why did Sydney go? Perhaps it was the prospect that he would be six thousand miles away from his father. What seems self-evident, though, is that Alfred's efforts to change Sydney's mind about joining A. G. Schiff & Co. were doomed from the start. He simply could not grasp that his son equated a career in banking with the loss of his soul.

Whatever Alfred's intentions and expectations might have been, Sydney's first several months on the ranch appear to have been happy. He enjoyed caring for the horses, he didn't complain about loneliness or lack of comfort, and the owners, his father's friends Sir John Lister-Kaye and his wife, Natica Yxnaga del Valle, made him feel at home. But some months later the Lister-Kayes were suddenly called back to England and left Sydney in charge of the ranch, a responsibility the nineteen-year-old was not eager to accept. Moreover, by then he had been there for almost a year and was getting restless. In any event, he packed up and headed for Cincinnati, three thousand miles to the southeast, to visit his father's brother Charles, a railroad executive there.

Sydney's most detailed and extensive account of his sojourn in Cincinnati occurs in *The Other Side*, the last book he wrote, which appears in its entirety in his multivolume autobiographical novel *A True Story*. In it he offers a fictionalized account of the logistics surrounding the last great bare-knuckle boxing match in America, between John L. Sullivan and Jake Kilrain. Charles Schiff almost certainly authorized one of his railroads to provide transportation to the fight's site in Hattiesburg, Mississippi, but Sydney's sugges-tion that he played a role in getting his uncle to comply is fiction. The date of the fight is not consistent with his time in Cincinnati.

Charles Schiff and his Nashville-born wife, Mamie, welcomed Sydney warmly and like the Lister-Kayes made him feel at home, but he interpreted certain elliptical remarks by his uncle to mean that his stay was intended to be long and possibly open-ended, a prospect he found disconcerting. He concluded his father had con-spired to get rid of him and his uncle was complicit. For a while he was given the freedom to explore his new surroundings. Eventu-ally, though, Charles Schiff received a letter from his brother that prompted him to put Sydney to work. He gave his nephew a few more days to settle in and then told him there was a job waiting for him in the railway's head office. When Sydney found out what was in store for him, he considered leaving Cincinnati and travel-ing. But he soon realized he had no idea where he would go, so he accepted the job. The next day he began training as a clerk in his uncle's office. The work, checking other people's addition, was mind numbing. He only had to do it for a week, but the immediate future didn't seem any brighter.

Soon thereafter Sydney told his uncle he didn't think he was cut out to work in a railroad office. Charles Schiff, carrying no paternal baggage, was much more sympathetic to his young nephew than his brother Alfred would have been. He took his nephew's resigna-tion in stride. He also concluded that Sydney would not benefit from spending more time in Cincinnati. While not exactly throw-ing him out, he advised him to see more of the United States, a suggestion Sydney by then was ready to accept.

A MISERABLE MARRIAGE

Sydney made his way to Louisville, Kentucky, little more than a hundred miles southwest of Cincinnati, but culturally much more southern. He must have had at least one introduction to someone there because he almost immediately met Marion Fulton Canine, whom many years later he would portray as Elinor Colhouse in *A True Story*. She was the dark-haired, olive-skinned eighteen-year-old daughter of a once-prominent dentist named James Fulton Canine whose taste for alcohol had decimated his practice. Sydney was instantly smitten by her beauty—by some accounts, she was the belle of Louisville. Less obvious to Sydney, who was twenty and not especially sophisticated, was that she was willful and single-minded. She was dead set on finding a husband who would dramatically improve her social and economic prospects. Here's how Sydney described Elinor's initial reaction to Richard Kurt in the novel *Elinor Colhouse*:

"Her first impression of Richard as he rose from an arm-chair beside the fireplace to meet her was that he was tall and slim and looked like a boy. The shutters were partly closed, but she could see that his hair was light, his eyes were dark and that he had a fair mustache. His accent, she thought approvingly, was very English." In contrast to Sydney's shy demeanor and lack of experience, Marion was womanly, self-assured, and socially adept. His immature appearance and social awkwardness, if he had been an otherwise eligible suitor from Louisville's professional class, would have guaranteed that his first meeting with Marion would have been his last. But Marion, perhaps because of her family's straitened circumstances, had perfected her own fiscally sound standard for calculating a young man's eligibility. It was instantly apparent to her that Sydney had advantages to offer that the young men of her Louisville circle could not hope to match. He was an English gentleman, which to her way of thinking placed him cuts above the best local society. But more significantly, there was this elegantly simple fact: his family was rich on a scale unattainable, at least by her, in Louisville. She told her mother bluntly that Sydney met her well-defined requirements for a husband, no one else did, and she was not going to let him get away.

Within a couple of months of the day they met, Sydney and

Marion eloped. They were wed in St. Luke's Church, Sault Sainte Marie, Ontario, Canada, on August 29, 1889. Both Sydney and Marion lied about their ages, he claiming to be twenty-five (he was four months shy of twenty-one) and she twenty-one. Sydney listed his profession as gentleman, his residence as London, England, and his parents as Alfred G. and Carrie Schiff. Marion gave her full name as Marion Fulton Canine and those of her parents as James F. Canine and Elizabeth Canine.

Sydney and Marion returned to Louisville a married couple, but considering that Marion had not asked their permission to wed and had denied them the pleasure of seeing her as a bride the reception they received from her parents was not necessarily warm. On the other hand, given the economically parlous condition of the Canines, an alliance with a wealthy English family might have mitigated their disappointment.

The young couple stayed only briefly in Louisville and what happened next is somewhat murky. Sydney and Marion might have traveled to Cincinnati to introduce Marion to Charles Schiff and his wife because Sydney wanted his uncle to break the news to his parents, whom he still hadn't told he had a wife. The *Cincinnati Commercial Tribune* reported the marriage on September 12 under the headline: "Marriage of a Well Known Young Railroader to a Louisville Lady."

Sydney knew his father would be apoplectic when he found out his son had married without his consent and was even afraid Alfred might disinherit him. He also knew his new wife's unimpressive social status—American of no particular background and very modest means—would make matters worse. But his greater concern was for his mother, the former Caroline Mary Ann Eliza Scates, with whom his relationship was as warm and close as the one with his father was cool and distant. She had been diagnosed with valvular heart disease, a condition for which at the time there was no treatment, and he worried the news might come as a devastating shock to her.

Even Alfred, who continued to have serial affairs despite his wife's illness, was concerned enough to buy a villa in the south of France to get her away from the bustle of London. He chose a house in Roquebrune, a historic town set on a tranquil hillside that was for centuries the property of the royal family of Monaco. It is hard to say whether the quiet life was good for Caroline's health, but the proximity to Monte Carlo was disastrous for Alfred's gambling habit. He made multiple daily trips to the casino during their eight-month annual stays and ultimately squandered half his fortune at the gaming tables, which, it is not hard to imagine, must have been distressing for her.

Sydney's concern that his parents would be incensed by his marriage was not unfounded. Alfred and Carrie, as all who knew her called Caroline, were extremely upset when they found out about the marriage. But between the time they learned of the wedding and Sydney and Marion's arrival in London, they managed to repress their anger and disappointment. They welcomed the young couple with well-bred civility, if not familial warmth. Sydney and Marion settled into a small but comfortable flat found and paid for by Alfred, who also gave Sydney a small allowance and a job at the bank. Sydney, for his part, for once did what was expected of him. He accepted the job. What he fervently hoped, however, was that his tenure would be short and at the end of it he would get enough money from his father to pursue his still-developing interests in art, literature, and high culture generally, without having to earn a living.

While he was not exactly happy with the arrangement, Sydney resigned himself to it. Marion, however, would have none of it. She had arrived in London with grandiose expectations unrelated to culture or, it seems, reality, and demanded instant gratification. She began whining almost immediately about their small, unfashionable flat, her husband's meager income, and the failure of the senior Schiffs to bestow on her the diamonds and furs she believed were the perquisites of her recently acquired status. What's more, she drove Sydney's mother to distraction by "making all kinds of [unspecified] mischief involving friends and family," all the while seeming oblivious to the self-destructive effect her behavior was having.

Although she probably could have gotten away with complaining to her husband about how deprived she felt, her frequent shrill bitching to his parents quickly wore out their grudging welcome. The only thing that kept Alfred from withdrawing all support from Marion—and Sydney—was his concern about aggravating Carrie. But before long Marion's provocations became intolerable and he decided to put an end to them. He probably would have liked to cut off the two of them completely and send them away empty-handed, but Sydney was Carrie's favorite child and a gentler solution had to be found. His pragmatic accommodation was to give Sydney enough money to take Marion away from London and keep her away for as long as necessary.

Sydney, while troubled by his mother's illness, was pleased with his father's decision. He was eager to travel with the leisure and comfort Alfred's money would afford. One might easily imagine, though, especially at that particular moment, that Marion was hardly his ideal traveling companion, if only because of the insufferable way she had treated his mother. But it went deeper than that. He makes clear in *A True Story* that his doubts about committing to a life with her began as soon as he proposed. It even appears likely he shared them with her almost immediately afterward. But having bagged her quarry she was not about to lose it. And despite his strong doubts, once having made a commitment his own youthful sense of honor would have prevented him from breaking it even if he sensed a disaster in the making.

So Sydney, cash and credit in hand, fluent in French and German and eager to explore European art and architecture, and Marion, financially and linguistically dependent and with little awareness of or interest in anything European but Paris and the Swiss Alps, set off for the Continent. What pleasures, if any, they shared during their wanderings, which consisted mostly of flitting from chic spa to elegant resort to cultural icon, are unknown. But somehow they managed to do it for more than five years, leaving no trace of their travels and returning to London only when Carrie died in 1896 at fifty-two. They stayed just as long as was absolutely necessary, which probably was not their choice, but Alfred's.

As soon as seemed decent after Carrie's death Alfred Schiff settled a sum of money on his wayward son sufficient to provide a gentleman's income for the rest of his life, but less than his full inheritance. He then bought a large villa on Lake Como for the couple not to own but to occupy and gave them money to furnish and refurbish it, which they did. They then lived in it—unhappily—side by side, but not together, for the next thirteen years.

In *Elinor Colhouse*, the second volume of *A True Story*, Sydney provides a kind of psychobiographical account of his dismal life on the lake in which he meticulously records his feelings but takes liberties with everything else. For several months he and Marion worked to restore the lakeside villa to its former gracious state, a project that united them for once in pursuit of a common goal. They were obsessed, possibly for the only time in their lives, with the same thing, which led to something resembling intimacy, a condition previously unknown to them. As they worked together toward a common goal they experienced mutual satisfaction, probably for the first time in their lives. They didn't even clash over matters of taste. They reveled in the villa's slick marble walls, the green and gold brocade chairs they fastidiously set against them, the laurel scrolls, garlands of flowers, and quivers of arrows, all in stucco, the Louis Quinze gilt brackets, and more, much more, all illuminated by a stunning array of electric lights. Was it over the top? For today, probably, but for their class in that time and place perhaps not.

Predictably, when the work on the villa inside and out neared completion, so did the tenuous period of comity between Sydney and Marion. She soon resumed regular outings with her entourage of admirers and reverted to the testiness and disdain that had long characterized her behavior toward him. But this time Sydney was less vulnerable, even indifferent to her torments. This was because nearing forty he had found a source of consolation of his own, a woman he called Virginia Peraldi, whose family and Sydney's actually were acquainted. She was a strange girl, half English, half Italian, seventeen or eighteen years younger than himself and a religious Catholic. In *A True Story* Sydney wrote that this relationship ended unsatisfactorily during a trip they took together to Milan to meet his father, who was sick and would soon die. The news of his father's illness stirred up a brew of conflicting feelings in Sydney, but most of all he wanted to tell Alfred that he had come to realize his own shortcomings and understood that his father's judgment of him had been more just than he had realized. Soon after his father died in 1908 he worked up the courage to leave Como forever, but not to divorce Marion.

A NIGHT AT THE OPERA

In the spring of 1909, Sydney arrived in London after several months of traveling in Europe. The city had been transformed during his generation of wandering in North America and Europe. With Queen Victoria's death on January 22, 1901, in the sixty-fourth year of her reign, a new century and a new age had begun. Gaslights had been replaced by electric lights and horse-drawn vehicles were rapidly giving way to automobiles and motor buses. In 1887, the year Sydney left for Canada, central London's streets—although not those in the Schiffs' neighborhood—were choked with coal wagons, carriages, and carts of all kinds. Cattle, sheep, and pigs were driven through those same streets to markets at Islington and Smithfield, as a result of which millions of tons of manure were dropped annually. The stench was poisonous, perpetual and omnipresent. And then there was the noise, a rumbling, inescapable din from the trampling and rattling of horses, cattle, and carts on the cobblestones. By 1909, though, the city had become cleaner and quieter. Theaters were showing silent films, the Victoria and Albert Museum had been completed, and so had Westminster Cathedral and the Imperial Institute.

The passing of the crown to Edward VII marked an intellectually disconcerting transition from Victorian customs, practices, and mores, both overt and covert, to an evolving Edwardian ethos. A new temperament, for better and worse, was being fashioned, partly by the advent of automobiles and assembly lines, telephones and moving pictures, Marxism and feminism, relativity and quantum physics, and, of course, psychoanalysis. Mechanization, innovative uses of electricity and other scientific and engineering advances were rapidly replacing Victorian-era transportation, communications and manufacturing techniques, while radical social ideas were challenging class and role rigidity and reshaping how people thought about the universe and their place in it. At the same time, new values and ideas were also transforming literature, music, and the plastic arts in ways that would come to be known collectively as modernism and would radiate around the world, changing the cultural environment of cities as distant from one another and as disparate as New York and Shanghai.

London was meant only as a way stop for Sydney on a trip designed to clear his head and help him figure out how to end his dolorous marriage—with propriety and honor—and begin a new life. As a result, he would not have expected to stay long or to be much affected by these social and cultural changes. But about both of these things he would be wrong. Modernism and its values would alter his future in ways he could not possibly foresee. But that time was still to come. For the moment he was profoundly unhappy not only with Marion, but because by his own sad reckoning he had lived forty years and accomplished nothing. He was desperate to find an escape route.

Part of his problem in ending his marriage was that the chivalry he portrayed in Richard Kurt, his fictional self, which he displayed as a mere boy and that seemed so naive at the time, turned out to be bred into Sydney Schiff. Despite all the pain Marion had caused him, and the changing mores of the times, he seemed incapable of branding her with the stigma his Victorian upbringing had taught him was the fate of divorced women. There can be no doubt that he desperately wanted to be rid of her. She had treated him almost from the outset with indifference, mockery—especially of his nascent literary efforts—and contempt. She was unavailable to him physically, emotionally, and intellectually. But by his rigorous standards of decency, and perhaps his concern for how polite society would judge him, none of this was enough to release him from his perceived obligation to protect her from any social retribution that might result from a divorce. He had been struggling with this conundrum for years and was no nearer a solution when he arrived in London except for one thing. He was in possession of his full inheritance and therefore could make Marion financially secure.

Sydney had few friends if any in the city. He had been something of a loner as a boy and with the exception of two unpleasant years away at school he had been educated by tutors. As an adult he had lived in London only briefly and sporadically. For all practical purposes he had been away for twenty-two years. His parents were both dead. Sydney was staying with his sister Edith, who would one day become the Countess Gautier-Vignal. She enjoyed many of the same things he did, and she tried to keep him distracted by arranging evenings at the theater and opera during his visit. Mostly these outings were uneventful, but one evening, during a performance of *La Bohème* at Covent Garden, something unexpected happened.

The Puccini opera was performed five times that season, all between June 15 and July 30, and the performance Sydney attended could have been any of the five. If Edith had her choice, though, it probably would have been the one in which Marcello was sung by one of the greatest baritones of the day, Antonio Scotti. And there is reason to at least speculate that she and Sydney saw the Scotti performance because Sybil Seligman was in her box in the Grand Tier that evening. Sybil, wife of the American banker David Seligman, was a daughter of Samuel and Zillah Beddington, whose house at 21 Hyde Park Square, was home to one of the most sought-after musical salons in London. Scotti, his good friend Enrico Caruso, and Nellie Melba, the greatest soprano of the era, came when they were in town. Paolo Tosti, singing master to the royal family—and the Beddington girls—and Sir Arthur Sullivan were regular attendees. Zillah, who was considered to be one of the best amateur pianists in London, played a Steinway grand chosen for her by Paderewski, and Samuel, a violinist, played a Guarneri del Gesù. Sybil's special friend, who always visited when he was in London and often played the piano when one or another of the girls sang, sometimes in a duet with Caruso, was Giacomo Puccini. Had she been attending just one *Bohème* during the season chances are she would have chosen the June 25 performance featuring Scotti over the alternatives, the respected but second-tier Mario Sammarco and the comparatively undistinguished Angelo Scandiani.

What made the evening unforgettable for Sydney, though, had nothing to do with who sang Marcello or the performance over-all, however brilliant it might have been. Under the Royal Opera House's grand cerulean blue dome that evening the music of Puccini and the tempestuous romance of *La Bohème*'s star-crossed lovers served as but a backdrop.

Sydney's sister Edith was acquainted with Sybil Seligman, and during intermission she took her brother to meet her and a guest in her box, Sybil's sister Violet Beddington. Violet was thirty-four years old, never married, and therefore by the conventions of the time a spinster. Nonetheless, as the youngest of the four Beddington girls (there were five boys), she was known as "Baby" in the family. By several accounts she was the wisest of the children and her parents' favorite, especially her father's. She was said to sing with extraordinary musicality, although the quality of the one recording that exists is too poor to confirm that judgment. Tosti once said, however, that while her voice lacked the perfection of Sybil's, she sang like an angel. Violet was also a discerning reader of contemporary literature (her passion was Henry James) and a keen analyst of human nature.

Sydney fell in love with her, instantly and overwhelmingly in love for the first time in his life. And unlikely as it may seem, in those very few minutes they were together, Violet felt an attraction, perhaps for the first time in her life, as powerful as his. But falling in love with Violet and knowing that she shared his passion did not make it easier to divorce Marion. More likely it added to Sydney's confusion. In any event, for reasons of propriety, potential legal exposure, and Violet's self-respect, after two brief meetings during which they affirmed their desire for a life together, Violet told Sydney she would not see him again until he and Marion were divorced. Things would have moved much faster, but Sydney was still struggling with his conscience, which led to procrastination. Finally, however, after dithering for many months, he worked up the courage to ask Marion to initiate divorce proceedings. She agreed in a flash and probably would have done so a lot sooner had she been asked because her lover at the time, a rich man named Sadleir Jackson, wanted to marry her. Even though she was marrying money Sydney gave her the house on Lake Como, which he had inherited when his father died, and half his income for the rest of her life. Marion later became a Christian Scientist and eventually died of a stroke.

As for Violet, she waited while almost two years passed between the night at the opera and the final decree. Fifteen years later, in his 1926 novel *Myrtle*, Sydney reimagined, or more precisely, reinvented the opening scene in that lonely and agonizing period in his life. He fictionalized his meeting with Violet, shifting the setting from Covent Garden to the Beddington mansion but precisely re-creating his misery and her empathy, which generated an instant connection between them. As he constructed the story, the fictional version of the Beddington family was about to set off for Folkestone, a resort and seaport on the English Channel where the real-life Beddingtons regularly vacationed and Zillah dined on chickens Samuel had brought in daily from their provisioner in London. Violet, recognizing Sydney's desperate condition, urged him to join them in Folkestone, which he did.

In the novel Sydney is portrayed as speaking freely to Violet about how unhappy his life on the lake with Marion had been and also about Virginia, and she listened without judging. She tried to convince him that there was life worth living ahead of him. But unsurprisingly she could not penetrate in a few minutes a penumbra of hopelessness that had been thickening around him for forty years.

After they said good-bye and agreed to correspond surreptitiously, Sydney indulged in a kind of silent soliloquy of ambivalence that pitted his fresh love for Violet against his inhibiting sense of obligation toward Marion. He doubted his capacity to love and thought of himself as someone who had lost all hope, all sense of self-worth. Violet's sympathy, her wisdom, her understanding, even her frank eyes and the way she walked, were restorative. But there was so much to restore. At first everything seemed so uncertain to him. He still had no answers, only questions. But then in a lightning bolt of insight he realized answers were not what he needed. What he needed was hope. Although it is fiction, in its psy-chobiographical context *Myrtle* has the texture of truth. Sydney knew Violet loved him and was waiting for him. Why wouldn't that give him the strength to hope, to confront Marion and to survive during the two long years Violet and he were apart?

CHAPTER 2

FAMILIES

⤜∶ʘʘ ∶⤛

(W)hatever it was in that brief interlude between acts of *La Bohème* that ignited Sydney and Violet's passion, it must have been supremely powerful to keep the flame burning for two long years. Sydney felt reassured in Violet's presence. He also sensed she might understand him, something he felt no one else—not his beloved mother, nor his sisters, and certainly neither his wife nor his father—had been able to do. Considering his contentious life-long relationship with his father and his twenty bleak years with Marion, it is hard to overestimate how gratifying that feeling must have been. But it would not have been enough. The impenetrable mystery called love was the sine qua non.

For Violet, who was also in love, it likely would have been her gifts of sympathy, equanimity, and patience, qualities she exhibited even as a child, that made her two-year wait for Sydney tolerable. Whatever the reasons, though, one has to admire the confidence and forbearance that enabled them both to endure such a long separation. In the age of texting and Twitter such constancy seems virtually inconceivable.

Unlike Marion, with whom he had little in common, Sydney

grew up in an environment quite similar to Violet's. Both were reared in large, affluent, cultured homes governed by traditional Victorian fathers. They were nouveau riche by the standards of the British aristocracy, but in both families, wealth had been passed on for generations. They lived in nearby fashionable areas of London, were cared for by nannies, educated by tutors, and learned classical and modern languages. Each of these similarities helped shape their characters and interests, but so did a few significant differences.

Violet, whose surname would have been Moses if her grandfather had not changed it to Beddington, was brought up Jewish. Her father, Samuel, often read from the Old Testament after dinner, and several Beddingtons, but not her father, were active in London's Central Synagogue, where Rothschilds and Montefiores worshipped. Sydney's father was Jewish, but his surname never changed. Sydney's mother, however, was Anglican, and he was baptized and brought up in the church. Although religion played a relatively minor role in both their lives, even after marrying Violet Sydney remained a committed Anglican. Violet's actual commitment to cultural Judaism is unknown, but it seems to have been marginal at best and with respect to religion it appears she was agnostic.

There was one other important difference between the two families: Samuel Beddington believed his children, male as well as female, should be free to live lives of leisure if they chose, which most did. Alfred Schiff, on the other hand, despite, or perhaps because of, his Jewish heritage, subscribed to the Protestant Ethic. He believed his sons had an obligation to work hard and his daughters to marry well. His daughters did not disappoint him.

The Schiff family history is something of a blur, but enough can be pieced together to provide a general sense of Sydney's origins. His great-grandparents, Samuel and Gutel Schiff, came from Mannheim, Germany. Their son, Leopold, who was born in Frankfurt, moved to Trieste, a teeming Austro-Hungarian city of mixed races and cultures, multiple languages, and frequently changing political masters. A possession of the Hapsburg Empire with varying status from 1382 on, Trieste had as tumultuous a history as any city in the world before settling into its role as an important commercial hub in the mid-nineteenth century. Leopold decided to take his chances in Trieste in the early 1830s because of the commercial opportunities rapidly opening up there, but he also had every reason to believe the cosmopolitan seaport would provide a more promising environment for an enterprising Jew than any place in Germany. The Triestine attitude toward and treatment of Jews had not always been benign. But Jews had lived in Trieste for hundreds of years, and in the early eighteenth century, in recognition of their important economic role, the Hapsburg emperors removed many legal restrictions, including the requirement that they live in ghettos.

Leopold's judgment about Trieste proved correct. He arrived in a wave of immigration that increased the city's Jewish population sixfold to about six thousand by the beginning of World War I. Many of these immigrant Jews, including the young Leopold, became successful merchant bankers. Not long after his arrival, on November 2, 1832, he married Johanna Wohlheim, who belonged to a well-established Jewish Triestine family. He and Johanna eventually had three sons, Alfred, Ernest, and Charles, all of whom would do as their father did and leave home while still young to make new lives abroad.

Alfred settled in London in 1860 and at twenty-six was admitted to membership in the stock exchange. He was good-looking, vigorous, and intelligent and was as successful socially as he was in business. But his life as a carefree bachelor did not last long. In 1865, the year before he was admitted to the exchange, he met the woman who would become his wife. There was a hitch, though. She was already married and had a year-old daughter. Her name was

Mrs. John Scott Cavell, formerly Caroline Mary Ann Eliza Scates. Based on two paintings and a photograph, she was dowdy as a girl, imperious looking as a young wife, and mean-spirited as an older woman. But she was English, from a respectable country family, an excellent horsewoman, French educated—a quality that would not have been lost on Alfred—and Anglican, a condition that did not deter him any more than her looks or married state.

In 1867 Cavell filed for divorce on grounds that in 1865 Caroline had committed adultery with an unknown man, had a daughter from that relationship, and had cohabited with Alfred Schiff since some time in 1865. Alfred was named a corespondent in the suit, which dragged on for two years. Finally, on August 14, 1869, shortly after the divorce decree was granted, Alfred and Caroline were able to wed, which they did at the register office in Kensington. Alfred is identified on the marriage certificate as a merchant and Caroline as a spinster, which of course she was not. Their fathers, Leopold Schiff and John Scates, were listed as gentlemen. Sydney, whose actual birth date has proved untraceable—not an unusual circumstance in the case of Victorian children born out of wedlock—was perhaps eight or nine months old at the time of the marriage. His parents told him later that he was born December 12, 1868, and there is at least one piece of circumstantial evidence suggesting that this date might be approximately correct. A portrait of Sydney by Alessandro Ossani, dated 1874, depicts a boy with a sensitive mouth and light brown or dark blond hair who looks to be about six years old.

After the wedding, Alfred, Caroline, and their two children, Carrie Louise, who was close to four years old by then, and her half brother Sydney, settled into a lavish house at 30 de Vere Gardens in Kensington. The Schiffs had four more children, a son, Ernest, and three daughters, Rose, Edith and Marie. With the exception of Carrie Louise, who was cool in the English manner, the other children were not lacking in temperament. As Sydney and his full sisters were growing up they had no idea of the circumstances of their parents' marriage, nor did they know that Carrie Louise, whom they all called Sissy, was a half sister. But then one day a maid let it slip, and Alfred and Carrie elected to handle the situation by lying to the children. They said Carrie had been a widow with a young child when she married Alfred. That became the "official story." But Sydney and his brother Ernest were never quite convinced because no one would ever tell them what their mother's surname was when she married their father.

Their comfortable life in Kensington consisted of Alfred spending most of his time at the bank while Carrie spent most of hers riding, shopping, socializing, and planning elaborate entertainments. These included a regular Sunday open house frequented by writers, publishers, painters, musicians, and financiers. Part of the household ethos was that birthdays and anniversaries were never celebrated and feelings had to be expressed and gifts given spontaneously, never out of a sense of obligation. Carrie did not have to concern herself too much about the children because their nannies looked after them except when their tutors were teaching them. They also had music lessons, which the sisters took seriously, and they were encouraged to read good books. A pattern of appreciation for literary fiction could be seen developing early in the girls that would enrich the rest of their lives. Sydney read avidly too, but his preferences were more eclectic than those of his sisters. He liked Dickens and Swift, but his favorite writer as a youth and even as a young man was Edward George Bulwer-Lytton, the much-maligned author of "It was a dark and stormy night . . ." This taste for over-the-top romanticism hardly suggested that one day he would idolize, befriend, and translate Marcel Proust and that T. S. Eliot, who like the modernists in general held romanticism in contempt, would value his critical comments on unpublished poems.

Although private tutors were not uncommon in well-to-do English families, boys of Sydney's social and economic class typi-

cally spent eleven or twelve years at boarding schools where sports
were emphasized and academics were fairly rigorous, but discipline was more so. These severe academies typically provided the
most important formative experience in their lives and a network
of friendships that served them well over a lifetime. But Sydney,
a highly sensitive and mildly effete boy who retained these characteristics as a grown man, was forced to endure only two years
of boarding school. This probably limited the scars, but also the
friendships and toughness acquired over a decade in the "public
school" system. At twelve he attended G. T. Worsley's, a preparatory
school, and a year later Wellington College. He was sent to Wellington because it was a school for boys destined for military careers.
Although it seems wildly inconsistent with his nature, to which his
mother was not indifferent, Carrie Schiff apparently hoped her son
would become an officer.

Sydney's childhood is vividly described in *Prince Hempseed*, the
first volume of *A True Story*, and a book warmly praised by Thomas
Mann. It is full of sadness and loneliness. Sydney especially disliked
his two nannies and his older half sister Carrie Louise. He men-
tions no friends at all. Most surprisingly, perhaps, he discloses that
his beloved mother Carrie was less than a paragon of virtue. This is
the kind of scandalous information Victorian families suppressed
at all costs, which makes it very odd that he would allude to it in an
autobiography only thinly disguised as a novel. Obviously, though,
it would have been even odder for him to have invented it.

But by the time he wrote *Prince Hempseed*, Sydney was a confirmed modernist and on his way to sharing Violet's belief that
art was transcendent. All of this entailed pursuing literary truth,
precisely conveying feelings material to his literary purpose, which
in this case was to reveal his inner life and all that influenced it.
His mother's extramarital relationships fit this criterion. Furthermore, his parents could not have been disgraced or embarrassed by
the disclosure of his mother's affairs because by the time he wrote

Prince Hempseed they both were long dead. Sydney's use of a pseudonym was designed to disguise the autobiographical nature of his novel, which would have worked for the general public but hardly would have been enough to prevent anyone who knew the Schiffs from recognizing the family.

Sydney's father also had many affairs, a documented fact never mentioned in *Prince Hempseed*. There is no hint in the book as to when, or if, Sydney knew of his father's extramarital liaisons. Yet it seems unlikely that someone as intelligent, observant, and sensitive as he was could have remained completely unaware of Alfred Schiff's multiple relationships. And if he was aware of them, why weren't they as relevant to his literary purpose as his mother's? Perhaps he left them out because in the Victorian era a father's affairs were less scandalous and therefore less interesting than a mother's. In any event it does seem possible that the rigorous concept of honor that kept Sydney tethered to Marion for twenty years developed at least in part in reaction to both parents' numerous illicit sexual adventures.

Although it is absolutely clear that Sydney's relationship with his father was conflicted by the time he was eighteen, it is less certain when the conflict began. In *Prince Hempseed* he suggests it might have been during a visit to Heidelberg with his father when he was about twelve. No record remains of such a trip, but as always the feelings expressed in the novel can be taken as genuine. Before describing the trip to the site of Germany's premier university, where he unburdened himself of his bitter feelings toward his father, Sydney had already expressed his dislike for his German governess, the German language, and Germany itself. Though two generations and two countries removed from Germany, Alfred Schiff was still fundamentally Teutonic. Sydney said he was always frightened of his father, but while they were at Heidelberg he began to hate him, which reinforced his love for his mother. There is every reason to believe this acute dichotomy between love and hate, mother and father, represented Sydney's true feelings—with rare moments of ambivalence about his father—even as an adult.

The schools he attended briefly as a boy are known, but once again, apart from *Prince Hempseed*, almost nothing is known about his experiences while attending them. Judging from his account, though, his first semester was not particularly pleasant, but probably no worse than that of the average English boy—some hazing and bullying, two tolerable canings, and a bit of fun and companionship. But when he went back to school for the second semester, things got worse.

It began when he was coerced into doing Latin homework for an older boy. Both were caught and caned and things spiraled downward from there. His mother visited him briefly and it was wonderful to see her, but when she left, the parting was so painful he couldn't bear it anymore and ran away. His father, simmering with anger and contempt, subjected him to unremitting cold, punitive silence during their trip back to the school together. He expected to be expelled, which would have been a mixed blessing, but his father persuaded the headmaster to take him back, substituting caning for expulsion. His father then left, taking with him his son's most treasured possession, a photograph of his mother in a ball gown.

After Sydney returned to school this time, things brightened considerably and he was looking forward to staying on, at which point his father decided to take him out. At home they hired a good-looking young tutor who taught him classics in the original Latin and Greek, and French. Then, perhaps because the tutor turned out to be too fond of Carrie, Sydney's father sent him off without consultation to a different tutor named Pellew in Bournemouth, where he lived in with five other boys. He found Pellew disagreeable and seemed to think he was gay and had made oblique advances, which made him uncomfortable. Another boy arrived who was more compliant, but when the two boys became close friends Pellew dismissed Sydney from his class. His next stop was what seems to have been a pleasant but uneventful sojourn in Vevey, Switzerland, in a kind of finishing school for young men.

It wasn't long after he returned from Switzerland that father and son had their disagreement about Sydney preparing for a learned profession at Oxford. As far as Sydney was concerned his father confused life with work, while he believed life only meant work when it was necessary for survival. He said the only advantage he saw in being his father's son instead of the gardener's was that he didn't have to work for a living.

This of course takes us back to where we began. But before exploring the early life and family history of Violet Beddington, the woman Sydney loved and would finally marry in 1911, consider what Sydney had to say near the end of *Prince Hempseed* about marriage, his state of mind, and the ineffable qualities he sought from life. It helps to explain the damage Violet would have to repair. He said he would never marry because he would never find anyone who understood him. And he blamed himself. "I think I was born to be solitary," he wrote. He was discontented as a young child and was afraid he would always be discontented because what he wanted from life was unobtainable, at least for him. There were things he liked that other people liked—some books, some games, riding, hunting, rowing, swimming—but he didn't like any of them whole-heartedly. There was always a side of him that wanted something different, something he couldn't explain, but that he had experienced and couldn't remember. Many things vaguely reminded him of it, "like the scent of a flower or the rustle of leaves or a broad sunbeam or the glistening of a calm sea when the sun sets."

THE BEDDINGTONS

Violet Beddington came from a distinguished line of Sephardic Jews on her mother's side. The memory, if not the full story, of perhaps her most illustrious ancestor, Baltazar Orobio de Castro, is still honored by her living descendants, all of whom are now English Christians. Orobio was born in 1617 into a family of what have been variously called crypto-Jews, conversos, Marranos, and Chuetas. These were Jews who professed Catholicism to avoid persecution, but many of whom secretly practiced Jewish rites and observed Jewish law and customs. It took forty-five trying and sometimes harrowing years, but Orobio was ultimately able to fully embrace Judaism. His ancestors, who were Spanish, had settled in Braganza, Portugal, four generations before his birth. It seems likely they left Spain to escape the Inquisition, but to the detriment of their great-grandchildren, by the end of the sixteenth century the Portuguese tribunals had surpassed their more notorious Spanish counterparts in the avidity with which they persecuted Jews. As a result, most of Orobio's extended family moved back to Spain in the 1620s. His parents settled in or around Málaga.

It is impossible to know whether the move to relatively gentler Spain saved their lives, but the impeccable records of the Inquisition make it clear that although they were not killed, many family members, including Orobio's grandparents and parents, were hounded, imprisoned, and tortured by the Spanish Holy Tribunals. On July 21, 1654, Baltazar himself, by then a respected professor of medicine, although most likely lacking a doctorate, was arrested and accused of observing Jewish law and mocking the Christian faith. For a year and a half he denied any lingering adherence to Judaism and professed allegiance to Christianity, but on January 13, 1656, under torture on the rack, he confessed and betrayed several other crypto-Jews. Sometime later in 1656 he was deemed to have repented and was released from prison.

By the middle of 1660 Orobio managed to flee Spain for France where, not long afterwards, he obtained a professorship in surgery and pharmacy at the University of Toulouse and established a reputation as a philosophical thinker as well. But two years later he left France for Holland with his wife and children, parents, a brother, two sisters, and two brothers-in-law. Orobio's biographer, Yosef Kaplan, speculated that this was solely because he wanted to live openly as a Jew and Amsterdam was one of very few places in Europe where this was possible. Also, the transition would be smooth because there already was a well-established community of Spanish and Portuguese Jews in the Dutch capital. He soon changed his name to Isaac and all of the other family members also took names from the Hebrew Bible.

Orobio thrived in his new environment, involved himself in the synagogue, and ultimately became one of the most respected members of the congregation. He read deeply in Jewish sources and before long had won a reputation as a theological and philosophical scholar and a stalwart defender of Orthodox Judaism. While he continued to earn a living from medicine, these scholarly pursuits soon became his dominant occupation. His crowning achievement was a brilliant response to Baruch Spinoza's radical critique of Judaism, which substituted reason for revelation, rejected the notion that Jews were God's chosen people, and treated the Torah as a cultural artifact with multiple authors, not the word of God.

Isaac Orobio de Castro died in Amsterdam on November 7, 1687, not long after a debate with Philip van Limborch on the truth of the Christian religion. John Locke attended the debate, and when van Limborch was preparing a summary for publication Locke read both manuscripts and offered suggestions for improvements. Now, some 325 years later, one can only wonder what Orobio would make of his Christian descendants. The same question might be asked about Sir John Simon, Violet's maternal grandfather and a lineal descendant of Orobio, whose forebears immigrated to the British colony of Jamaica, probably in the early eighteenth century.

John Simon was born in Montego Bay on December 9, 1818. His father, Isaac Simon, was a merchant who was active in the emancipation movement and by one account was the first Jamaican to free his own slaves, a year before the Abolition of Slavery Act in 1833.

His mother, Rebecca, was the daughter of Jacob Orobio Furtado. When John was fifteen his parents sent him to Liverpool to continue his education and while there he studied Hebrew on his own. He wanted to become a rabbi, but his father disapproved. Unlike Sydney Schiff, he complied with his father's wishes and attended University College, London, from which he was graduated with a law degree. A year later, in 1842, he became the second Jew admitted to the English bar and the first to practice at the common-law bar. The same year he joined the recently founded Reform Synagogue of London, in which he remained an active member for the rest of his life. And in 1843 he married Rachel Salaman, sister of Charles Salaman, a composer and pianist who had been elected to the Royal Academy of Music at the age of ten. Charles Salaman was especially well known for his Jewish devotional music. He was also active in Reform Judaism and wrote *Jews As They Are*, a book intended to debunk myths about Jews and Judaism. He was a friend of the Beddingtons and regularly attended their Sunday musical afternoons.

After their wedding John returned to Jamaica with Rachel and for the next two years practiced law in Spanish Town, then the capital. Their daughter Zillah was born in Jamaica in 1844, the first of five children, not long before the family immigrated to England because Rachel found the Caribbean climate unbearable. John opened a law office on the northern circuit where his practice flourished and included a successful defense of Simon Bernard, who was accused of complicity in an attempt to assassinate Napoleon III. In 1858, the same year as the Bernard trial, he became the first Jew in England to sit as a judge. Subsequently he was appointed serjeant-at-law and then Queen's Counsel. And in 1868 he was elected to Parliament from Dewsbury, a mill and market town in West Yorkshire. In a photograph that might have been taken around this time he looks magisterial in full-length black law robes and a tightly curled wig that extends below his shoulders. His expression is serious, but not hard, his eyes are deep set, his nose large, and his forehead high and broad. John Simon served for twenty years as a liberal MP, and even though he didn't have a single Jewish constituent he was widely referred to as "the member for Jewry." One interpretation of this designation would be that it resulted from his advocacy on behalf of oppressed Jews. He was knighted on August 24, 1886, two years before he retired from Parliament. He died on June 24, 1897.

The historical record on Violet's paternal side is considerably thinner, probably because there is no ancestor of comparable stature to Isaac Orobio or John Simon. Her grandfather was Henry Moses, who sometime in the 1860s changed the family name to Beddington, apparently after the town of Beddington in the county of Surrey, where he owned property. He continued to live openly as a Jew after the change, which makes clear that he did not do it to pass as a Christian. He might have thought it would make it easier for his children and grandchildren to get on in Britain, or perhaps he just wanted to identify more as an Englishman. Whatever his motives though, the Moses name had not kept him from becoming a successful wool merchant and real estate investor. He was so successful, in fact, that his son, Samuel Henry Beddington, did not have to work a day in his life, although during his lifetime he acquired a substantial amount of property in England and Australia and dabbled for a while in brokering precious stones.

In December 1861, Samuel married Zillah Simon. He was thirty-two, she just seventeen. She came from *yiches*, a Yiddish word that in this context means from a family deserving respect, he from *gelt*, which always means money. Together they settled into a grand mansion at 21 (now 20) Hyde Park Square. In a portrait of Zillah at age thirty-five by Sir John Everett Millais, she looks young and beautiful at a time when women her age often looked matronly. If this is unusual, as I think it is, it is all the more so because she already had eight children. She was short and plump, her features were regular, her complexion pale, and her auburn hair was usually piled high. Her gaze is direct in the portrait and there is a hint of sensuousness in her full lower lip.

Zillah's first love was music, her instrument was the piano, and she devoted more time to practicing and playing than to her children or, it would seem, to her husband. She was said to have been extremely gifted, but she only performed once in public. At Paderewski's request she joined him in a piece for four hands. She was also a creature of habit. She always ate fried sole for lunch and roast or boiled chicken for dinner, accompanied in both cases by champagne.

Samuel Beddington's looks are more a matter of conjecture. He was extremely private and might have been unwilling to be photographed. The only physical description of him I've come across is in a brief memoir written by Violet's nephew Frederick Beddington, which was composed in the form of a letter to his friend Nicolas Bentley. "No doubt he was handsome," he wrote of his grandfather. "[He] always held himself erect, straight as a poker and had a commanding presence." The presence was not a facade. Like Alfred Schiff he was a traditional Victorian father. He also suffered from what we would now call OCD. He washed his hands incessantly and wouldn't touch coins that had been handled by anyone else until they had been set on a table long enough to lose their germs. His bow ties were cut daily from yards of fresh white linen and his dressing gowns were all white so that any speck of dirt would be noticed immediately.

While Violet's parents were imposing, the house she grew up in was if anything more so. It was very large and faced Hyde Park Square in front and Sussex Square in back. A wide entrance hall with café-au-lait walls, varnished oak woodwork, and floors carpeted in dark blue and red led to the main staircase. To the right was a morning room furnished with leather chairs, a table covered with a red cloth, bookshelves displaying the *Encyclopaedia Britannica,* and a small grand piano. The spacious dining room, protected by a massive wooden screen designed by Samuel to keep out the draft, occupied the whole of the rear of the house. The decorations included several oil paintings and a large sculpture of a woman holding a conch shell to her ear.

The stairs, situated under a skylight, swept up to the second floor in three flights, and in a folly of sorts, there was a fern garden with a miniature waterfall on one of the landings. The third flight gave access to a very large double drawing room, a long, wide picture gallery, and a billiards room. There was little doubt as to whom the drawing room belonged: It was dominated by the Millais portrait of Zillah and her grand piano. Eventually electric lights replaced gas lamps in the wall brackets throughout the house, and around 1908 an elevator was installed that could carry two persons to the third-floor bedrooms. And somewhere, although I'm not sure where, there must have been quarters for servants, including Leggatt, the bewhiskered long-serving butler with big gaps between his teeth; Lily Cameron, who looked after Violet from childhood to old age; and Kate Hudson, Zillah's paid companion and trusted manager of the household.

Frederick Beddington spent an evening at his grandparents' house as a child. Five of Samuel and Zillah's children and three or four grandchildren were at the table. "As always, an empty place was set for any unexpected guest or in case Signor Tosti should drop in." After dinner they all moved to the drawing room, where Zillah played, most likely Chopin, whose vast and demanding range of piano music she loved and had mastered, and Sybil and Violet sang, probably arias by Puccini or other Italian composers, Tosti's art songs or German lieder. The music stopped when Samuel Beddington definitively pronounced, "That will do, dear," after which he solemnly read from the book of Job, concluding the evening.

The Beddington family was large, but exactly how large remains a matter of conjecture. There were eight children, more likely nine, or just possibly ten. No one seems sure. It is likely that a ninth or tenth child would have died at or soon after birth. Of the children whose existence is certain Violet was one of four girls and the youngest of all. Beginning with the brothers, Frederick's father, Charles, appears to have been the most interesting, or at least it would seem so from an anecdote in his son's memoir. Charles and his wife, Stella, were spending a few weeks at Oxford with their friends Brandon and Margaret Thomas. Brandon and Charles were at Pembroke College, Oxford, at the same time and had the distinction of being sent down together. Brandon Thomas was writing a play, which, as Frederick tells it, turned into a collaborative effort with Charles, who "did much cutting out of the sentimental scenes." In the end, though, the two men quarreled and Charles withdrew from the project. The play, *Charley's Aunt*, opened in London in 1892 and went on to be performed 1,466 times, which made it at the time the longest-running play in British theatrical history. The first Broadway production was in 1893, and *Charley's Aunt* became as big a hit in America as it was in Britain. Charles eventually became a divorce lawyer. Violet's brother Frank's distinction was his passion for rowing. He twice made the semifinals of the Diamond Sculls, a race for single sculls at the Henley Regatta. Her brother George was known as a "wit and charmer," but died at about twenty-two of typhoid. And finally, there was Arthur, who suffered a mental breakdown at an early age, never fully recovered, and was put under the care of a doctor near Brussels, with whom he lived for the rest of his life.

Of Violet's sisters, especially Sybil and Ada, there is a great deal more to be said. For one thing, the girls got most of the musical talent. They all played the piano and three of the four, including Violet but not Ada, were accomplished singers. Ada, however, and Sybil had long and interesting relationships with two of the most important figures in the arts of their era. Sybil was seven years older than Violet. Her husband, David Seligman, came from a well-established San Francisco banking family. For twenty years she was Giacomo

Puccini's closest confidante and for several years his lover. Ada, who was thirteen years older than Violet, married Ernest Leverson, a diamond merchant. She wrote six novels, contributed humorous articles to leading magazines including *Punch*, and Oscar Wilde, with whom she was close, called her "the Sphinx." The fourth sister was named Evelyn. Frederick Beddington thought she was the "most gifted" of the girls. She was said to have been a superb singer. But she had more than her share of unhappiness. Her first marriage to a cousin ended when he cheated on her with his young niece, then committed suicide. Her second marriage was to Walter Behrens, president of the British Chamber of Commerce in Paris, with whom she had twin boys, Walter and Edward. But she died of breast cancer in 1910 when they were thirteen. She would have been about forty-five years old.

⌇

To turn to Sydney again briefly, it seems clear that he was an embryonic aesthete whose refined sensibilities and developing tastes for fine art and literature were alien to his finance-oriented father, who made no effort to hide his disdain. His mother did not seem totally insensitive to his instincts for beauty and culture, but his father ruled. In a kind of rebellion, unacknowledged perhaps even to himself, Sydney married a woman he knew his parents would disapprove of, which condemned him to twenty years of misery. That plus his parents' serial affairs easily could have soured someone of much less delicate sensibilities than his on ever marrying again. On the face of it, therefore, there is little in his background that would make him a likely candidate to lurch blindly into another marriage. He had two years to mull it over, of course, but very little to mull. What he knew about Violet was nominal.

For the first time in his life, though, he sensed a soul mate. Violet Beddington was in relevant ways the opposite of Marion

Canine. To begin with there were all the things she and Sydney had in common that Marion lacked, foremost among them a love of literature, a cultured, sophisticated worldview, and a fascination with the vicissitudes of human nature. Like Marion, Violet had shrewd insights into people, but unlike her, she valued them for their own sake. Sydney shared Violet's abiding interest in people and would have recognized and appreciated it in her. And Violet was attractive in a way that was quite different from Marion. Her face was alive with intelligence, her steady gaze and ever so slightly lifted brows registered her frequent skepticism, and no one ever would have mistaken her for an Anglo-Saxon. I don't know whether her Jewish appearance and affect appealed to him, but they might have. In the end, though, for Sydney it was probably that undefinable, inexplicable inner something that reminded him of "the scent of a flower or the rustle of leaves or a broad sunbeam or the glistening of a calm sea when the sun sets."

What Violet saw in Sydney is perhaps a more interesting question. He was excessively polite and refined to a fault by some accounts, but given her insight, she might have attributed these finicky characteristics to his extreme shyness. Although many years later she said that at first she had been unaware of Sydney's love of literature, she could not but have noticed that they had been educated in much the same way and that they were both cultivated in the manner of their class. And Sydney was emotionally needy but also knew who he was, a combination that almost certainly would have attracted her.

It is also worth considering that Violet was thirty-four years old and single. She was self-contained and self-sufficient, but it is not unreasonable to think she viewed someone like Sydney Schiff as a last, best hope for a happy marriage. At forty, he was neither too young nor too old. He was financially independent. And he was not unattractive. As far as the Jewish question was concerned there is no indication one way or the other whether the fact that he was the Anglican son of an Anglican mother concerned Violet or her parents or that his father's Jewish origins mattered.

In any event, and whatever the reasons, on May 10, 1911, two days after Sydney's divorce decree became final, he and Violet Beddington were married, like his parents, at the register office in Kensington. During their honeymoon in Venice a cholera epidemic broke out. It was the same one that inspired Thomas Mann to write *Death in Venice*, but neither Sydney nor Violet became ill. Their marriage lasted until Sydney's death thirty-three years later.

CHAPTER 3

THE MODERNIST WORLD

When Sydney and Violet launched their leap of faith, what little they knew about each other—not what they felt, or intuited, or guessed, or suspected, but what they knew—would not have filled a teacup. No matter how intense their feelings for one another, the specter of failure must have loomed ominously in the background. Sydney would have worried because he already had made a disastrous mistake. Violet, who by then was thirty-six years old, no matter how self-possessed and self-confident she was, would have worried that she could not afford a mistake. They were making a high-risk bet whether they knew it or not. Among other things they would of necessity begin building their life together on unstable ground, not through any fault of their own, but because the world they inhabited was in turmoil. Their wealth would shelter them from some of it, but rapidly changing values, unsettling scientific and technological advances, pressure on the class structure, and world war would shape their environment and inevitably their lives.

A decade had passed since the death of Queen Victoria, and Gavrilo Princip's shot that began World War I, the war to end all wars, was just three years off. More men would be killed than in any previous war. The Paris Conference to divide the spoils in 1919 would dramatically change the political geography of Europe and the Middle East and scatter the seeds of the next war. These events on a global scale had consequences that affected Sydney and Violet personally. Among other things the war created or deepened fissures in the London community of artists and intellectuals. Some, like Bertrand Russell and many of his Bloomsbury friends, were pacifists and did not fight. Others, like Wyndham Lewis, who did fight, and T. S. Eliot, who tried unsuccessfully to enlist, gravitated toward ultraconservatism, authoritarianism, and fascism, ideologies they believed were better suited to preserving order and culture and to avoiding another war and more social upheaval. And still others, like Isaac Rosenberg, a now largely forgotten poet and painter of considerable talent, fought and wrote painfully moving verse about it.

Each of these others, Lewis, Eliot, and Rosenberg, would play an important role in the Schiffs' life. Eliot's and Lewis's would be long and consequential. Rosenberg's would be short, but significant. He was born in London and lived in South Africa because he believed the Cape Town air was better for his diseased lungs. But soon after the war began in 1914 he returned to England and enlisted in the army. Sydney and Violet met him in 1915. They liked him, admired his work, and provided him with small amounts of money and art supplies without requiring anything in return. He visited them during leaves and found them easy to talk to, including about the anti-Semitism he encountered in the army. Toward the end of the war Rosenberg was serving in the King's Own Royal Lancaster regiment on the Somme. He was returning from a night patrol on April 1, 1918, when he was shot and killed. He was twenty-seven years old. Rosenberg is less well remembered than his friends and fellow war poets Wilfred Owen, Rupert Brooke, and Siegfried Sassoon and his friends and fellow painters Mark Gertler and David Bomberg, but he was a good poet—Eliot thought so—and perhaps an even better painter. He most likely was the first beneficiary of Sydney and Violet's patronage.

In the years leading up to and during the war, the creative and philosophical currents that would give content to the Schiffs' intellectual lives, form their literary tastes, determine who were their friends and who their adversaries, and that would provide the theoretical substructure for Sydney's writing were swelling from faint underground rumblings to a rolling thunder. While Sydney and Violet were both sensitive, intelligent, aware adults who would have had their own critical thoughts about the seismic shifts that were occurring around them, it is hard to know exactly when they tuned in to the signs of modernism's arrival, at first inchoate but well developed by the war's end. It seems likely, though, that at the very least they would have thought and talked about the implications of the industrial revolution, a question that animated the thought and work of Eliot and Lewis, with whom they would form intellectually fruitful, but in Lewis's case extremely contentious, personal ties.

Eliot, Lewis, Ezra Pound, and others, including Virginia Woolf and her Bloomsbury friends, talked a lot about how the industrial revolution was leading to a loss of support for creative work, a decline in respect for the arts, decreased education in the humanities, and the devaluation of craftsmanship, all of which led to a general coarsening of life. It would have been surprising if Sydney and Violet didn't share at least some of these views. Most well-educated people of their class did and they would turn out to be right. All they worried about happened. And in some ways it was a shame, especially for those who could not survive without support for their creative work, who depended on respect for the arts to earn a living, who had benefited from an education in the humanities, and who could afford to buy art and other handcrafted objects. The more one learns about these people, though, the more it becomes clear that the real reason so many of them vehemently opposed mechanization and the rise of a new, less cultured middle class had little to do with the general welfare. What troubled them most was that it threatened their way of life.

It apparently escaped their notice that railroads, automobiles, and large-scale manufacturing would improve the living conditions of millions of workers and their families whose lives had always and inevitably been coarsened by poverty and that a large, thriving middle class was essential to the functioning of an egalitarian democracy. Egalitarianism, however, was a value whose benefits the modernists in general, including the Schiffs, failed to recognize.

In the spring and summer of 1911 Sydney and Violet were busy choosing mirrors, wallpaper, and paint colors and having expensive contemporary furniture made to order for their new home at 18 Cambridge Square, a short walk from Violet's parents' house in Hyde Park Square. Unlike the traditional and lushly furnished house in Como where Sydney once thought he could be happy, but whose memory he now was desperate to erase, everything in his new home was going to reflect Violet's taste for the cool, the clean, and the modern. In a letter to Proust nearly a decade later Sydney wrote that he had wanted to remake his life in every way, and as a result of Violet's influence his taste had turned toward everything modern and he had learned to appreciate "the charm and satisfaction of simple tastes and objects without value."

Violet's twenty-three-year-old cousin Irene Ash called at 18 Cambridge Square in 1929 and described her visit. She was received at the front door by Ali, Sydney's Indian valet, who was "immaculately dressed in one of Sydney's old suits." After taking note of Ali's attire she looked up and saw a fierce-looking self-portrait of Wyndham Lewis glaring down from the landing above. Hurrying up the stairs past it she entered a long room with a high ceiling whose walls were painted with gold leaf and hung with pictures. There was "a great placid woman's head from Picasso's blue period," a large painting by Giorgio de Chirico, and a painting by William Roberts of "fat, elongated figures in a cinema watching an elongated screen." There were also works by Mark Gertler, John Currie, and Stanley Spencer as well as several busts by Jacob Epstein. At each end of the room were fireplaces topped by mirrors that reached the ceiling, an electric fire burning in one and a log fire in the other. The lighting was hidden in a strip around the ceiling, a Steinway grand piano stood at the far end of the room, and several round tables were piled high with books. There were also a few smaller tables, two enormous sofas with black silk cushions, and several armchairs.

Shortly after arriving Irene noticed a tall, thin man enter the room. It was Aldous Huxley. Not long afterwards Violet's nephew Edward Beddington-Behrens came in. He kissed Violet before joining Sydney and Huxley. Irene noticed that Violet did not turn her head away when he kissed her. This was inconsistent with her normal practice, which she believed reduced her chances of getting infections. Beddington-Behrens said nothing to Irene but looked at her in a way that warmly acknowledged her presence before turning his attention to the conversation between Sydney and Huxley, which went on for some time. Eventually though, one by one, Huxley and the other guests said their good-byes and left.

After all but Irene and Beddington-Behrens had departed, Sydney, relaxing in an armchair, his long legs stretched out in front of him and ignoring the others, said to Violet, "Thank goodness they've all gone at last and I have you to myself, my darling." But moments later he included Irene and Beddington-Behrens. "You know," he said, "I am always jealous when she is giving all her attention to other people, even when it's you, Edward. Sometimes those interminable telephone sessions you have together make me quite unreasonably impatient and I have to get out and walk across the park."

Violet smiled but said nothing. She rang an electric bell on a cord draped over the arm of her chair. A maid appeared and she ordered tea for herself. Sydney ordered brandy. The conversation continued and somewhat incongruously Sydney said, "I cannot like Aldous. I have tried to, but everything about him is antipathetic to me." Beddington-Behrens nodded agreement and Violet smiled enigmatically. She poured tea into her cup, added cold water from a little jug, squeezed half a lemon into it, and then added several teaspoons of glucose from a small crystal bowl. "He's a pure intellectual," Sydney said. "He has no heart. All that erudition is no use unless there is feeling as well." Violet remained silent.

❦

But to return to 1911: Sooner or later, before or after the paint was dry, the wallpaper hung, and the chairs and mirrors bought, Sydney and Violet would have become aware that Henri Bergson and T. E. Hulme, among others, were laying the philosophical foundations of modernism. Maybe it was around the time Eliot and Pound separately explained the big idea of modernist writing. Eliot said writers had to find "objective correlatives," that is, concrete images that transmit without explanation what writers want their readers to feel. Pound put it even more simply. If you want a reader to feel something about a tree, for example, describe the tree so that she feels it, don't tell her how to feel about it. There is, of course, a great deal more than this to modernist aesthetics, and there are a great many books on modernism for those who would like to pursue the subject. But for our purposes here just a few words on modernism in the social and political spheres will make it easier to fully grasp the rapidly evolving world the Schiffs inhabited.

The key sociopolitical distinction the modernists made was between classical (conservative) and romantic (liberal). Hulme was convinced all human beings were one or the other by temperament. Romantics, he believed, think humanity's inherent goodness justifies liberty for all. Take the shackles off mankind, do away with oppressive laws and customs, and you set loose the forces of prog-ress. The classicists, however, believed human beings are limited animals with a fixed nature. Tradition and organization, which I suspect a romantic would not distinguish from oppressive laws and customs, are necessary to get the best out of them. And for the classicists, progress, at least as far as human nature is concerned, is a myth. Modernists of the Pound, Eliot, and Lewis school were clas-sicists. In this sociopolitical sense, many others were still roman-tics. The Schiffs, although personally and intellectually close to Eliot and Lewis, fell somewhere in between.

～

Of all the gaps in Sydney and Violet's story, perhaps the biggest is from the time of their marriage in 1911 until about 1915. There are few letters and nothing significant in Sydney's work about that four-year stretch of time. It was presumably a period in which they learned a great deal about one another. Of the relatively few things we know for sure, one is that they had a great deal in common. Apart from the visceral love they shared, both were intellectually curious, passionate about literature—although Violet did not know this about Sydney until after they were married—and connoisseurs of human nature. And it was their good fortune that besides what they had in common their differences were often complementary. Violet's tough-minded practicality, for example, compensated for Sydney's otherworldly sensitivity and refinement. And his taste in the visual arts complemented hers in music. They were in short thoroughly compatible. We also know that with Violet's fervent and unswerving support to motivate him a grateful and newly con-fident Sydney started to write seriously.

It was also during this period that the Schiffs began to invite to their home the kinds of people who when they achieved criti-cal mass would amount to a salon. There is no way to tell whether they purposefully went about creating a salon or whether it was a natural outgrowth of their tastes and predilections.

One evening in March or April of 1912, Filippo Marinetti was in London for a lecture series. Enrico Caruso was also in town. Marinetti was the theologian of futurism, the violent Italian variant of modernism fixated on speed, industry, and technology and best remembered for its painters, especially Umberto Boccioni, Giacomo Balla, and Gino Severini. Marinetti, with his florid mustache, flowing tie, spats, bowler hat, and bombastic personality, was the model of a music-hall Italian. Most likely speaking in French because he spoke no English, he sprayed invective at his audience in Bechstein Hall, calling England "a nation of sycophants and snobs, enslaved by old worm-eaten traditions, social conventions and romanticism." His tirade earned him headlines. According to the *Times*, "some of his audience begged for mercy," but the *Daily Chronicle* reported that "the long-haired gentlemen in the stalls and the ladies with Rossetti eyes and lips rewarded him with their laughter and applause." Although he might easily have been dismissed as an offensive clown, his effectiveness, measured in twenty-first-century terms—which is to say, by press coverage—could not be easily dismissed. In six weeks he racked up 350 articles in newspapers and little reviews.

Who—or what—brought Marinetti to 18 Cambridge Square on the evening mentioned above is not known. But most likely it was one of his Italian compatriots such as Caruso, who was there for sure, or Tosti, the royal singing master and master of the art song, who probably was. Whoever it was, he had given Marinetti, the professional promoter, another opportunity to stage his carnival act. He had an audience, admittedly just a fraction of the one at Bechstein Hall, but probably more elite, and he was not about to let it go to waste. He took the floor and launched into a lengthy and obscure oration on the theoretical substratum of futurism the details of which reside in the waste bin of history. What else we know is just this: Caruso, wearing a false nose and hiding in plain sight under the Schiffs' piano, but unnoticed by Marinetti, kept the audience from being bored to death by mocking the futurist seer with a running pantomime of ridiculous faces and gestures. No, we don't know whether Marinetti ever discovered he'd been made a fool of. We do know, though, that performances, games, and other entertainments requiring a thick skin became fixtures of evenings at the Schiffs'.

Sydney enjoyed the socializing, but from the day he married Violet until the day of his death in 1944 he lived mainly for two things—her love and his novel. The former satisfied all his needs but one, for which the latter proved indispensable. It provided a catharsis for his unbearable and seemingly ineradicable memory of life before Violet. The record of their thirty-three-year love affair is subtly woven into his book. They spent long hours together at Cambridge Square and Ilchester Place, Abinger, Eastbourne, and Lye Green, painstakingly revising difficult passages, searching for the most accurate and evocative imagery, refining meaning, eliminating flaws in rhythm and pace. And they spent even more hours alone, Sydney writing legibly in longhand, and Violet, whose handwriting was always difficult to decipher and deteriorated in her old age, editing and typing. The novel from beginning to end was a collaboration between an inspired writer with a painful personal story to tell and an intelligent, sympathetic, but unsentimental editor who was dedicated to his success.

Sydney had published nothing before marrying Violet in 1911 and arguably would never have published anything had he not met and married her. But that year in response to her urging him to write about what he knew best—himself—he began *Richard Kurt*. He soon set it aside, though, to write *Concessions*, a novel with much more circuitous autobiographical implications than *A True Story*. Why he stopped working on *Kurt* is not known. Perhaps he thought he didn't know himself well enough yet; or maybe he wasn't quite ready to tell the full truth, which would have made the task futile.

After *Concessions* came out in 1913 Europe was on the verge of war, and everybody's mind was on when it would begin, when Britain would be drawn in, because it seemed almost inevitable that it would, and how horrible it was going to be. The imminent threat of a devastating conflict might have made it difficult to concentrate on a project that for the times might have seemed self-regarding and even frivolous. The book he wrote instead was *War-Time Silhouettes*, a collection of short stories with war-related themes. He published only one other book of short fiction, *Celeste and Other Sketches*, which was issued in 1930. "Celeste," the title story, was first rate and the others as slight as the word "sketches" suggests. All of the stories had previously appeared in literary magazines.

Sydney probably returned to *Kurt* in 1916. That was the year Violet read *Swann's Way*, was enchanted by it, and urged him to read it. When he didn't get it the first time, she persevered, as was her way, and made sure he read it again. Had she not, he very likely would never have recognized Proust's genius and would not have written the letter that kindled their relationship. And if he had failed to share her love of Proust, it surely would have altered not only *A True Story*, but their relationship.

How much of *Kurt* was already written when they read *Swann*, what state it was in, how much if any was revised or scrapped, is not known. Nevertheless, it is undeniable that *A True Story* was influenced by *In Search of Lost Time*. But even though the similarities are numerous and obvious, they are hardly peculiar to Marcel Proust and Sydney Schiff. Both books are largely autobiographical; both are composed of several individual but closely related novels; both are mainly character rather than plot driven, with an interest in time, an obsession of many modernists of the Bayswater and Bloomsbury persuasions. And in both many of the characters are based on real people.

But the differences in style and scope are vast. Sydney, benefiting from Violet's acute editorial judgment, achieved clarity in the traditional way through straightforward plotlines and short sentences with simple structure. Proust achieved it much more originally—despite a maze of subplots—through perfectly crafted, unusually long sentences that are remarkably lucid despite their length and complexity. Moreover, Proust's three-thousand-page novel is encyclopedic in its interests, while Sydney's, which is one-fifth its size, is much more narrowly focused. *Richard Kurt* is a relatively uncomplicated tale in which the narrator is the protagonist and the narrative rarely strays from the narrow path of his life. In *Swann*, Marcel, the narrator, is not the protagonist; indeed, in the novel taken as a whole, there is no protagonist and complications abound. Furthermore, Proust's work is a compendium of art, music, philosophy, medicine, history, social mores, sexual deviation, fashion, theater, and much more. Theophilus Boll, an insightful interpreter of Sydney's fiction, suggested Sydney learned from *Swann* how to seamlessly combine analysis with description, which he did effectively. But without access to early drafts of *Kurt* it is impossible to know for sure that Proust was his master even in this respect. It could have been Violet or just his own development as a writer.

Richard Kurt was the first of seven explicitly autobiographical volumes published between 1919 and 1937 in which Sydney combined fictionalized events with actual ones and inserted invented characters alongside real ones. He exploited this technique to express his own feelings and beliefs in an effort to come to terms with himself, which was his principal motive for writing. But he was not entirely self-absorbed. His own interest in other people had been intensified by Violet's. Throughout the novel he conveyed the essential qualities that defined all of the significant characters and delineated their human relationships subtly and convincingly. He used characteristics such as religion, ethnicity, class, race, and intellect to describe characters in his fiction but never to evaluate them, a quality that emerged most explicitly in his last book, *The Other Side*, which Somerset Maugham thought was remarkably real, a "chapter from [Sydney's] life." *A True Story* was published in three separate editions in 1930, 1948, and 1965. The last edition was composed of *Prince Hempseed, Elinor Colhouse, The Other Side*, a drastically cut version of *Richard Kurt*, and the last chapter of *Myrtle*.

Bernard Bergonzi, a British poet and critic who specialized in the modernist period, wrote in the March 17, 1966, issue of the *New York Review of Books* that the final rendering of *A True Story* "may not be the forgotten masterpiece of English fiction that the publishers claim it to be; but it is still important enough for its reprinting to be welcome." Roger Dooley, however, writing in the *Saturday Review* of January 1, 1966, found Hudson's style "as flatly unimaginative as his titles." The only section of the book he thought worthwhile was *Richard Kurt*, which he found "absorbing and soundly constructed."

Violet was always careful to point out after Sydney's death that he began *Richard Kurt* in 1911 because she was sensitive to criticism that he shamelessly modeled his work on Proust's, which she maintained would have been impossible because the Schiffs did not read the first volume of *In Search of Lost Time* until years after he began *Richard Kurt*. But *Kurt* was not published until 1919. Lacking an original manuscript there is no way to know how much might have been written or rewritten in the three years between his first reading of Proust and its publication. And while hardly dispositive, it does not seem totally irrelevant that the book was dedicated to "M.P.," initials that would have meant nothing to all but the handful of his readers who were writers themselves.

In those early years of the twentieth century a small group of writers and artists, many of whom would become the Schiffs' friends, including Proust, were on the cusp of cultural dominion. And Sydney Schiff, under the spell of the former Violet Beddington, was absorbing the zeitgeist and beginning to mutate into Stephen Hudson. *Concessions* appeared under his real name, but *War-Time*

Silhouettes and each book after it were signed Stephen Hudson. He took the name "Hudson" because it was the surname of the Beddingtons' secretary and he was using their address to communicate with his publisher in an attempt to hide his identity from his family and former wife. He chose Stephen as a given name, it has been suggested, because St. Stephen was a martyr.

Eight novels and a collection of stories was a considerable output considering that Sydney did not begin writing seriously until he was forty-three years old. What he would have written without Violet's early encouragement and long-term influence is an imponderable, but there is no doubt that her moral and intellectual support was crucial to the quality of his work and to their relationship. He told Edward Beddington-Behrens that "if it were not for her divine companionship, his literary output might have been much larger, but in their interminable conversations together, many long novels had been dissipated." Not all writers necessarily need a muse, but they all know in their heart of hearts that the only gift as valuable as talent is a good editor. Sydney knew his was better than good. She was by his side day and night and he trusted her implicitly. And perhaps more important, she prodded him to aspire to a level of creativity that without her very likely would have been beyond his reach.

There is no way to know precisely what or how much Violet contributed. However, *Richard, Myrtle and I*, which was published in 1926, and in which Richard is Sydney and Myrtle is Violet (the "I" in the title is Sydney's alter ego), provides some clues. It is constructed as an extended conversation between Richard, Myrtle, and the coldly analytical "I." The book—or story, more precisely, because it is only forty-three pages long—strongly suggests Violet played a seminal role in Sydney's writing and that he rarely if ever rejected her revisions.

Perhaps the best clue to the nature of her contribution to Sydney's novels is in the notes she wrote when she was in her seventies suggesting changes in various works by Julian Fane, the young English writer she befriended a little over a decade before she died. They give a clear indication of her critical sensibility and the attention she paid to the little things that animate fiction. They also demonstrate that she could be generous with praise, using phrases like "so charming" and "beautifully suggested" where she thought they were deserved, but acerbic when criticism was necessary. She unequivocally recommended that Fane delete pages and details and leave some things to the reader's imagination. She instructed him that he was writing for an intelligent public, not children, and added bluntly, "I do not care for the description of Dorothy. It is unpleasant and has no interest."

Violet became more short-tempered as she grew older, and although she was gentler with Sydney, the man she adored, this was a woman whose ideas about writing, as about most everything else, were clearly formed, who spoke her mind, and who did not suffer fools. If there is a distillation, or a summing up, of what she thought and how she felt about writing, it is probably this quotation from André Maurois's *Reflections* that she passed on to Fane:

"To adopt an artist's calling is to accept a kind of religion. You must set above all pleasures, all honors, the satisfaction of a well-written page, a well-made sentence, a word that is the only right word. Like love and friendship, art demands from you all that you have to give. And like love it will repay you a hundredfold." This attitude and sensibility, which Violet and Sydney shared with James and Proust, is reflected to a considerable degree in *A True Story*.

Violet was also musical, which Sydney was not, which would have given her a feel for the rhythm and phrasing of language. The modernists were hardly the first to recognize the relationship between music and felicitous language. But they believed this relationship transcended beauty, that it was more than a pleasant sensation independent of meaning. Many of them believed that along with concrete images musical elements were indispensable for communicating feelings as precisely as possible. Henri Bergson, perhaps the most influential philosopher of modernism, went further. He believed music was even more important than images and urged writers to find language that by its musicality helps convey exactly what they want their readers to feel. One of the most powerful influences on Sydney's writing, however, was Violet's literary taste. Her favorite writer when she married Sydney was James, and he remained her sole favorite until five years into their marriage she read *Swann's Way*. Eventually Proust's work and their friendship with him transformed their understanding of literature and, to a degree, their lives.

And as one might expect of someone whose literary assessments were so acute, Violet's judgments of people were similarly keen. She could be empathetic, sympathetic, snobbish, or acidic in her reactions, but she was always incisive in her analysis. Her ability to identify hypocrisy and deceit, to differentiate genuine from false emotion, in life as well as in print, must have been enormously valuable to Sydney, who, when she married him, was a middle-aged novice writer with the desire but not the confidence to embark on an ambitious literary enterprise. Sydney, as it turned out, was an equally acute observer and equally blunt in his appraisals, which meant that neither was oblivious to the other's flaws, nor likely silent about them. His fussiness must have gotten on her nerves and her acerbity must occasionally have abraded his delicate sensibilities. Although their love for one another was never in doubt, at times they must have found each other irritating. Violet could be willful and Sydney petulant and by some standards petty.

More important, though, they were matched in a way that brought out the best in both of them. And in a world where wives didn't always count, it was as a couple that they were accepted and even courted by modernist royalty. It seems more likely than not that on their own, or with other mates, they would not have met Proust and Eliot, Wyndham Lewis and Katherine Mansfield,

Aldous Huxley, and Edwin and Willa Muir, or achieved the intimacy they did with these writers. And in their wildest dreams they
would not have imagined inviting Proust, Picasso, James Joyce,
Igor Stravinsky, and Serge Diaghilev to dinner and having them
all appear. Their wealth certainly facilitated these relationships,
but their patronage was always on a small scale, so it could hardly
account for the closeness of many of their friendships. They were
gracious hosts, but not lavish. They did not orchestrate elaborate
country weekends the way Lady Ottoline Morrell did at Garsington. They preferred quiet dinners with Tom and Vivienne Eliot or
Wyndham Lewis, who never took his wife anywhere, or small parties with intimate friends who often knew each other well.

From about 1916 on, these relationships and Sydney's literary
career more or less defined their lives. Sydney wrote modernist novels, published in the most prestigious journals, translated works by
leading German, Swiss, and French writers, and funded and helped
edit a prominent journal. Still, the Schiffs' status among the modernist elite was not completely secure. Although Lewis praised
one of Sydney's novels, his overall assessment of him was that he
was no more than a rich amateur. Muir, on the other hand, in a
minority view, thought his books had as good a chance as those of
Joyce, Virginia Woolf, and D. H. Lawrence of becoming part of the
canon. Whatever anyone thought, though, these were the people
with whom the Schiffs spent their time, whose books they read,
who reviewed Sydney's books, with whom they discussed politics,
painting, poetry, and the rapidly evolving world they were trying
to understand, explain, and depict. According to Lewis, who didn't
suffer from diffidence, "It was . . . a new civilization that I—and a
few other people—was making the blueprints for."

CHAPTER 4

THE WAR YEARS

In July 1914 a twenty-five-year-old Harvard graduate student a dissertation short of a PhD in philosophy, but with literary aspirations, passed through London on his way to Germany. His name was Tom Eliot and he planned to return to England after participating in a two-month summer program at Marburg University. But on August 1, just before the program was due to begin, his plans abruptly changed. Germany had declared war on Russia and was no longer a safe or welcoming place for Americans. Eliot returned to London.

A week or two after arriving he called on Ezra Pound at the suggestion of his college friend Conrad Aiken. He showed him several poems, including a draft he had been struggling with for four years. Pound, who was just three years older than Eliot but well established in London, had already published five volumes of verse. After reading Eliot's poems he wrote to Harriet Monroe, the editor of *Poetry* magazine, that he had never seen a better poem by an American. It was "The Love Song of J. Alfred Prufrock" and Monroe published it in 1915. It was, of course, one of Eliot's best poems and a twentieth-century masterpiece. Pound also wrote to

H. L. Mencken praising Eliot's intelligence and urging Mencken to keep an eye on him, and introduced Eliot to others in his circle, including Hilda Doolittle, the American poet who signed her work "H.D.," and her husband, the essayist and critic Richard Aldington.

On the strength of "Prufrock" and Eliot's obvious intelligence, Pound invited him to his flat at the foot of Notting Hill to meet the acid-tongued painter, writer, intellectual gadfly, and founder of Vorticism, Percy Wyndham Lewis, who hated his first name and never used it. When the two men didn't seem to hit it off, which Pound attributed to the younger Eliot's reserve and lack of confidence, he tried to break the ice. "Yor old Uncle Ezz is wise to what youse thinkin," he said to Lewis in the hillbilly drawl he liked to affect. "Waaal Wyndham I'se telling *yew*, he's a lot better'n he looks." Years later Lewis described Eliot that day as "a sleek, tall attractive transatlantic apparition," a description at once detailed and opaque, which is characteristic of much of Lewis's prose.

Whether Pound's corny dialect helped or not, Lewis and Eliot quickly became friends. Despite their contrasting temperaments, each respected the other's intellect and they shared a taste for scathing humor. Moreover, it was a cardinal principle for both that authority, firmly exercised, was a precondition of civilization. The only difference was that Eliot's views were skewed toward religion and authoritarianism and Lewis's toward authoritarianism without religion. Lewis thought democracy was the death knell for discipline, by which he meant the destruction of culture and society. Both admired the French nationalist, monarchist, and anti-Semite Charles Maurras, whose mantra, *"classique, catholique, monarchique,"* Eliot later adapted to his own purposes as "classicist in literature, royalist in politics, Anglo-Catholic in religion." Maurras, a rabid supporter of the Vichy regime, was arrested in September 1944, charged with complicity with the enemy, convicted, and sentenced to life in prison. In March 1952 he was transferred to a hospital and he died on November 16.

Eliot and Lewis had all this in common plus an expansive sense of self-importance. At thirty Eliot considered himself the most influential critic in England, which, to be fair, he might have been. Lewis, in his 1937 autobiography *Blasting and Bombardiering*, in a chapter grandiosely titled "The Period of 'Ulysses,' 'Blast,' and 'The Wasteland'"—*Blast* being the title of a Vorticist journal he edited that died after its second issue—proclaimed, "I was at its heart. In some instances, I was it." By "it" he meant nothing less than the entire modernist movement. If that were not enough, he also said that by August 1914, the month World War I started, "no newspaper was complete without news about Vorticism and its arch-exponent Mr. Lewis." In anyone else's case you would think they were being arch, but in Lewis's his remarkable gift for bluster casts some doubt. "I might have been the head of a social revolution, instead of merely being the prophet of a new fashion in art," he declared.

Eliot considered Lewis a better painter than he was a writer, but what he especially admired was his erudition and gift as a conversationalist. A few years later in a review of Lewis's novel *Tarr*, which has its moments, although mostly the characters deliver short lectures and strain to sound witty or aphoristic, Eliot called him "the most fascinating personality of our time." This view of Lewis was widely held in Bayswater, but he was reviled in Bloomsbury and after a visit or two rejected by its Garsington branch. He of course thought no better of the Woolf-Bell-Strachey-Keynes crowd, accusing "the really malefic 'Bloomsburys' . . . of having a destructive influence upon the intellectual life of England." Without them, he wrote, "The writing and painting world of London might have been less like the afternoon tea-party of a perverse spinster." He also accused "the Bloomsburys" of blocking him from publishing any literary journalism and of accepting his books for review, then "neglecting" to review them. Whether or not this was true I don't know, but it doesn't seem far-fetched.

Bloomsbury was not alone, however, in its distaste for Lewis. Ernest Hemingway once dismissed him as someone who "just looked nasty," a man with the eyes "of an unsuccessful rapist." Sydney and Violet however were in the admiring camp and would in time form as close a relationship with Lewis as they would with Eliot. Eventually, though, a disagreement about money and a scathing chapter on the Schiffs in a satirical novel by Lewis all but ended it. In *Blasting and Bombardiering*, a book that is at its best when describing life at the front during World War I, he gave the Schiffs only one brief mention. He did not even include their first names despite their having supported him with gifts and loans, bought his paintings, funded and published in his journal the *Tyro*, subsidized his health care, and provided him with many a meal and multiple diversions in the city and in the country.

In October, Eliot, by then a fledgling member of the Bayswater chapter of the modernist club, went off to Oxford, where he had a fellowship. While there he worked on his dissertation and studied Aristotle, but as the year wore on his interest in philosophy, a vocation leading to the academic career his father and his Harvard mentors wished for him, wore off. He was more and more drawn to poetry, even though the professional prospects were considerably vaguer, and by the time his year at Oxford was over he had pretty much made up his mind to pursue his literary ambitions in London, if only for a time.

London during the war was a grim city. Sporadic bombing raids, first by zeppelins, then bombers, and finally primitive missiles, began in May of 1915 and continued until the armistice in November 1918. Between six and seven hundred Londoners were killed by the German bombs. There were also food shortages and frequent blackouts. By and large, though, there was remarkably little discussion of the fighting or deprivation in the letters Sydney and Violet exchanged with their friends. And Lewis was the only one of their intimate circle who saw combat, serving first as a noncommissioned officer, then as an artillery officer and a war artist. Never a man to leave his resentment unexpressed, even though in this case it simmered for more than twenty years, he wrote contemptuously, although understandably, in his autobiography that "the 'Blooms-buries' were all doing war work of 'National importance,' down in some downy English county, under the wings of powerful pacifist friends; pruning trees, planting gooseberry bushes, and haymaking, doubtless in large sunbonnets."

Sydney—once characterized by the Bloomsbury princeling-by-marriage and sun-bonneted gooseberry planter David Garnett as a rich Austrian with the acquired manners of an actor playing an English colonel—was too old to fight. Nevertheless he was deeply interested in the progress of the fighting. He told Edward Beddington-Behrens, a captain and later a major in the army who saw action in the Battle of the Somme and elsewhere at the front, that he wanted to know all about the war, both the light and the dark side. Beddington-Behrens took him at his word and in his letters recounted gory details including descriptions of body parts being picked up and dumped into sacks and of the three or four hours he spent searching for and burying the dead within sight of the German trenches a couple of hundred yards away. "It is the only way to get an idea of this war," he wrote. Sydney and Violet corresponded regularly with Beddington-Behrens throughout the war and sent him packages including everything from socks, a cap, and a waterproof jacket to Devonshire clotted cream from Fortnum & Mason. Violet wrote to her nephew that if she and Sydney had a son they would want him to be like Beddington-Behrens. They were not as close to his twin brother Walter, who was killed in action on July 10, 1917. He was twenty years old.

The only one of Sydney's books in which he gave some idea of his dejection during the war was *Richard, Myrtle and I*. He projects a sense that his world was crumbling around him, that civilization was in ruins, and that even Proust belonged to the past and his writing had little or no value anymore. "The whole thing is broken," he told his alter ego, who was trying to convince him otherwise. "No one will have time for anything except work. There'll be no room for people like me. . . . In the old leisurely world one could do what one pleased. Those who wanted to spend their time hunting or shooting or playing golf could do so. No one minded. The same thing with reading. But all that's changed now. First, the war isn't over. When it is do you think those millions of men who've been living in hell all these years, will put up with the old state of things? I can tell you they won't." In the end, though, Violet and his alter ego conspired to convince him that Proust still mattered, which seems to imply that while civilization as Sydney knew it was being transformed, quickly and radically, it would survive.

Although he was too old for the army Sydney managed to play a small part in the war effort in a rather mysterious way. From early in 1915 until the armistice in 1918 he carried on a correspondence with Basil Thompson, a son of the Archbishop of York and a former prison governor. Thompson was then assistant commissioner and chief of the Criminal Investigation Department at New Scotland Yard. During the war the CID functioned as part of military intelligence. It is not clear how or why Sydney and Thompson made contact. Although they both attended G. T. Worsley's School they were there six years apart. Only Thompson's letters and those of an agent in Rotterdam have survived. Their language is oblique, but the letters suggest Sydney was trying to do his patriotic duty as a noncombatant.

Thompson was anti-Semitic and deeply conservative. He was also relentless in pursuit of anyone he thought posed a threat to Britain. His principal targets apart from German spies were suffragettes, Irish nationalists, and British Marxists. Thompson's first letter to Sydney with a specific request for assistance was dated March 23, 1915. He asked if "there would be any objection to one of our people in Switzerland calling upon Dr. Kuhlmann-Ristner. I think he might be very useful to us. . . . Perhaps you could prepare Dr. Kuhlmann-Ristner in very guarded language. After all, he can but refuse." It's not clear if Sydney was being asked to recruit a spy, but he would continue to be solicited by Thompson to provide various vaguely described services throughout the war.

In a second letter, Thompson wrote to Sydney that a Mr. Lang had sent him a collection of German propaganda papers, "and I am able to tell you confidentially that action has been taken from them. I am surprised to see from his letter that he has not yet been called upon, and I am taking steps to have this remedied." The correspondence continued in this vein throughout the war, and in one of the last letters, in January 1918, Thompson wrote to Sydney that "the admiralty is quite alive to the probability of a Naval action, but I will see that your suggestions are brought before the right quarter." Was Sydney offering strategic or tactical advice? If so, based on what expertise? Did Thompson actually pass it on, and was it followed? I don't know, but the Thompson correspondence makes clear that the war was never far from Sydney's mind and that he knew what side he was on.

In 1919 Thompson was named head of the Directorate of Intelligence, which gave him authority over all British intelligence, military, foreign, and domestic. But in 1921 his office was found to be an unnecessary layer in the intelligence bureaucracy and he was forced to resign.

Although the Schiffs' nephews fought in the war and one was killed, among their close friends only Lewis did. In 1914 national service was far from Eliot's mind. The personal hardships and geopolitics of war were outweighed by the cultural ferment in London and its abundant and, to him at least, welcoming community of native and expatriate writers. And then there was the added attraction of the pretty and by Eliot's standards socially desirable Vivienne Haigh-Wood, whom he met through an old school friend in 1915. Not the least among the qualities he found endearing was her enthusiasm for his poetry. Although not generally given to snap decisions he married her three months later.

Many years afterwards, however, Eliot singled out his first meeting with Pound as the real turning point in his decision to stay in England. It "changed my life," he wrote. "He was enthusiastic about my poems, and gave me such praise and encouragement as I had long ceased to hope for." By that time Pound had become Eliot's mentor, in the full meaning of the word. He was a wise and trusted counselor and an influential senior sponsor. And if you set aside William Butler Yeats, the greatest of all modernist poets, it seems fair to say that only Pound could have filled that role for Eliot, who arguably became the best known of all modernist poets and critics.

But if Pound's early mentoring of Eliot made sense and therefore was unsurprising, it comes as a colossal surprise that Lyndall Gordon, the deservedly respected author of the standard Eliot biography, has unambiguously asserted that Sydney Schiff was Eliot's mentor. I have read every bit of the Eliot-Schiff correspondence and I feel obliged to say I think Gordon overstated Sydney's influence on Eliot's work. What Eliot's letters to Sydney reflect, rather than mentorship, is a certain dependence Eliot developed on the Schiffs and was not loath to exploit. For one thing, Sydney had connections Eliot valued, among these, Lady Rothermere, who put up the money for Eliot's journal, the *Criterion*. Sydney also published Eliot in his journal, *Art and Letters*, and was always a potential patron. Additionally, Eliot liked being invited to the Schiffs' houses in town and in the country. And most of all, perhaps, Vivienne found the Schiffs more sympathetic and compatible than most of Eliot's friends. Eliot did seek Sydney's opinion on at least one important poem, but he often sent drafts of his poems to friends and there is no reason to think he valued Sydney's critical sensibilities more highly than those of his other friends.

The Schiffs' friendship yielded Eliot tangible benefits, a serious intellectual relationship, and a warm and respectful friendship. There is a sense of ease in many of Eliot's personal letters to the Schiffs that is rare in his correspondence with others. It is also likely that Sydney and Violet were the only friends with whom the young Eliots had a genuine "couples" relationship. The idea that Sydney and Violet could engage each of them without estranging the other seems all the more remarkable because Eliot and his wife were spiritually and physically, though not intellectually, estranged within weeks of their wedding day.

There are various accounts of exactly what triggered their alienation, but all of them point to Bertrand Russell, philosopher, pacifist, do-gooder, and Eliot's professor at Harvard. Russell, who feared his four-year affair with Lady Ottoline Morrell was running out of steam, is said to have caused the rupture by seducing Vivienne, whom he had characterized to his Garsington friends after first meeting her as "faintly vulgar." While there is a fairly widespread assumption that an affair occurred, there is no hard evidence and little agreement on how long it might have lasted if it did occur. Accounts vary from one night to three years. Lady Ottoline wrote rather circumspectly in her memoir that Russell "was convinced that the Eliots were not really happy together, but by a little manipulation on his part everything would come right between them."

Vivienne was beginning to suffer from a series of ailments that would distress her for the rest of her life, but also would endear her to Violet, whose empathy gave her comfort. Eliot meanwhile was doing his best to support them any way he could. First he taught several subjects including Latin, French, German, and drawing at two boys' schools, High Wycombe and Highgate Junior School. Then, in 1917, through a friend of Vivienne's family, he got a job in the Colonial and Foreign Department of Lloyd's Bank. Full-time employment compromised his ability to write but provided a regular source of income, which he badly needed. Pound and Sydney, among other friends, tried to get him to quit, but he stayed on for eight years.

Russell, who had eased Eliot into the Bloomsbury circle of modernist society by introducing him to Garsington, soothed his conscience by providing a small amount of financial support to the young couple. Those who believe the relationship with Vivienne lasted for three years accuse him of fomenting depression in her by abruptly breaking it off in the winter of 1918–19 and moving on smartly to another mistress. What Eliot knew, believed, or thought about Russell's relationship with his wife is not known. He did, however, mock Russell in his 1916 poem "Mr. Appolinax" as "Priapus in the shrubbery," a man with "pointed ears" and "centaur's hoofs." The marriage in any event endured, but Eliot grew more and more distant from his wife, although he continued to show concern about her health and respect her opinion of his work. She eventually retreated into drugs and had other affairs.

The Schiffs and Eliots probably met sometime in 1919. In a letter to her friend Mary Hutchinson written on May 10 while she was on her way to Garsington, Vivienne referred to poems Eliot had asked Leonard Woolf to send to "a man called Schiff" of whom she obviously had never heard. Between Vivienne's May letter to Mary Hutchinson and early July, however, the Schiff-Eliot relationship flowered. Eliot wrote three letters in nine days to the Schiffs. He told Sydney he had read *Richard Kurt* "with great interest" and was looking forward to discussing it with him. He also thanked Sydney for his careful study of "Gerontion." To Violet he wrote, "I was really glad of the bad weather as it gave excuse for more conversation. There are very few people to whom we could say that sincerely." And in a letter to his mother on August 9, 1920, he wrote: "We spent the weekend at Eastbourne, visiting some friends called Schiff—very nice Jews." By 1918–19 Eliot was already an adornment to any drawing room with modernist literary pretensions, and he was invited regularly to the Schiffs' houses in Cambridge Square and at the seaside in Eastbourne on England's south coast.

The letters they exchanged regularly began quite formally, but by mid-1920 Eliot was writing to "My dear Sydney" and signing himself, "Affectionately, T.S.E." In another 1920 letter, Eliot wrote, "With love from both of us to you and Violet." A year later it was "aff., Tom," which is especially meaningful because only Eliot's closest friends received letters signed "Tom." And in 1921 Vivienne wrote to "My dear Violet" and signed off "With love." They wrote about where they planned to spend the summer, commented superficially on each other's work in generally flattering, but occasionally mildly critical terms, and alluded to financial matters, and many of the letters contained more than anyone would want to know about their multitude of minor ailments and discomforts.

In later years, Violet, who suffered from fevers of unknown etiology among other things, referred to herself as a valetudinarian, a rather arcane word that means someone who is excessively, perhaps even morbidly, concerned with his or her health. She had a sense of humor about it, though, once signing a letter to the Schiffs' friend, the English writer and caricaturist Max Beerbohm, "V. Valetudinariana." It is a word that accurately described not only Violet but the Eliots and almost everyone else with whom the Schiffs corresponded.

Those were the days in which the Schiffs were hosting parties in Eastbourne in which the guests took part in role-playing games. Tom Eliot and Vivienne especially liked these evenings, and he wrote to their friend Mary Hutchinson that "London life would be more tolerable if there were more people like the Schiffs. They won't have anyone . . . they don't really like. One result is that everyone is ready to . . . play the fool if necessary." The Eastbourne gatherings were so successful that Sydney and Violet duplicated them at Cambridge Square. What Eliot called playing the fool Sydney referred to benignly in a letter to Proust as "an exchange of personalities." Each guest, as well as Sydney and Violet, had to impersonate someone known to all of them, who often was in the room, and the others had to guess who it was. This may sound innocent enough, but as Sydney explained it to Proust it was clearly more wicked than innocent. The goal, it seems, was to expose their friends' weak points. He wrote that the game was "diabolically entertaining and illuminating at the same time" and that he was very bad at it, but that Violet was brilliant. During one of those evenings Eliot did a caustic impression of Wyndham Lewis, who turned out to be as thin-skinned about being parodied by his friend as he was thick-skinned about parodying everyone else.

These evenings were important to Eliot not only because he found them distracting, but because Vivienne, who was depressed and took pleasure in very little, enjoyed the acting. It seems that an entertaining evening at the Schiffs' made Eliot's life with Vivienne just a bit easier to bear, if only temporarily. Also, it would have been out of character for him to flatter Sydney and Violet in a letter to another good friend unless he meant it. On the other hand, it could have been that the normally shy and restrained Eliot, who was a fan of rowdy, even raunchy British music hall, comic strips, detective novels, and boxing, also enjoyed acting out in a relatively nonthreatening environment.

During the austere war years Sydney and Violet were able to ingratiate themselves with Eliot, Lewis, and other modernist luminaries because they had the means to be good hosts and they were good at bringing the right people together. But, as Eliot's letter to Mary Hutchinson indicates, there was more to it—and to them—than that. Neither of them was outgoing, but what they would not or could not do alone, they did well together. This applied not only to their social life but also to Sydney's work. United with Violet, Sydney was finally becoming the man—and the writer—he dreamed of being. After surviving his father's contempt for his aestheticism, and twenty poisonous years with Marion, he found himself in the nurturing embrace of someone who loved him, understood him, appreciated his sensitivity, accepted his excesses, and, most importantly, believed in his incipient talent. And Violet, middle-aged for her time and unmarried, had met and wed a man who loved her unconditionally, who responded with perfect pitch to her sensibilities and intelligence, and perhaps of most importance desperately needed her nurturing. To her he was the person whose needs perfectly matched the gifts she had to give. Each gave the other a sense of completeness and fulfillment.

No one knows for sure what would have become of Sydney without Violet, or Violet without Sydney, but it seems likely he would have remained unhappy and unfulfilled and she would have carried on her life with equanimity. Together, however, between 1913 and 1919, above and beyond their social success, Sydney wrote and Violet midwifed, edited, and typed three books, all of which were published. The first, *Concessions*, deconstructed his personality into three parts, each represented by a separate character. Violet also appears, as two characters, one a brilliant pianist like her mother and the other a woman named Zillah, Violet's middle name as well as her mother's first name. And like Violet, the character named Zillah was an accomplished singer.

The direct style of *A True Story*, using the simplest possible language to convey complex insight and emotion, was yet to emerge. But one defining characteristic of Sydney's later work is evident in this first effort. Without masking his identity, he was as brutally honest about his weaknesses as the pseudonymous Stephen Hudson was in *A True Story*. The Scottish poet and critic Edwin Muir, who was to become a good friend of the Schiffs, wrote some years later that in *A True Story* Sydney "pushed his honesty . . . so far . . . that he was less than just to himself." Two of the three aspects of himself he drew in *Concessions* emphasized character flaws: the artist possessed of the childish selfishness not infrequently found in creative persons and the hopelessly naive man lured into a loveless marriage. The third was generally positive: a man capable of selfless love because he had received it from his mother. It doesn't take too much imagination to recognize that a composite of these three characters amounts to a self-portrait of Sydney. In a letter to Proust in 1920 he explicitly referred to himself as selfish, but beyond question what he gave to Violet was selfless love.

In Sydney's second book, *War-Time Silhouettes*, two of the stories were based on his relationship with his uncle, Sir Ernest Schiff, and one on a nephew of Violet's great-uncle, the composer Charles Salaman. But the five others, although probably not pure invention, have no obvious family connections. The stories on the whole are slight, but entertaining, and stylistically they are a bit closer than *Concessions* to the autobiographical volumes that make up *A True Story*.

Richard Kurt was his third book. Soon after its publication Eliot wrote to tell Sydney that he had "read [it] with sustained interest" and that it was "a book which seemed to me a very accurate study of a *monde* which is almost unknown to me . . . there was no moment of boredom." His only criticism was that "the canvas was more crowded with events and people than was essential to the effects." The letter ends with the Eliots' plans to visit the Schiffs in Eastbourne on the weekend. Nine days later, Eliot wrote again and by then he had received at least a draft of *Elinor Colhouse*. He said he had not begun reading it yet, but that he wanted to see "at what point if any, it joins the curve of development of *Richard Kurt*. I see in R.K. a process of crystallization in the latter part of the book which interests me and which I think may in future lead you further away from or *beyond* your theory of the novel than you may think." Just what Sydney's "theory of the novel" was regrettably is unrecorded. But by then Sydney and Violet had developed a profound regard for the radically innovative work of the still little-known Proust, and they had begun to correspond with him. It would not be unreasonable to think therefore that Sydney was pursuing some sort of Proustian design.

Between 1916 and Proust's death in 1922 the great French novelist was at the center of their universe. *Swann's Way* was published in

Paris in 1913, but few French-language copies crossed the channel. Sydney and Violet were not the first in Britain to read it or to recognize Proust's greatness nor were they the first to proselytize for his novel, but they were spellbound by his mastery, and proselytize they did.

They admired other writers, but Proust was their idol. He also eventually became something resembling a friend, which if it were anyone but Proust would be a circuitous way of putting it. But in principle Proust didn't believe in friendship. Samuel Beckett wrote that according to Proust, "Friendship is a social expedient, like upholstery or the distribution of garbage buckets. It has no spiritual significance. For the artist, who does not deal in surfaces, the rejection of friendship is not only reasonable, but a necessity." So Proust, although he did have a few real friends such as Reynaldo Hahn and Paul Morand despite his principles, managed these relationships carefully, especially in the last years of his life. He saw less and less of those he knew and certainly was not interested in getting to know anyone new. Mostly he was afraid they would slow his work, which he felt he could not afford to have happen because he expected to die young—an expectation that was realized—and the novel he had conceived was so vast and ambitious that any delay would mean leaving it unfinished.

But inexplicably Sydney and Violet seem to have been treated as exceptions. Although at first he did not want to meet them at all, and they met in person only a few times, a strong case can be made that with the exception of Morand and Hahn, Proust's brother Robert, Céleste Albaret, his extraordinarily devoted housekeeper, and possibly Prince Antoine Bibesco, toward the end of his life Sydney and Violet were closer to him than anyone else. During his last year Proust worked steadily and rarely left his room, except for occasional midnight excursions to the Ritz for dinner alone. He spent most of his time in bed under blankets and furs writing. He consumed only croissants and coffee and the ice-cold beer

Céleste's taxi-driver husband, Odilon, collected from the Ritz at any hour Proust wanted it. Yet he made the effort to see the Schiffs on their few brief visits to Paris and he wrote to them frequently. And while the Schiff-Proust letters, all twenty-five of them written between 1919 and the year he died, 1922, are not totally transparent, there is an unmistakable intimacy in many of them suggesting if not friendship as it is generally understood, then something very much like it.

Proust was a person of interest for the Bayswater modernists with whom the Schiffs were closest, but none shared their adoration of him. He had his admirers, but the more macho and anti-Semitic members of the club such as Lewis and Pound derided him as a rich, effeminate little half Jew of no literary importance. Eliot too was unimpressed by Proust. He wrote to Pound in 1923 that he was publishing a short essay by Proust in the *Criterion*, but that Proust was "not to my taste, merely a necessary sensation," and that he would publish nothing else by him. And for the most part the other literary magazines Eliot and his friends published in such as the *Athenaeum*, the *Little Review*, and the *Egoist*, of which Eliot was assistant editor, ignored Proust's work. This mattered, although less financially to the relatively well-off Proust than most of the others, because these literary journals, although usually underfunded and short-lived, kept their work and names in circulation. Both poets and fiction writers, whose long works the journals excerpted, in most cases depended on them for both income and recognition. Their novels were often privately published or published by small literary houses in editions of fewer than a thousand copies. Poetry collections were generally issued in even smaller editions. And the situation was no better in France. *Swann's Way* would have languished unpublished if Proust hadn't paid for it himself. Sydney's books were all commercially published, but few copies were printed and fewer were sold, which might have affected his ego but had no effect on his lifestyle.

While he was hardly a literary star, by early in 1917 Sydney had published two books and was nearing the completion of a third. He also had an unpunched ticket into the arena of literary journalism— discretionary income. His interest had been aroused and he would soon use his access. The challenge was to find or create the right vehicle, which, whether he knew it or not, was in the process of being born. It was conceived by Frank Rutter and Herbert Read, both art critics. Read was also a poet and literary critic. In accord with the professional background of its four coeditors—Rutter and Read, and two painters, Charles Ginner and Harold Gilman—the magazine was designed to give more emphasis to art than the typical literary journal. They called it *Art and Letters: An Illustrated Quarterly* and the first issue was published in July 1917. It lasted exactly a year in its original incarnation, suspending publication after the fourth issue in June 1918 because of increased costs and the war-related duties of three of the editors.

Sometime between the last issue and the armistice that ended World War I on November 11, 1918, in an effort to restart *Art and Letters*, Read met with the Sitwell brothers, Osbert and Sacheverell, to discuss the prospects of their investing in the magazine. The deal went through, but the details are fuzzy. What is known is that Osbert Sitwell became a part owner, that he and Read served as the magazine's literary editors, and that Sydney, anonymously, became the magazine's most powerful financial backer, a status that apparently gave him a significant amount of editorial control. It is less clear how heavy a hand he exerted on the content of the magazine, but many of the contributors already were or would become friends of the Schiffs. The first issue of the revamped magazine, now called simply *Art and Letters*, included poetry by Edith Sitwell, Siegfried Sassoon, Ford Madox Ford, and Aldous Huxley and prose by Wyndham Lewis, Read, and Rutter. There were drawings by Picasso, Lewis, and Gaudier-Brzeska. Later issues included work by Eliot, Pound, Katherine Mansfield, Wilfred Owen, Isaac Rosen-

berg, Ronald Firbank, and Stephen Hudson. Among the other artists whose work appeared were Matisse, Modigliani, and Severini.
The magazine also published drawings by numerous British artists
including the Nash brothers, John and Paul, William Roberts, and
Jacob Epstein, all of whom were friends or acquaintances of Sydney
and Violet and whose work they collected.

The summer issue in 1919 was notable for the publication of
"Burbank with a Baedecker, Bleistein with a Cigar," one of Eliot's
most blatantly anti-Semitic poems. Although Sydney and Violet never mentioned it in their letters, anti-Semitism inevitably
touched their lives, given the temper of the times, the London intellectual milieu they inhabited, and their tenuous but not irrelevant
Jewish identity. Sydney, of course, was not Jewish by birth because
his mother wasn't Jewish. And he was Christian by upbringing
and belief. But he had two problems—a Jewish name and a Jewish father. Violet was brought up Jewish but was nonpracticing
and had a non-Jewish name. As far as most of the Bayswater and
Bloomsbury modernists were concerned, though, they were both
essentially Jewish, which was not a social asset. Pound was an out-
spoken anti-Semite, as was Lewis, despite his occasional denials.
His halfhearted effort to right matters in a nominally pro-Semitic
book with a title only he or Goebbels could have dreamed up—
The Jews: Are They Human?—was laughable. Eliot's anti-Semitism,
however, which also cannot be denied, was more complicated and
less frequently expressed, and some of his rationalizations for it in
later years seemed sincere. Nonetheless, despite the interesting if
convoluted arguments made by thoughtful critics such as Ronald
Suchard, it is hard to read poems like "Burbank with a Baedecker,
Bleistein with a Cigar" and "Gerontion" without concluding that
no one but an anti-Semite could have come up with such virulent
characterizations of Jews.

As it happens, during Sydney's tenure at *Art and Letters* Eliot sent
him these two poems, both of which have figured prominently in
the critical reassessment in recent years of Eliot's attitude toward

Jews. In "Burbank with a Baedecker," Eliot characterizes Bleistein as "Chicago Semite Viennese," staring from "the protozoic slime." And Eliot, as we know, had asked Sydney for his critical comments on "Gerontion." In a separate letter to Violet referring to "Gerontion," he asked the Schiffs not to show it to anyone else. Both poems contain language that would be considered prima facie evidence of anti-Semitism today, but of course they were not written in this relatively enlightened age. Stephen Spender opined that in 1918 or 1919 using a Jew to symbolize capitalist-industrialist exploitation, as Eliot did in "Baedecker," hardly represented bigotry. I don't know whether Spender intended this as a justification or an excuse for the use of anti-Semitic imagery. But I have no doubt that many of the most refined, best-educated people back then would not have been troubled by the selection of a Jew to represent the entire class of oppressors of working men and women. This is probably why Eliot felt comfortable sending the poems to the Schiffs. He was eager for Sydney to publish "Baedecker," a poem he considered one of his best at the time. And publish it Sydney did without the slightest suggestion that he or Violet found it offensive.

In Eliot's letter expressing his appreciation for Sydney's comments on "Gerontion" he added that he would be "glad always to hear anything further you may have to say about it." If Sydney or Violet had expressed an objection to anything in the poem on grounds of anti-Semitism, Eliot surely would not have let it pass without comment. It seems likely therefore that Sydney and Violet read the following passage without registering a complaint:

> *My house is a decayed house,*
> *And the jew squats on the window sill, the owner,*
> *Spawned in some estaminet of Antwerp,*
> *Blistered in Brussels, patched and peeled in London.*

Gradations of anti-Semitism such as those exhibited by Lewis, Pound, and Eliot were commonplace among the modernist aristocracy in the pre–World War II years. But it was also true of Eliot and Lewis—literally—that some of their best friends were Jewish, and there is no reason to think they did not include Sydney and Violet. The Schiffs never did become friends with Pound, but there is no evidence one way or the other whether their Jewishness had anything to do with it. A decade or so later they were the subjects of a brutal satire by Lewis called *The Apes of God* that included anti-Semitic references, but nastiness, even viciousness, was not unusual in modernist satire and nothing was sacred. Others who were not Jewish were just as savagely skewered in the same book.

In March 1920 Eliot wrote to Sydney at the Schiffs' house in Roquebrune near Monte Carlo promising to send him a short prose piece for the next issue of *Art and Letters* and possibly a short poem. This was probably in response to Sydney's complaint to Eliot a week earlier about how difficult it was to find good material. Eliot seemed of the same mind. "Certainly no new material of any merit has come into my sight lately," he said. Eliot also encouraged Sydney to shed his preoccupations and work on his novel for six months without worrying too much about the magazine or anything else. Then, perhaps to suggest that Sydney not bother their mutual friend for a contribution to *Art and Letters*, he wrote, "Lewis of course ought to devote himself to painting for some time to come. His drawings . . . give me a conviction of permanence that even his best writing does not." He went on to say that Sydney's comparison of Lewis's work with that of the great fifteenth-century Italian painter Andrea Mantegna interested him because he felt the same way. The remark was probably stimulated by Eliot's recent visit to Lewis's exhibition at the Adelphi Gallery in London, which came about at least partly as the result of a suggestion by Sydney. Rutter, who ran the gallery, was by then coeditor of *Art and Letters* with Osbert Sitwell.

Six issues of the magazine appeared during Sydney's tenure, making ten in all, not bad by the standard of the time. But *Art and*

Letters should not be judged solely, or even principally, perhaps, by its relatively long life and distinguished roster of writers and artists. Under Sydney's editorial control it became the model for the most important journal of them all, Eliot's *Criterion*. Herbert Read called the *Criterion* the "sequel" to *Art and Letters*'s "forgotten experiment." "Art and Letters," Read wrote, "in its two years' existence had precipitated the first crystals of a new literary substance, and it was out of this substance, intensified, to some extent purified, and amalgamated with new ingredients, that the new review was moulded." But since Sydney regularly took Eliot's advice in shaping the second coming of *Art and Letters* it is hard to know to what extent Eliot drew on Sydney's ideas as opposed to his own while conceptualizing the *Criterion*.

Eliot's explanatory note in the first issue of the magazine said in part: "The object is not to create more experts, more professors, more artists, but a type of man or woman for whom their efforts will be valuable and by whom they may be judged. . . . A cultured aristocracy cannot indeed create genius, but it can provide genius with an immediate audience, it can keep the national intelligence vigorous and it can check what is crude, tedious and impudent." In other words, the *Criterion* was designed to mold new readers for the works of Eliot, Pound, Lewis, and their friends, including Sydney, and keep everyone else—the "crude, tedious and impudent"—at bay. There are no guarantees, but this statement of purpose has the clarion ring of Eliot's thought and style. Indeed, Eliot might well deserve the bulk of the credit for the design and conception of the *Criterion*, but who knows whether there would have been a *Criterion* had Sydney and Violet not introduced Eliot to Lady Rothermere.

CHAPTER 5

A VOLATILE RELATIONSHIP

~∴ ᎾᏳ ∴~

*D*espite the occasional lengthy hiatus in Sydney and Violet's relationships with Eliot and Lewis, usually resulting from Lewis's financial problems and Vivienne's poor health, by 1922 they were among the Schiffs' closest friends. Their social, professional, and, in Lewis's case, financial lives were entwined with the Schiffs. They were seeing each other frequently and exchanging letters on an almost weekly basis. Sydney and Violet would tell Lewis about visiting Picasso in Paris, and he would tell them James Joyce thought that he, Lewis, was the only prose writer in England worthy of notice.

The Schiffs knew Joyce by then. Their relationship was more casual than the ones they had with Eliot and Lewis, but they saw him socially, promoted his work, and introduced him to friends such as Katherine Mansfield and her husband, John Middleton Murry. Murry, who at different times edited two highly regarded modernist journals, the *Adelphi* and the *Athenaeum*, was a desirable contact for the always impecunious Irish novelist. Lewis, who knew Joyce well, responded to Violet's account of the Schiffs' first meeting with him by noting approvingly that Sydney had recognized

Joyce's urbanity and his strong sense of family. He added, though, that he hoped Sydney had also noticed Joyce's condescension. Then the blissfully unself-aware Lewis condescendingly character-ized Joyce as "a pleasing delightful fellow, with all his schoolboy egotism and Irish nonsense."

As for Mansfield, Lewis held her in contempt and eventually came between her and the Schiffs. Her relatively brief and often volatile relationship with Sydney and Violet began on April 1, 1920, when the Schiffs were staying at the Villa Violet, their house in Roquebrune. Mansfield wrote asking if she might call on them or whether they would like to visit her in Menton for tea and to talk about *Art and Letters*. She wrote at the suggestion of the publisher Grant Richards, but she didn't really need an introduction because she had already had professional dealings with Sydney.

It appears, however, that they were unpleasant. Virginia Woolf, who admired Mansfield's work and liked her, wrote in her diary that Katherine "told me a long and to me rather distasteful story about her dealings with a man called Schiff." Sydney wanted Mans-field to write something for *Art and Letters*, but when he offered advice about what she should write she reacted huffily. Sydney eventually published her poignant and personal short story "The Man Without a Temperament" in the spring 1920 issue. It recounts how a wife's illness shapes her husband's feelings as his thoughts fluctuate between the happiness they experienced together before she became sick and the hostility-engendering misery of their cur-rent lives. Mansfield was writing from experience. She suffered from tuberculosis and died at thirty-four.

In any event, Sydney promptly and personally delivered a posi-tive response to Mansfield's request and several days later took a horse-drawn carriage to Menton to pick her up. He was greeted by a young woman with dark eyes, a penetrating gaze, short dark hair with bangs, and an air of cultivated plainness. Mansfield was in her early thirties at the time and Sydney was in his mid-fifties.

She was pleased he had come in a carriage rather than a car, and he was thoroughly entranced by her. Her first impression of him, however, was less positive. She had written caustically across the bottom of his hand-delivered response: "Marie told me un m'sieu tres grand was waiting for an answer & I went into the salon to discover the most soigné creature in the world—in the false grey flannels—waiting for me. . . . He seemed *horrified* by me & I don't know what he had expected. He kept saying 'sit down, I *implore* you. Pray forgive me imagining you could take a tram.' I wish people didn't always expect me to be on the point of death. It's horrid." But just before being picked up by Sydney on April 7 she wrote to Murry much more enthusiastically, "I'm off to lunch at Roquebrune with the Sydney Schiffs and to see their Gauguins and their Picassos."

Later, as Stephen Hudson, Sydney wrote a surprisingly over-the-top sketch for the *Cornhill* magazine called "First Meetings with Katherine Mansfield." The florid romance-novel prose quoted here is typical of the sketch but bears little resemblance to his normally cool, understated style:

"The door opened softly and Katherine Mansfield, young and seductive, came towards me holding out her hand. . . . She held the index and second fingers, long, delicate and tapering, of one hand palm outwards between her face and mine. The sensitive gesture silenced me; I watched the fingers close slowly and her hand fell softly to her lap. . . . Her features were mobile; she arrested their movement and sat very still, gravely considering me. . . . As I helped her to her feet, my hand under her bare fore-arm . . . I could detect no wastage there nor in her frame, slight as it was; her throat and breast outlined under her silk bodice were full and firm."

Mansfield and the Schiffs got on so well that first afternoon that they offered her the use of an apartment they owned in Roquebrune. There was, however, one awkward exchange between Sydney and Katherine resulting from the fact that she had no idea Syd-

ney Schiff was Stephen Hudson. On assignment from Murry, who
was editor of the *Athenaeum* at the time, she had reviewed *Richard
Kurt* five months earlier. She told Sydney she had been reading a
book called *Richard Kurt* by Stephen Hudson and asked him if he
had heard of it. Then, without waiting for an answer, she said the
book had really irritated her. "I'm not sure it's altogether a bad
novel," she continued. "The author knows the people he writes
about. Jack considers it worthless as literature because it's autobiographical. . . . I can't find a category for it. It is written as though
one were overhearing conversation in a train or at an hotel. People
come and go for no special reason. There are two characters that
are alive. I think its discursiveness irritated me and I don't see what
the writer is driving at."

Sydney, unperturbed, said, "Perhaps he's driving at nothing, just
delivering himself of experience," which seemed to confuse Mansfield. "What made you say that?" she asked. "Do you feel that yourself? I mean do you feel that you want to be delivered of something
that oppresses you?" To which Sydney responded, "Yes—I wrote it."

Mansfield was mortified, but Sydney, trying to alleviate her
discomfort, told her that one reason he wrote the book under a
pseudonym was to get honest criticism. The main if not sole reason, however, was to provide at least minimal cover for his family.
He went on to say that for him it had no value as a novel, "It has
only the value of truth." She was deeply embarrassed, though, and
in trying to mitigate the damage she gushed unconvincingly, "It's a
thousand-fold more. It is a work of art. I know it is. I do want you
to believe me." And had she been less effusive and more circum-
spect he might have. While her unsigned review in the *Athenaeum*
was not a rave, it was favorable enough to have pleased all but the
touchiest of writers. She seemed puzzled by the odd construction
and plotless nature of the novel, but she didn't appear to be too
troubled by it and she marveled at how Sydney had conveyed Elinor's "brilliant and horrible little personality" as if through a con-

versation between two people who had known her all their lives. She also said she found Elinor, and Virginia, "amazingly real."

As soon as Mansfield got home she wrote to the Schiffs to tell them that for health reasons she would not be able to live in "that darling little flat" they had offered her and to thank them for a lovely day: "I'm lying here living it over and seeing in my mind's eye your garden and house & hearing the torrent—and—much more important than those things—delighting in the fact of having met you." Then, just four days later, she wrote to Murry, who lived apart from her, an arrangement that seemed to suit them because they were both difficult to live with and it facilitated their serial affairs. "It makes another great joy in my coming back here this winter to know I'll have the Schiffs at Roquebrune," she said. "Do I take violent fancies? . . . I must say at present, I love Violet Schiff. I think you would too. [You] would certainly find her very beautiful, as I do. I want you to see her and to talk to her. She's extremely sympathetic."

And by the latter part of April, Mansfield, who was by then totally enamored of Violet, had revised her initial impression of Sydney. In a letter to Murry on the twenty-second, she listed some people she considered genuine and worthwhile friends. About the Schiffs she said: "Violet Schiff Id [sic] include and Schiff without the smallest hesitation or doubt. I like him as much as I do his wife but in of course an entirely different way. He attracts me *tremendously* and his great kindness, sensitiveness, almost childishness, endear him to me. In fact Id [sic] head my list with those 2 but thats [sic] because I look at people from a different angle to what you do." And finally, in a letter to her husband dated April 24–25, she wrote: "Mr. Schiff is a kind of literary fairy godfather to me. He looks after me so perfectly and so gently and Violet Schiff seemed to me the last time far more beautiful and more fascinating than before. . . . And their house is always for me the house where *lovers* dwell. He loves her perfectly. . . . They are so real and dear and beautiful to me and they understand one's work."

Between the beginning of May and the end of November, how-ever, there appears to have been a gap in their correspondence, at least from Mansfield's side. She also wrote to Murry between September and the end of November that she was "dead off" the Schiffs. She called Sydney "hectic and arrogant," and expressed her irritation with Violet for having had the nerve to touch her hair. She referred to them both as "a trifle grotesque" and called Sydney "overpoweringly deaf—deaf to everything."

By December 1920, however, their epistolary conversations resumed without the least trace of pique. Mansfield's letters undu-lated between the pinnacles of European literature—from Tolstoy, whose work she knew well, and Proust, whom she didn't feel quali-fied to speak about—and the marvels of the mundane: "I have an old servant, a butter and sugar thief who is an artist in her way, a joy. Her feeling for hot plates and what dear Henry James might call the *real right* gravy is supreme. These things are so important. I don't think I could love a person who liked gravylene or browno."

Although Sydney's letters to Mansfield are lost, we know the Schiffs lent her several volumes of Proust. They also introduced her to Joyce and to his work. She was initially repelled by what seemed to her the smuttiness of *Ulysses* and found it impossible to make sense of. She was also unimpressed by its linguistic acro-batics. In an entry in her scrapbook headed "An Unposted Letter," which almost certainly was intended for the Schiffs, she wrote: "I must reply about 'Ulysses'. . . . It took me about a fortnight to wade through, but on the whole I'm dead *against* it. . . . that is certainly not what I want from literature." Sydney and Violet persisted, how-ever, and convinced her to read it again. She never became a com-plete convert, but she did acknowledge its importance. "It shocks me," she wrote to Sydney, "to come upon words, expressions and so on that I'd shrink from in life. But now it seems to me that seeking after Truth is so by far and away the most important thing that one must conquer all minor aversions." Despite Mansfield's reservations and difficulties in decoding the book, Joyce told Violet he thought she understood it better than her renowned-critic husband.

Nevertheless, Mansfield never really got over her queasiness with respect to Joyce's work. In a letter to Sydney she wrote:

> About Joyce and my endeavor to be doubly fair to him
> because I have been perhaps unfair and captious. Oh, I
> can't get over a great deal. I can't get over the feeling of wet
> linoleum and unemptied pails and far worse horrors in the
> house of his mind—He's so terribly *unfein*; that's what it
> amounts to. There is a tremendously strong impulse in me
> to beg him not to shock me! Well, it's not very rare. I've had
> it before with men and women many times in my life. One
> can stand much, but that kind of shock which is the result
> of vulgarity and commonness one is frightened of receiving.
> It is as though one's mind goes on quivering afterwards. . . .
> It's just exactly the reverse of the exquisite rapture one feels in
> for instance that passage which ends a chapter where Proust
> describes "the flowing apple trees in the spring rain."

Whatever Sydney and Violet made of Mansfield's distaste for the vulgar, despite their own well-bred refinement and delicate sensibilities, there is nothing to suggest that either of them was ever repulsed by Joyce's sexual or scatological references.

In December 1921, this time addressing Sydney as Stephen Hudson and overflowing with enthusiasm, she wrote: "I read your *Elinor Colhouse* more than twice, and I shall read it again. I do congratulate you sincerely from my heart. It's amazingly good! So good one simply cannot imagine it better. One pushes into deep water easily, beautifully, from the first sentence, and there's that feeling—so rare—of ease, of safety, of wishing only to be borne along wherever the author chooses to take one. . . . Why aren't you here—that we might talk it over and over." Perhaps to make up for having been denied the pleasure of praising him in person, she pressed on ful-somely: "It's your presentation of Richard which I admire so tre-mendously. I don't mean only his boyish charm—though Heaven knows that is potent enough—or even his naturalness—which at times takes my breath away. But it's Richard's innocence of the wiles and arts of Life! It's the sight of him, in the midst of all that scheming and plotting and his horror, finally, that this should hap-pen to him. . . . Of course all the detail, so fastidious, so satisfying, is beyond praise. Elinor *lives.* I see her, recognize those fingers with the long pointed brilliant nails, look into that little brain. Yes, I honor you for it. It's an achievement. I rejoice in your success."

Mansfield was a woman who when she chose could be as tart-tongued, cruel, and duplicitous as Bloomsbury's best, which makes one wonder what she said or might have said to Murry about *Elinor Colhouse.* But then like many of her modernist peers she was also mercurial. Her critical judgment might have reflected what she was feeling about Sydney that particular day, or perhaps for a change her bunions weren't bothering her. The trick would be to know what she would have made of the book if she hadn't known who had written it.

In the end I don't know if there's any way to tell whether Mans-field was more hypocritical or less stable than the average modern-ist or whether modernists as a class were more hypocritical and less stable than their intellectual forebears or followers. It's a good bet, though, that they were not less so. And on the evidence avail-able, about modernists in general and Mansfield in particular, it is better than an even bet that her assessment of *Elinor Colhouse* was either a gross exaggeration or a flat-out lie. I think this is so even after discounting her extraordinary gift for hyperbole. *Amazingly good! One simply cannot imagine it better. Beyond praise. Takes my breath away.*

Mansfield takes my breath away. Sydney Schiff, while a talented man, was not the second coming of Cervantes.

The relationship between Mansfield and the Schiffs was both friendly and stable during the first half of 1922, but resulting from a coalescence of her fragility and their poor judgment that would soon change. Sometime in September Sydney and Violet introduced Katherine to Wyndham Lewis, with whom they were in unusually close contact at the time because Sydney had commissioned him to paint Violet's portrait, a project that would prove frustrating to all of them. The Schiffs should have known better. The meeting took place at 18 Cambridge Square just weeks before Mansfield traveled to the Institute for the Harmonious Development of Man at Fontainebleau outside Paris. The institute was run by George Ivanovich Gurdjieff, a Russian-Greek-Armenian mystic who taught that every person was born without a soul and had to develop one by following teachings like his, or he or she would "die like a dog." She believed Gurdjieff's institute was her last best hope for a cure. At the time, in a sign of her desperation, she also was immersed in a now-long-forgotten book of spiritual nonsense called *Cosmic Anatomy*, which she apparently thought might help her in some way.

Although they had not met until then, Mansfield and Lewis knew a fair amount about one another's work. His opinion of her stories was dismissive, and although she admired his draftsmanship and fiction, she was put off by his general negativity and, by her lights, his contempt for any conception of a human soul. Although Lewis's respected biographer Jeffrey Meyers wrote that "Lewis could not have known very much about her desperate condition," it is a bit hard to imagine that he wouldn't have. Her illness was widely known in the gossipy circles they all inhabited, and it seems unlikely that Sydney and Violet, knowing Lewis and Mansfield as they did, would not have prepared him for the meeting. And, as dense as he was about certain things, it is hard to believe that he would not have noticed the debilitated state of a woman on the verge of dying from tuberculosis.

Lewis's callous behavior toward her that day, whatever he knew or didn't know, was both characteristic of him and inexcusable. He went on at length about the triviality of her stories and mocked Gurdjieff. He called her putative savior a "Levantine psychic shark." I don't know what expectations Mansfield had of Lewis, but just as it is hard to believe he knew very little about her condition it seems unlikely that she was unaware of his reputation for crudeness and cruelty. Of course expecting cruelty does not necessarily palliate it. Lewis made a feeble attempt to excuse his behavior, but to the Schiffs, not to Mansfield, who was furious at the Schiffs for not defending her.

After the lunch at the Schiffs', Lewis received a note from Mansfield. There is no indication he responded, but he did write to Violet: "I don't see how, short of possessing such powers of divination as [Gurdjieff's] Institute would provide you with, you could have foreseen the rather comic denouement of my meeting with the famous New Zealand mag. short story writer, in the grip of the Levantine psychic shark. I am rather glad not to be troubled with her, though I hope she won't be too venomous." In another letter to Sydney he accused Mansfield of picking a quarrel with him and making a fuss "both with you and Violet and me, about nothing in particular." He then went on to malevolently disparage her work: "she is nothing but a writer of 2 books of short stories, as she puts it, which have been advertised and pushed cynically out of proportion to their merit. I find them, as I have always said, vulgar, dull, and unpleasant." Finally, in a stingy attempt at an apology, he gave with one hand and took away with the other: "I'm afraid I must have been too uncouth," he wrote, "or perhaps, who knows, too sincere."

Sydney and Violet had sat silently through Lewis's savage verbal assault on their sick friend and now he was shifting the blame to her. Apparently they tried to apologize to Mansfield, but it was too little too late and she wasn't having it. The evidence that the Schiffs failed to defend Mansfield lacks specificity but, given the timing, seems persuasive. In a cryptic diary entry on September 17, 1922, she wrote: "Lunch with Sydney and Violet. Odious." She also wrote to Murry on September 22 that "Schiff continues his epistolatory bombardment. I refuse to reply anymore. He is a silly old man." There were no more letters from her to the Schiffs, but many years later Murry confirmed that she was devastated by Lewis's behavior and Sydney and Violet's failure to stand up for her. He wrote to Violet that after the lunch Mansfield was "a naked nerve quivering upon the air." He said Lewis had outraged her and she felt Sydney and Violet didn't protect her as she thought they should have. According to Murry, she "quivered for days afterwards." Three and a half months later Mansfield was dead. It wasn't Lewis's fault, as much as his callousness and monumental lack of self-awareness would make one want to think it was, but it probably wasn't Gurdjieff's either, as has frequently been alleged.

CHAPTER 6

ANNUS MIRABILIS

The Schiffs' relationships with Mansfield, Eliot, Lewis, and Joyce were genuine even if at times contentious, but for quality and intensity, none of them rivaled the almost pathological attachment and affection they shared with Marcel Proust. This was true despite the fact that their intimacy was achieved almost entirely through letters. They met in person at most four or five times over three and a half years. The amount of time they spent in each other's company is best measured in hours. And most of those hours together took place after midnight during one brief period just months before Proust's death. They were among the very few *friends* the eccentric French novelist was willing to see during the last year of his life.

The year 1922 would have been notable in the history of literature if only for Proust's death and the completion of his novel. But 1922 was much more than notable, it was the annus mirabilis of modernism, the year of the century in letters. And three of Sydney and Violet's friends—Eliot, Proust, and Joyce—were the writers who made it so. Each published or completed a work many critics still consider one of the three greatest literary achievements of the twentieth century. Eliot's *The Waste Land* appeared in the first issue of the *Criterion*, which turned out to be the most important and longest-lasting of all the modernist literary magazines, in February 1922. Sylvia Beach published one thousand copies of Joyce's *Ulysses* the same month. And Proust finished correcting the last pages of *In Search of Lost Time* three days before he died in November. All this is of interest here mainly because, Zelig-like, Sydney and Violet kept popping up.

⤳⸳⤳

Their friend T. S. Eliot was not poor like Wyndham Lewis. He earned just enough at Lloyd's Bank evaluating World War I debt obligations to cover his modest living expenses. But he spent so much time and energy on bank business and slight literary journalism to supplement his income that he had little left of either for poetry or criticism. He was so physically and mentally exhausted toward the end of 1921 that he took three months off to recuperate, which led some of his friends to worry about his health, state of mind, and dwindling poetic output. The perpetually self-absorbed Lewis, on the other hand, wrote to the Schiffs that he hadn't seen Eliot for a long time and, oblivious to his friend's physical and mental state, blamed Eliot's absence on "his Bloomsbury cultural groove, combined with the wife obsession."

The ever big-hearted Ezra Pound, however, was genuinely concerned and acted reflexively and to some extent recklessly. Without telling Eliot he began to solicit ten-pound annual subscriptions from his friends to provide enough of an income to allow him to leave the bank. The scheme, which Pound called Bel Esprit, was not unusual at the time. Lewis often lived on similar subscriptions. But it was perfectly designed to embarrass Eliot, who, in line with the Protestant Ethic, was brought up to be self-sufficient, not a charity case. At first it attracted few subscribers, but Pound was persistent.

Meanwhile, convinced Eliot was the best poet of his generation,

Sydney and Violet, in a generous gesture more suited to Eliot's temperament, had introduced him to Lady Rothermere. She was the wealthy wife of the English press baron Harold Harmsworth, Viscount Rothermere, and had an idea for a modest project of her own, a London-based literary journal. The timing could not have been better. Eliot had been pondering how he might get financial support for a successor to *Art and Letters*, a journal in which he had published two important poems and that he admired, especially during Sydney's tenure as what today might be called its chief financial and creative officer. Eliot needed the money, but he also craved editorial control of a literary magazine and Lady Rothermere needed an editor of Eliot's stature. But despite the apparent good fit and Sydney and Violet's best intentions it was not a marriage made in heaven. They had different concepts of what the magazine should be like, and notwithstanding Eliot's literary credentials the lady with the money left no doubt about who would have the last word.

Eliot, whose needs took precedence over his cravings, was determined to make it work, but this turned out to be a lot harder than he expected. He and Lady R., as Eliot and his friends called her among themselves, quickly agreed it would be a quarterly, but about the rest there was little agreement, only long, tedious negotiations Eliot found debilitating. During this period he wrote to Sydney in frustration, if not utter despair, that he was "about ready to chuck literature altogether and retire." And editorial disagreements with Lady Rothermere were not the only problem. Under the bank's rules Eliot could not simultaneously hold another paying job. His income for editing the journal would be about the same as what he was earning at the bank, but his bank salary was relatively secure and the average life of a new literary quarterly was about four issues. This was a risk he could not afford to take, which brings us back to Bel Esprit, whose history is eternally entwined with the birth of the *Criterion*.

Eliot wrote to Pound, who was living in Paris, to tell him about his discussions with Lady Rothermere and offer him an opportunity to make regular contributions to the new journal. But Pound refused to have anything to do with it and told Eliot that England didn't deserve a good review. He then added rather obscurely, "Of course if Lady R. is willing to cooperate with me in a larger scheme, which wd. mean getting you out of your bank and allowing you to give up your whole time to writing, I might reconsider . . . I cant [sic] see that editing a quarterly will give you any more leisure to write poetry." Pound's response could have been motivated by jealousy or self-interest. Pound, like Eliot, was eager to edit his own journal and if Eliot didn't take the job it just might be offered to old Ez.

Pound enclosed in his letter to Eliot the template for Bel Esprit, which he was getting ready to send to potential donors. He might have hoped that an endowment would entice Eliot to give up both the bank and the journal. The template said in part that "the greatest waste in ang-sax letters at the moment is the waste of Eliot's talent. . . . He must have *complete* liberty" to devote his entire time to literature, which meant his own writing. It sought thirty contributors of ten pounds a year to endow Eliot for life. Pound, Richard Aldington, and the novelist May Sinclair were the first subscribers. Other subscribers were not so easily found, although twenty-two eventually signed up. Eliot wrote to Aldington that Pound wanted everybody in England, including the Schiffs, to deal with him about subscriptions.

Eliot was uncomfortable with the idea from the outset but did not immediately reject it. In time, although he remained conflicted, his desire for more freedom to pursue his writing free of economic concerns eroded his principles about accepting charity. He did, however, want to make sure that if he accepted the endowment it would provide a sufficient and secure income. He wrote to Pound in mid-July that a vague guarantee of three hundred pounds a year would hardly suffice for him to risk leaving the bank. Two weeks later he wrote to Sydney that "those who are accustomed to small or precarious incomes [Pound, for example] cannot take my circumstances into account and realize why I should need more money or more security."

At the time Eliot did not specify why he would need more, but the main reason was Vivienne's worsening health, for which he felt some responsibility. Furthermore, Eliot valued privacy and was distressed by the spotlight the ongoing discussions about Bel Esprit were putting on his personal circumstances. And when he accidentally came across one of the circulars soliciting funds for Bel Esprit it clearly upset him, mainly because it strongly suggested that Lloyd's Bank interfered with literature. "If it is stated so positively that Lloyd's Bank interferes with literature," Eliot wrote to Pound, "Lloyd's Bank would have a perfect right to infer that literature interfered with Lloyd's Bank." He wrote that he needed time to decide what to do and that if there was any more publicity for Bel Esprit he would publicly repudiate it. There was and he did. In November the *Liverpool Post* published an article on the scheme, which embarrassed Eliot terribly. He wrote to the paper saying he disapproved of it and had not accepted it.

While Eliot was still engulfed in controversy with Pound about Bel Esprit and Lady Rothermere about the *Criterion*, Pound, in his predictably inept fashion, tried to get Eliot to ask his titled angel to contribute to the endowment fund. Eliot, although overworked and under pressure, refused. He was focused above all on putting together volume one, number one, the reception of which, he knew, could determine the success or failure of the entire enterprise. Sydney had contributed a short story called *The Thief*, which was scheduled to appear in the first issue. But for reasons most likely related to Eliot's desire to achieve maximum impact, at the last minute it was held for the second. It was one of several contributions he and Violet would make to the magazine over the years. They also helped Eliot solicit original work from others. But their efforts at Eliot's request to get a contribution from Proust for the first issue, to be translated by Sydney, were unsuccessful.

Despite the long labor and intense birth pangs, the *Criterion* was destined for a life Eliot would not have dared to imagine—seventeen years, longevity unheard of for a little modernist quarterly. Its most distinguished contributors populate the Who's Who of modernism. They include William Butler Yeats, Luigi Pirandello, Ezra Pound, E. M. Forster, Virginia Woolf, Marcel Proust, W. H. Auden, Paul Valéry, Jean Cocteau, Aldous Huxley, Hermann Hesse, and Hart Crane. At the time Stephen Hudson did not seem particularly out of place in their company. Apart from his novels he published short stories, essays, and translations from German and French in the leading journals of the day. But in the end he was just one of a multitude of forgotten contributors to the *Criterion* who were well-regarded in their time.

The first *Criterion*, in an edition of six hundred copies, appeared October 15, 1922, flush with articles and stories by distinguished contributors. But more than anything else it is remembered because it was the vehicle for publication of *The Waste Land*, the signature poem of modernism. Eliot most likely began *The Waste Land* early in 1921. He continued working on it during his convalescent leave from the bank in Margate on the southeastern English coast and finished it in Lausanne, Switzerland, where he had gone for treatment by a renowned Swiss physician named Roger Vittoz who had developed a treatment based on mental exercises that was designed to cure anxiety. When Eliot returned to London, however, he found that his poem was not finished. What remained was the fairly drastic cutting and editing done in collaboration with Pound and with a little help from Vivienne that resulted in the first published version.

Even before *The Waste Land* appeared in the *Criterion*, however, Eliot had sold the rights in book format to the American publisher Horace Liveright. The offer was made at a dinner in Paris arranged by Pound that included Joyce and, of course, Eliot. Imagine Pound, Eliot, and Joyce sitting around the same table—at the time it could easily have constituted "the most extraordinary concentration of talent," as Jack Kennedy famously said about a White House dinner for Nobel Prize winners, since "Thomas Jefferson dined alone." But if it was, the distinction was short-lived. Ten months later an even more stunning concentration of genius coalesced around several tables in a Paris hotel at Sydney and Violet's invitation.

In the meantime, the Schiffs followed the progress of *The Waste Land* from Cambridge Square, Eastbourne, and their house at Roquebrune near Monte Carlo through correspondence with Wyndham Lewis and Eliot himself. Sydney, who was finishing up *Elinor Colhouse* with Violet's help, was the first to write in praise of it. Vivienne was so moved by his letter, which the Eliots received the day after the poem appeared, that she wrote back immediately to express her gratitude for Sydney's understanding and appreciation of the work, which undoubtedly also reflected Violet's critical sensibility. Eliot wrote the same day, saying, "You could not have used words which would have given me more pleasure or have so persuaded me that the poem may possibly communicate something of what it intends. But I cannot expect to find many critics so sympathetic." About this, of course, Eliot was wrong.

The Schiffs also monitored the evolution of the *Criterion* from the perspective of matchmakers with an interest in seeing their undertaking flourish. There was no guarantee that the magazine would land with a bang, not a whimper, indeed the odds were heavily against it, especially given the friction between Eliot and Lady R. But it did. Although like almost all literary magazines it never made money, measured by the standards of the day—quality and survival—the journal was a great success. It was talked about, even respected, in the right circles. And its owners—Lady Rothermere for the first four years and then the book publisher Faber & Gwyer, which in 1929 became Faber & Faber—were willing to accept the losses it consistently incurred.

None of this meant, however, that during the time she owned the *Criterion* Lady Rothermere was content and would always let

Eliot do things his own way. Indeed after the first issue appeared to general acclaim, she wrote three biting letters to her editor complaining about what she viewed as its shortcomings. The letters were written from Gurdjieff's recently opened institute, and the Eliots seemed more troubled about what Lady Rothermere was up to there than her criticisms. Vivienne wrote to Pound that the institute was an "asylum for the insane" and that Lady Rothermere was doing "religious dances naked with Katherine Mansfield," who had gone there in a last-ditch effort to cure her tuberculosis. Vivienne's concern, it seems, was not that Lady Rothermere was doing naked devotional dances, but that she was doing them with Mansfield, whom the Eliots abhorred. In the great tradition of the modernists Eliot satirized her (as Scheherazade) in his only short story, "Eeldrop and Appleplex." He and Vivienne not only disliked Mansfield personally but were contemptuous of her short stories, which were part of the literary canon for decades but now are infrequently read.

The Schiffs had pampered Mansfield and were her favorite friends in 1920 and 1921, except when they weren't, as a result of her frequent mood swings. By the time Lady Rothermere "danced with her" at Gurdjieff's institute, however, her health was declining rapidly. Vivienne worried that Mansfield would turn Lady Rothermere against them and she would fire Eliot from the *Criterion*. To short-circuit any such possibility Vivienne offered to put up half her dowry—five hundred pounds—to try to buy the magazine. Eliot liked the idea and suggested collaborating with Pound, but Ezra thought it was a pipe dream and told Eliot so. He also told him that Mansfield was intelligent and she wasn't a threat to him or the *Criterion*, which really got under Eliot's skin. He responded to Pound that Mansfield was "simply one of the most persistent and thick-skinned toadies and one of the vulgarest women Lady R. has ever met and is also a sentimental crank." There was, however, no obvious evidence that justified the Eliots' concerns. In fact, in a letter to Violet on August 24, 1922, Mansfield had only praise for Eliot and the *Criterion*. "I see Eliot's new magazine is about to appear," she wrote. "It looks very full of rich plums. I think Prufrock by far, by far and away the most interesting and the best modern poem."

Although Mansfield's preoccupations in the last six months of her life were mostly about her health, she hadn't lost interest in literature, nor had she lost the wicked sense of humor so characteristic of the modernists that occasionally still resonates today. In at least one instance a few lines she wrote foreshadowed a politically incorrect but hilarious Mike Nichols and Elaine May routine. She wrote to Lady Ottoline Morrell: "I can't walk yet—absurd as it sounds—only a few puffing paces, a most humiliating and pug-like performance. . . . I have got Fat—Wyndham Lewis I hear is also fat, May Sinclair has waxed enormous, Anne Rice can't be supported by her ankles alone."

Mansfield died January 9, 1923, of a pulmonary hemorrhage while running up a flight of stairs to show Murry how well she was doing. The *Criterion* published a brief tribute in its April 1923 issue, but any doubt about its insincerity can easily be removed by skimming Eliot's letters. For example, on June 10, 1923, he wrote to Richard Aldington about Mansfield that "I think her inflated reputation ought to be dealt with." And on December 21, 1924, he sent a correction to his printers asking them to change a sentence that referred to modern young intellectuals to include a distinction between really modern young intellectuals and those who thought Katherine Mansfield's stories were required reading.

A PORTRAIT OF VIOLET

Despite the Wyndham Lewis episode's destructive effect on the Schiffs' relationship with Mansfield, it did not seem to have any detrimental effect on their relationship with Lewis, which by the

slippery standards of the modernists could fairly be called close
or even intimate. During 1921 and 1922 the Schiffs provided fund-
ing for Lewis's new journal, the *Tyro*, which focused more on art
than literature and lasted only two issues. Sydney published a
short story in the second issue called "Bugs" about a schoolboy
who was caned for asking a laborer if he had bugs in his hair. By
the end of 1922 neither of the episodes that would permanently
sour their friendship had yet occurred. Sydney and Violet continued to respect Lewis as a thinker, writer, painter, and designer.
They praised his books, bought his work, invited him to dinner,
and once asked him to design a room for them whose sole purpose
would be to display the drawings they had bought from him. At
one point Sydney even said Lewis was "the only definitely creative
artist this country possesses." Lewis's opinion of them is more a
matter of conjecture. At times he behaved as if he respected them
intellectually, and at other times he seemed contemptuous and
only interested in their money. He often complained to them about
his poverty, which resulted in poor working and living conditions,
evictions for nonpayment of rent, and escapes from creditors in the
dead of night. They responded with intermittent financial support
in varying amounts, sometimes in the form of gifts or loans and
other times as advances on Violet's portrait.

The agreed price for the portrait was one hundred pounds and
an additional thirty pounds for an oil study to be delivered before
the painting. Lewis handed over the study in March 1922, but
Sydney was not pleased with it. Nonetheless, he advanced Lewis
another twenty pounds on the painting and the work went on. A
few months later Lewis did a pencil sketch of Violet, which Sydney didn't much like either, but he paid him twenty pounds for it.
Lewis took the sketch back a while later and said he would find a
better frame for it. Instead he sold it to a critic named O. R. Drey
in whose house, to Sydney's consternation, he eventually saw it
hanging.

Meanwhile, with some effort Sydney had managed to sufficiently interest the important Paris art dealer Léonce Rosenberg in Lewis's work so that he considered giving him a show. As usual, however, Lewis was difficult and tried to set all sorts of conditions, which in the end scuttled the exhibition. Years later Lewis recounted the episode without mentioning Sydney at all. "That enlightened Parisian," he wrote referring to Rosenberg, "had seen some picture of mine, and had said to me when I was in Paris: 'Lewis, these things of yours are the only things being done in England today which would interest Paris'. . . . I might have set the Seine on fire. I should have been the only Anglo-saxon painter who ever set the Seine on fire."

As was usual with Lewis, he was running out of money so he wrote to Sydney from Paris asking for another thirty-pound advance on the portrait. Sydney sent him a check. He also suggested that Lewis visit Proust and make a drawing of him. Sydney had already written to Proust, who obviously liked the idea because he sent Céleste to find Lewis and bring him back. But Lewis was out. Proust caught cold that evening and explained in a letter to Sydney that his illness would likely last beyond the time Lewis would be in Paris. In any event, Lewis never did get to see Proust, who, in another radiant example of the excess typical of the modernists, wrote a note to Lewis saying, "to be drawn by you would have been my only chance of reaching posterity." With Proust it is sometimes hard to know whether his flattery was sincere, but the irony in this case, intended or not, is unmistakable. Proust's work, of course, is known to—if not read by—every literate person to this day, while Lewis's is forgotten by all but a scattering of devotees.

When Lewis returned to London Sydney sent him another thirty-pound advance on the painting, but this time he included an accounting of his payments. It added up to 130 pounds, the total amount agreed on for the painting and the oil sketch. Four years later Sydney, frustrated beyond the breaking point, asked

Lewis for the still-unfinished portrait, which Lewis finally turned over. "Never again in my life," Sydney wrote to him, "shall I enter into a business relationship with any artist, least of all with you." By then he had given Lewis 712 pounds altogether, a considerable amount at the time.

But no matter how exasperating Lewis was, and few people anytime or anywhere were more exasperating, neither Schiff—but especially Violet—ever completely gave up on him. Their respect for his intellect and creative output never waned and even after putting up with his inconstancy, unreasonable demands, and nasty temper they still seemed to like him and value what they deemed to be his friendship. For his part, he accepted their patronage, treating it as tribute money due him as a consequence of his creative genius. What he actually thought of them, setting aside the noxious prose portraits he drew in *The Apes of God*, remains hard to discern, except that he seemed to like Violet better than Sydney. But given his pathological hatred for the rich, especially those who supported him financially and those he thought had creative pretensions, it would be surprising if his resentment of both Schiffs didn't come close to canceling out any positive feelings he might have had for them.

THE ENIGMA OF WYNDHAM

Although Lewis was widely regarded as an intellectual force by the cream of the modernists, history's verdict on him has not been kind. As a writer he is remembered only by the modernist scholars who struggle to keep his name alive. Try asking anyone but a specialist on the period, even if they have heard of him, to name anything he wrote and you are likely to draw a blank. He is a bit better known today as a painter—his works are owned by the Tate Collection and other museums. But he is generally considered a minor artist. He is said by his friends and admirers to have been a brilliant conversationalist, but alas no record survives to support their assessment.

Nevertheless, no matter how unpleasant he was, and how often he was wrong, there is no question that he was a fascinating, erudite, complicated character who impressed and influenced many of the brightest and most talented artists and intellectuals of his time. For those of us who see much of Lewis's work as seesawing between the obvious and the obscurantist—and frequently badly written—his stature among his contemporaries is hard to comprehend. But it cannot be denied. Yeats likened his satirical wit to that of Swift and there can be no higher praise than that. And it was the conventional wisdom, in Bayswater at least, that his intellect was unparalleled among the modernists.

He was also antidemocratic, anti-Semitic, and a misogynist whose insecurities inflamed his feeling of victimization and fueled his anger toward anyone who was better off than he was. Yet even his outsized sense of entitlement, lack of gratitude, and roiling anger did not always drive away his benefactors. Despite their Jewishness and Violet's gender, each of which was associated with a virulent prejudice of his, Lewis continued to see them and correspond with them. Mostly it was because they supported him financially by buying his work and with loans and gifts. But it was also because he ate well and met interesting people in their house. He also seemed to have liked Violet. He corresponded with her long after he and Sydney had written each other off. In the early twenties, though, the Schiffs very likely had no idea how much he resented them, or even *that* he resented them and stereotyped them. Lewis himself probably had no idea how deep his anger and resentment toward them ran.

One must, of course, beware of the anachronistic flaw. Those were different times and people had different expectations. Lewis's social and political sentiments, which today would be considered retrograde, were relatively widely held and did nothing to taint his reputation among his peers, some of whom, including Eliot, shared his general outlook. In England, continental Europe, and even the United States in the 1920s, especially among the ruling and intellectual classes, anti-Semitism and other varieties of racial prejudice were commonplace. And sympathy for the rising fascist regimes in Italy and Germany was unexceptional, especially in Britain, where it was fed by fear of a rising working class. Even in this environment, though, Lewis was an outlier in the extremity of his views and the unrepressed bitterness and anger with which he expressed them. In 1931 he published a volume titled *Hitler* in praise of the up-and-coming Nazi dictator. He made an unconvincing attempt to take it all back in 1939 with two books, *The Hitler Cult* and the infamously titled *The Jews: Are They Human?* But having given the matter further thought, in his 1950 autobiography *Rude Assignment* he found a way to equate the execution of Nazi war criminals with the mass murder of six million Jews. None of this, however, seemed to compromise his social acceptance, which, in the Schiffs' case—especially Violet's—at times appeared to have bordered on affection.

Lewis was also a hard-core male supremacist. In an age and social set in which women, no matter how intelligent and talented—unless, of course, they were independently wealthy—were still treated first and foremost as sex toys, he was the objectifier-in-chief. He believed women were intellectually inferior and of value principally as receptacles for his sexual relief, although Violet appears to have been an exception in this respect. His long list of liaisons, punctuated by multiple bouts of venereal disease, was Casanova-like. And in the erotic arena, as in all others that interested him, he was fiercely combative and competitive. Examples abound, but in a particularly uneven match for the favors of Nancy Cunard, the shipping heiress, poet, and social activist who also held the record as mistress of modernist men, his brawny, dominating lovemaking easily bested the gentle, halting, and timid efforts of Aldous Huxley. Huxley, however, got even as best he could. In the modernist fashion he caricatured Lewis and Cunard as Casimir Lypiatt and Myra Viveash in his satirical novel *Antic Hay*.

Lewis was beyond doubt a Lothario of epic proportions, but it was in the domestic arena that he truly distinguished himself as a monumentally self-centered misogynist. His secret wife, the beautiful, intelligent, and talented Gladys Anne Hoskyns, was relegated to the bedroom and the kitchen. She was never to show herself when guests were in the house. Lewis went even further, demanding that she tell no one of their marriage. And she had to agree there would be no children. (Lewis's children from previous relationships were given away at birth.) She also tacitly consented to his ongoing series of affairs.

CHAPTER 7

A FRIENDSHIP IN LETTERS I

Tom and Vivienne Eliot, Wyndham Lewis, and to a lesser extent Katherine Mansfield and James Joyce can be described as Sydney and Violet's everyday friends. When they met, at least as far as the Schiffs were concerned, it was as equals. This was never the case with Proust. The Schiffs' friendship with Proust could not have been based on equality because they worshipped him. And it was not an everyday friendship because the total amount of time they spent in his physical presence over the three and a half years they knew each other added up to twenty-four hours or less. Their relationship consisted almost entirely of exchanging letters, which would not satisfy anyone's criteria for a normal friendship. Yet the letters they exchanged document a closeness that is almost impossible to conceive of in an age in which Facebook posts, texting, and tweets pass for intimacy. There is no way to know most of what the Schiffs and Proust said to one another on the few occasions they met face-to-face, but it could hardly have been more open, more candid, or more intimate than their letters. The correspondence began in 1919, perhaps because the Schiffs waited for the war to end before writing.

By the eighteenth century letter writing had been elevated to the status of art, at its best a form of literature that was private, relatively brief, sometimes wise, and reeking of style and wit. Among intellectuals and the leisured classes, time was set aside for it every day. And in the 1920s, despite the existence of the telephone, handwritten letters were still the principal means of non-face-to-face communication. Considering the time they took to compose they were exchanged remarkably often. In cities like London and Paris there was more than one mail delivery a day, and when a letter was deemed even moderately important it was sent by messenger. A reply might arrive within the hour. The denizens of Bloomsbury and Bayswater regularly used letters to trade gossip, lacerate social, political, and intellectual rivals, and, of course, burden their friends with extended accounts of minor discomforts and inadequate vacation housing. But whatever the self-regarding nature of many of these letters, the intimacy they frequently conveyed was unmistakable.

Letters were also an acceptable way to make contact with a stranger. It was not unusual, for example, for a reader who admired a book, or even disliked it or was offended by it, to write to the author and say so. A flattering letter, especially an intelligent one, might even stimulate a response or begin a casual correspondence, or, in rare cases, a friendship. This was how Sydney and Violet got to know Proust, the man they admired most in the world. A letter from Sydney began a correspondence, conducted entirely in French because Proust's ability to write English was minimal, that lasted until just a few weeks before Proust's death.

Sydney's first letter has been lost, but Proust's response, which appears to have been mailed a few days before April 14, 1919, provides a general sense of its contents. It was extremely flattering, which we know because Proust said so. Still, no matter how flattering it was, it is surprising that Proust, who was weakened by illness and was jealously husbanding his strength and time to complete his novel, answered at all. For one thing, he had no idea who the Schiffs were. The tone of his letter, the way he addressed Sydney—he wrote to "Monsieur"—and the fact that he referred to Stephen Hudson as Sydney's *"ami"* all clearly indicate that he was writing to a complete stranger. Nevertheless it is evident that Sydney's letter moved him. He wrote that he was extremely touched by it, admired the writer's delicacy of spirit and heart, and that he was especially sensitive to Sydney's thoughtfulness in "associating Mrs. Schiff" with the words he found so flattering. A good guess might be that he was reacting to Sydney's honest declaration that Violet had recognized Proust's genius before he had. Proust's letter also made clear that Sydney was seeking an excerpt from the latest volume of *In Search of Lost Time*, known in English as *Within a Budding Grove*, for *Art and Letters*. Proust wrote that he would have been honored to have a fragment in the journal, but that it was not possible because it would conflict with the book's upcoming publication. He also said he could not write anything new because of his poor health and overwhelming editorial responsibilities.

In Sydney's second letter, addressed to "Cher Monsieur," he told Proust that it was "impossible to say how much pleasure" his letter had given him and Violet. He then launched directly into a rapturous account of how Charles Swann, the central character of the first volume of *In Search of Lost Time*, had become more like a beloved soul mate to both Schiffs than a literary figure. "It seems to us that in your creation Swann," Sydney wrote, "we have an intimate friend whom we love and whom we understand as one understands those one has loved for a long time. My wife feels tender toward him and we never stop regretting that we haven't been able to find among our friends anyone who resembles him." And Sydney would, of course, have noticed the congruence between Swann and himself. Both had rejected their fathers' world of finance for a life of the mind. It is hard to imagine praise that would have pleased Proust, or perhaps any writer, more. Here were two people,

English, not even French, who reacted to a character he had created
as if he were a living, tactile person, a physical, emotional, and intellectual presence. But that wasn't all. Sydney went on to say Swann
"resembles my wife and only my wife of all the people I know."
His belief in Swann's particularity, his identity as an individual different from all other individuals except one, the woman Sydney
knew better than all others, would have pleased Proust even more.
And Proust among all writers, perhaps, would have been especially
gratified that the qualities to which Sydney responded in Swann
were androgynous.

All of this suggests a degree of compatibility between the Schiffs
and Proust that was often borne out in their unusually rich correspondence, although here and there Sydney was a bit tone deaf
or overstepped the bounds of propriety, which irritated Proust. A
glaring example of Sydney's presumptuousness was an invitation
he extended to Proust to stay with the Schiffs in London. Proust,
who had never even met Sydney and Violet and had been corresponding with them for less than a month, responded graciously
although negatively. He addressed himself to *"Cher Monsieur et ami"*
and apologized for not writing sooner, explaining that he had been
too ill. He wrote that he was moved, touched, and delighted by
the letter, but that unfortunately he was "uninvitable," because
it was hard enough to get through his crises when he was alone,
and it would be much worse in the presence of others. Later, when
they knew each other better, if only through their letters, Proust
did not hesitate to let his annoyance show. This time, however,
he went on to tell Sydney, in his own flattering or ironic way (it's
unclear which) that he had turned down a similar invitation from
the Duke and Duchess of Clermont-Tonnerre, but that the Schiffs'
offer "touched him a thousand times more because they didn't
know him." Finally, he added, "In any case, I have never received, or
almost never, a letter that has touched me so, you are for me, like
a friend."

If the exuberant warmth Proust exudes for the Schiffs at this early stage of their relationship seems excessive, it is worth noting that his categorical "never" is tempered by the phrase "or almost never" and that he carefully avoided saying Sydney was a friend, but rather said he was "like a friend." But even with these qualifications and Proust's well-known gift for graciousness there is still something remarkable about his manner of responding to Sydney and Violet given the short time they had been corresponding and the fact that they had never seen one another. The Schiffs' invitation at the very least was premature and presumed an unwarranted degree of intimacy. This would not have been out of character for Sydney, but it surely would have been for Violet.

The Schiffs and Proust met for the first time in 1919, although exactly when is unclear. Proust at first did not want to meet them but for some reason changed his mind. The meeting took place in a private salon at the Ritz. Sydney and Violet were dining at the hotel, and when they finished their meal the headwaiter came by to tell them that Proust was waiting for them. Sydney lingered to say good-bye to the French friend they were dining with, but Violet got up immediately and went to Proust's table. She introduced herself and expressed her surprise at how young he looked, "much too young," she said, "to have written *Swann*." "Swann is not me," Proust, who was forty-eight, answered. And when Sydney arrived at the table he told him, "Your wife does not believe that I have written my books myself." All the while Proust was eating asparagus in the French style, with fingers, not a fork. Violet thought he was "remarkably handsome and quite unlike anyone else" with his thick, dark hair and that he looked about thirty-five. He had on a fur-lined coat, which was open, displaying a colored waistcoat that was fastened up to his neck. When Sydney arrived a few minutes later, Proust chastised him for not bringing his friend to the table. He said it was "unkind to neglect an old friend for a new one." The friend, however, might have been just as happy to have been left behind because he thought Proust was a bad writer and a snob.

Proust then invited the Schiffs to his apartment. They were driven there by Odilon, who was always available to drive his master anywhere at any hour. Proust and Violet got out of the car first and went into a dark entrance hall that looked sordid. Proust said they had better wait for Schiff and Odilon because neither of them knew how to operate the elevator. When the two men got there they all took the elevator up to Proust's apartment, where they were let in by Céleste, who was young, graceful, and dressed in black. It was late and Proust sent Céleste off to rest, which she did knowing that when the Schiffs left, no matter what time it was, Proust would need her again. Proust, Sydney, and Violet sat together talking into the early morning hours. At some point during the conversation Proust noticed that Sydney was somewhat hard of hearing and insisted on making an appointment for him with an otolaryngologist he knew.

"The strange enchantments of the nights we passed with Marcel Proust made us believe that no daytime meetings could have equaled them," Violet wrote years later. "Nothing he said was trivial or unimportant, not that he was by any means serious all the time. His astringent satire left one with no feeling of sadness or bitterness. He put himself into his conversation as he did into his books, but not by talking about himself. He made it clear that what mattered to him was the motive of people's acts and words. He was always seeking the truth about everything and everybody. He was bored by insincerity."

At daybreak Odilon, who remained on duty waiting, drove the Schiffs back to the Ritz, where they were staying. Afterwards Proust liked to tell a story about how Sydney stopped friends on the street in London and told them that the most remarkable thing he had seen in Paris was Marcel Proust, the only man he had ever known who dined in a fur coat.

The next three letters from the Schiffs to Proust, which are also missing, apparently were written by Violet, the first sometime in June. She must have read *Within a Budding Grove* by then because in the first letter she expressed her disappointment that Proust had emphasized an unattractive side of Swann in this second volume of the novel. The Swann the Schiffs loved, admired, and believed in as a living person, Proust responded, was made to look "less sympathetic, even ridiculous" because he [Proust] wasn't free to "go against the truth and violate the laws of characters." He added that it wasn't easy for him to see Swann go in that direction and then noted wistfully that sometimes even the nicest people have hateful periods. Finally, he appended in Latin, *"Amicus Swann, sed magis amica veritas"* (Swann is my friend, but the truth is a better friend). Proust told Violet not to worry, though, because in the next volume Swann would become a "dreyfusard" and sympathetic again. But, no doubt in response to another immutable law of fiction, there was to be one last twist. In the fourth volume, Proust warned Violet, to his own great sorrow, Swann would die.

He concluded his letter with an overarching aesthetic principle in the form of a nine-word epigram: "Art is a perpetual sacrifice of sentiment to truth." Sydney, of course, had told Katherine Mansfield, who was somewhat dismissive of *Richard Kurt*, that truth was all he cared about in his novel. And Joseph Conrad, a godfather of modernism, wrote "truth alone is the justification of any fiction that makes the least claim to the quality of art." The work of Stephen Hudson is not comparable to that of Proust or Conrad, but he shared with them a firm understanding of the nature of literary truth—without any postmodern condescension—and its place as the preeminent value of art in general and fiction in particular.

The next letter from Proust was to Violet. He addressed her more formally and less affectionately than he did Sydney, simply as "Madame." The letter was filled with apologies because they had not received first editions of his books he had reserved for them and with further apologies that he could only send third editions in their place. It was written in August from an apartment at 8 bis, rue Pichat, an address he correctly characterized as "very temporary." He also alluded briefly again to the subject of Swann, telling Violet that he hoped Sydney "is as indulgent as she has been and gives him his permission to render Swann as ridiculous alas as conforms to his character."

After that several months passed before Proust wrote again, on November 17, this time from 44 rue Hamelin, an apartment near the Arc de Triomphe. He said he was "at least provisionally installed," possibly suggesting that he hoped to move to more comfortable quarters. In fact 44 rue Hamelin would be his final address, the place where he would struggle mightily to finish *In Search of Lost Time*, and where he would die. This letter to Violet is one of the most interesting in the early correspondence. Proust referred to a brief article about his work Sydney had written as Stephen Hudson for *Art and Letters* and to a copy of *Richard Kurt* the Schiffs had sent him and he had been reading. He expressed delight in both the article and the book, although he noted apologetically that he read English "with great difficulty." But as he went on it soon became obvious he was operating under what could properly be called a misconception, although in an important sense it was not entirely wrong.

Proust had concluded that Violet was Stephen Hudson. Therefore, referring to the highly flattering article, and believing that Violet had written both the article and *Richard Kurt*, he wrote effusively to her that *Kurt*, much more than *Swann*, deserved all the praise in the article. In his confused state he compounded his error by saying he now understood that the letters from the Schiffs, the article in *Art and Letters*, and the novel were all the work "of the same person: you." Violet's letters, Proust wrote, "confirmed my hypothesis and hope, that this pair of readers, as [Sydney] too modestly referred to you, was a household of artists and creators." Convinced he was right, Proust waxed on: "I have been able . . . to compose without any gap your moral and intellectual physiognomy." He then thanked Violet profusely for dedicating *Kurt* to him and apologized for the quality of the paper on which he was writing, explaining that it was the middle of the night and he couldn't call for his normal writing paper. He ended curiously by implying that because he believed Violet was Stephen Hudson he understood Sydney's life and his soul and sent him his respects.

After that letter there was a nine-month gap in the correspondence. It is not clear whether letters are missing or none were written. The correspondence resumed with a letter from Proust to Sydney written a little before August 30, 1920, and addressed with moderate formality as *"Cher Monsieur"* (dropping *"et ami"*). The letter began in typical Proustian fashion: "I have been so sick since seeing you—a little like the living dead—(and my vision continues to get worse) that I haven't been [able] to write to you or Madame Schiff, and this just at the time I was getting to know you." Proust then offered another of his elaborate apologies, this time for having used Sydney's name without his permission in a story he wrote for the Paris newspaper *Le Matin*. In a reference to the Italian diplomat Sydney Sonnino, whose "real name [was] Schiff," Proust wrote parenthetically, "nothing to do with the charming Sydney Schiff." This, he wrote to Sydney, was intended "as a little friendly visiting card for you." But just at the time the story was being prepared for publication, and before Proust had a chance to make sure Sydney didn't mind, he won the Prix Goncourt, France's most prestigious literary prize, which apparently completely disconcerted him. A month later, in mid-January 1920, the *Le Matin* article was reprinted in a magazine called *Feuillets d'Art*, again with Sydney's name. As a final word of apology-cum-explanation, before getting to the real purpose of his letter, Proust wrote that at that point, "I was in no condition to open my eyes."

Then, eyes wide open, presumably, Proust wrote: "Today I'm writing to you with a practical goal," which, editing out the flattery and excessive deference, amounted to a request that Sydney round up subscribers for a deluxe edition of *Within a Budding Grove*, which would include fragments of original manuscript. Proust complained that the publisher had underpriced it at three hundred francs a copy and told Sydney that André Gide thought it should have been a thousand francs. He also wrote that what upset him most of all was that they were only planning an edition of fifty copies, which he thought was "ridiculously small." When the deluxe edition was first discussed Proust thought an edition of twenty would be adequate, but that was before he won the Goncourt. Before moving on to another subject, he told Sydney not to worry if he couldn't find subscribers because fifty copies could easily be sold.

Sydney and Violet bought a copy for themselves—it is not known whether they found any other buyers—but Sydney, in keeping with his sometimes indiscriminate cult of honesty, made emphatically clear his disapproval of such editions generally. In a letter from Eastbourne to "Cher Monsieur Proust" dated August 30, he wrote: "I am not a friend of these bibliophile editions, which to me seem artistically unjustifiable. I am disgusted by the commercial exploitation of the personality and the intimate particulars of an author loved as you are loved." He went on to say he considered it a "sacrilege" to make original manuscript pages "a plaything or a commercial object," a bit of hyperbole to which Proust objected in his next letter. "Do you think it's necessary for authors to die of hunger?" Proust asked. "I wrote Swann in a hovel, it's true, but because of the rental crisis, this hovel cost 2,600 francs a month." After a couple of obscure allusions to Ruskin and Whistler, Proust allowed that he was in complete agreement that deluxe editions were of no interest and neither were autographs, which should have put an end to the matter but didn't. Sydney couldn't contain himself. He admitted somewhat guiltily in his response to Proust that he would have liked to have not just a fragment but the entire manuscript in his hands. And, driven to excess by the thought that "some idiot by paying 300 francs can think he loves your pages as much as I do," he added, "Yes, I would like many writers to die of hunger, but that the rare artists of value [would be] in your happy position of independence."

The deluxe edition was not the only subject of the sequence of letters exchanged in late August and early September of 1920. Nor was it the only source of disagreement. In Proust's letter dated a few days before August 30, he briefly noted that he was unaware Sydney was related to his young and relatively new friend, the writer Louis Gautier-Vignal. The relationship was not by blood but by marriage. Sydney's sister Edith was the second wife of Count Albert Gautier-Vignal, Louis's father. Proust said he would have liked to talk to Sydney about Louis, whom he admired for his kindness and intelligence and of whom he wrote, "I may not know anyone else so free of disagreeable qualities. His spiritual and moral purity are charming." Sydney, whose propensity for not letting well enough alone must have been obvious to Proust by then, once again could not restrain himself. Either from tone deafness or compulsive honesty he delivered a diatribe in his next letter in which he called Louis "artificial, superficial, [and] full of exotic tastes." And if that were not enough, after denigrating Louis's sisters in particular and his family in general, Sydney turned on Louis again, accusing him of liking "things rather for their appearance than for their intrinsic value."

Proust's initial response, had he been anyone else, would have seemed ironic. He said he was "enchanted" by Sydney's characterizations of the members of the Gautier-Vignal family and his "juicily and spitefully profound views on humanity." But being Proust, he probably meant exactly what he wrote even though he abruptly changed course and defended Louis. He said Louis had "more nobility of spirit" than Sydney gave him credit for. But that wasn't nearly enough to get Sydney to drop the subject. He couldn't resist attacking Louis in another letter, accusing him of being a congenital liar. "He always lies in the family and it is boring and tiresome. Nothing kills friendship like lying and even obligatory family affection can't resist it for long," Sydney wrote. It apparently never occurred to

LEFT: Violet Schiff's mother, Zillah Beddington, was the daughter of Sir John Simon, a member of the British Parliament. She was a noted amateur pianist whose only public appearance was at the request of the great Polish pianist and composer Ignacy Paderewski, with whom she played a piece for four hands.

BOTTOM: As a girl and a young woman Violet went regularly with her parents for seaside vacations in Folkestone. In his novel *Myrtle,* Sydney wrote a fictional account of having spent a few days there with the Beddingtons at Violet's invitation before he and she were married.

TOP: Sydney Schiff's father, Alfred, arrived in London as a very young man and soon set up a brokerage house with his brother Ernest. He became a member of the stock exchange when he was twenty-six. He hoped Sydney would join him in the business one day, which, to his great regret, was not to be.

BOTTOM: Sydney's mother, the former Mrs. John Scott Cavell, originally Caroline Mary Ann Eliza Scates, was still married to Mr. Cavell when Sydney was conceived. His relationship with his mother, unlike the one he had with his father, was very close, and he was devastated when she died of heart disease in 1896 at fifty-two.

TOP: Sydney commissioned this portrait of Violet by Percy Wyndham Lewis, which was the source of considerable friction between him and the Schiffs. He worked on it for years, during which time Sydney kept advancing him money on the unfinished work and finally demanded that he turn it over, even though Lewis considered it unfinished.

BOTTOM: This graphic rendering of Sydney was done by Sir William Rothenstein, a British artist best known for his portrait drawings of prominent persons. He was an acquaintance of the Schiffs and a friend of many of the young British artists in their circle.

TOP: T. S. Eliot and his first wife, Vivienne, shown here with Sydney, were among the Schiffs' closest friends from 1919 to 1924. After that, for various reasons, the relationship deteriorated and eventually petered out entirely. But when Sydney died and the war ended, Violet began seeing Eliot again, with his second wife, Valerie.

CENTER: The Schiffs regularly entertained friends at their summer house in Eastbourne on the southern coast of England. This group includes, besides the Schiffs, Wyndham Lewis; Vivienne Eliot; and the wife of Paolo Tosti, the composer of art songs and singing master to the royal family as well as to Violet and her sisters.

BOTTOM: Lady Ottoline Morrell's country estate, Garsington, was a gathering place for the bright lights of Bloomsbury, including Leonard and Virginia Woolf, Clive and Vanessa Bell, John Maynard Keynes, Bertrand Russell, and Roger Fry. In this group, from left to right, are Lady Ottoline; Aldous Huxley's wife, Maria Nys; Lytton Strachey; Duncan Grant; and Vanessa Bell.

TOP: Lady Ottoline Morrell, the grande dame of Garsington, was both adored and brutally satirized by her guests. They never admitted that she was the target of their satire and never refused her hospitality.

BOTTOM: Aldous Huxley, who was a regular guest, took part in the bucolic activities encouraged on the estate, including pitching hay, for which he dressed appropriately.

TOP: Croquet was a popular game at Garsington, which Wyndham played on one of his infrequent visits. Unlike Aldous Huxley, however, he lacked the proper attire.

CENTER: In 1922, the year Eliot's *The Wasteland* was published and the year Proust completed *In Search of Lost Time*, Sylvia Beach, owner of the Paris bookstore Shakespeare & Co., published James Joyce's *Ulysses* in an edition of one thousand. Adrienne Monnier, standing on the right, also owned a bookstore and translated Eliot's *The Love Song of J. Alfred Prufrock* into French with Beach.

BOTTOM: Marcel Proust wrote large chunks of *In Search of Lost Time* in bed, mostly late at night and into the early morning hours while subsisting in the last years of his life on coffee, croissants, and ice-cold beer, which his driver, Odilon Albaret, would fetch from the Ritz, often after midnight.

TOP: Katherine Mansfield, the noted short-story writer who died at thirty-four of tuberculosis, mostly lived apart from her husband, the essayist and literary magazine editor John Middleton Murry. The arrangement seemed to suit them both, judging from the plethora of letters they wrote to each other.

BOTTOM: John Quinn, third from the left, was a New York lawyer who collected modernist art and literary manuscripts from the likes of James Joyce, Ezra Pound, and Ford Madox Ford, pictured with him, as well as Joseph Conrad.

TOP: The Scottish poet, critic, and translator Edwin Muir and his wife, Willa, were close friends of the Schiffs during the mid- to late twenties. Edwin Muir ranked Sydney (Stephen Hudson) among the nine living writers whose work he believed would still be read decades later. The others included James Joyce, T. S. Eliot, D. H. Lawrence, and Virginia Woolf.

BOTTOM: Abinger Manor, in Surrey about an hour from London, was the house Sydney and Violet occupied during World War II. Part of the roof was blown off by a German rocket, which resulted in an injury to Violet's back that left her partly crippled for the rest of her life.

him that relentlessly attacking your friend's friend might be boring and tiresome and might even kill a friendship. In any event, with a heroic display of restraint Proust let the dialogue peter out with no apparent hard feelings.

Sydney's tactless unsolicited critique of Gautier-Vignal—a friend for whom Proust had clearly expressed affection and admiration—raises questions about his judgment and character. This is especially so in the context of his still developing relationship with Proust, a man he held in almost godlike esteem. It seems highly unlikely that he knowingly would have risked endangering a still fragile connection he valued more than any other except the one he had with Violet. Perhaps he thought Proust would not hold his blunt criticism of Gautier-Vignal against him, which would mean he believed Proust shared his unconditional commitment to truth telling, at whatever cost, in life as well as literature. But even so, his failure to at least temper his vitriolic tone when writing about Proust's young friend demonstrates either a conspicuous unawareness of or a lack of concern about how others might react to his blunt criticism.

Perhaps the best context for judging Sydney's abrasive comments and writings about Gautier-Vignal and a whole cast of other characters, including his parents and siblings, is the remarkably candid way he assessed and portrayed himself. The critic Edwin Muir's strongest criticism of Sydney's novels was that he was too hard on himself. The final version of *A True Story* seems unsparing of Richard Kurt, the fictionalized Sydney, but the version Muir read was even tougher. Violet's editing after Sydney's death eliminated some of the harshest self-criticism. Sydney was uncompromisingly self-critical in his books and of his books. He accepted Katherine Mansfield's criticism of *Richard Kurt* with equanimity and when asked to contribute an article on his work for a book titled *Ten Contemporaries: Notes Toward Their Definitive Bibliography*, he wrote that he "wanted to make an apology rather than to offer explanations [for his] unfinished novel," meaning *A True Story*. He called *Richard, Myrtle and I* "unsatisfactory" and labeled his 1923 novel *Tony* "a failure."

These severe assessments of his work probably resulted in part from insecurity induced by his father's lifelong disapproval as well as twenty years of abuse and mockery from Marion, but his quasi-religious commitment to truth telling can't be overestimated. Of course, when it came to acid observations about putative friends he was not out of step with the literary royalty of Bayswater and Bloomsbury. The only difference was that the residents of these rival intellectual neighborhoods lacked the courage of their convictions. Unlike Sydney, when confronted with their cruelly satirical representations of supposed friends, Huxley, Lawrence, Lewis, and company lied.

Sydney was rarely duplicitous. In his life as in his work he considered the truth sacred. And he believed complete honesty could not always be achieved without using disagreeable language, as a result of which he sometimes came across as self-righteous. He responded to Proust's late-August letter in a way that seems compulsively honest because it was so painfully revealing about his insecurity. "Looking for an explanation for your long silence," he wrote, "I thought you had been disillusioned by your perception of my personality. That didn't trouble me. I'm sure it would have been otherwise if the occasion had arisen for a more intimate acquaintance." It is understandable that Sydney was distressed by the long break in the correspondence, but since Proust's letters almost always began with disclaimers that his poor health and the demands of his book had kept him from writing, Sydney's self-regarding comment could easily be seen as almost childishly obtuse. Proust, who was either offended or disappointed by Sydney's lack of understanding, said he was "stupefied" that Sydney could have thought he failed to write because he didn't like him. "How could you possibly think I didn't like you right from the start?" he asked. "There is no one I would rather see."

A long, rambling paragraph later in Sydney's letter even more clearly indicates his insecurities and internal contradictions as he vacillates between intellectual arrogance and self-deprecation. It evokes his voice and feelings—petulant but poignantly honest:

We are by the sea—a spot of little interest, but healthy, having rented this house for six months to be able to invite some young people, relatives of my adored wife. It is very tiresome for me because I don't like being constantly with young people. I am distressed by their naivete, which I am afraid of corrupting or at least compromising. I have no patience for being restricted. I like to come and go, talk and be quiet, when I like. I am selfish, not extremely, but too much to put up with personal sacrifices, except some financial sacrifices. Any kind of reining in irritates me and generally speaking people bore me terribly because they understand nothing. My wife is an angel. She thinks it's for them that she likes the young, but it's for herself. I don't bore her because she loves me. If she didn't love me, she would prefer to be with young people. She is frightfully young and I am very old and I only live by her and for her. The human being sometimes interests me, but I don't like him because he has too little intelligence, but my wife to the contrary is not troubled by stupid people if they are sincere and honest. She finds all sorts of qualities that are really pale reflections of herself. If I could write adequately in French and if I were not certain that I would tire you I would tell you many things. I know life well, but I am ignorant; people's ignorance irritates me, they think one is full of knowledge because one has scratched the surface and one never listens to the little things one knows, the things life has taught you. To be able to imagine that I have for a moment the slightest bit of contact with you is a precious gift I don't want to abuse. I stop.

To begin on the bright side, it was a testament to Sydney's love for Violet that he rented a house for six months in a place he found uninteresting to entertain her young relatives, whom he found naive and boring and who limited his freedom. He admitted he was selfish, which indicated some degree of self-awareness, then tried to mitigate his admission by adding "not extremely," which would have been good news if he hadn't tacked on his unwillingness to make personal sacrifices. The single non-Violet-related exception he made for certain financial sacrifices must have, or probably should have, referred to his largesse in giving the despised Marion the villa on Lake Como and half of his income for life. His gifts to Lewis and others were insignificant compared to his wealth and ought not to count as sacrifices although he might have thought they were.

Toward the end of this outpouring of self-revelation, Sydney blurted out his contempt for young people as a class and the masses in general. It's hard to tell whether he was expressing firm convictions or momentary pique. And one has to wonder whether he thought Proust would share his views. If he did, he would have been wrong, which he soon found out. Proust told him rather gently not long afterwards that his intellectual work was an internal affair and, just as it did to Violet, sincerity mattered a great deal to him. As far as his fellow men were concerned, he wrote that he cared whether they were nice or not, but was somewhat indifferent to whether they were intelligent.

Finally, to conclude a letter that was essentially one long bleat, Sydney wrote that "since reading [Proust's] books he had less desire to write." He said Proust had "expressed a large part of what he felt" and that he didn't "know whether it was worth the enormous effort to continue writing." The entire letter suggests Sydney was feeling terribly sorry for himself, but especially so when he expressed his frustration and sense of futility about his writing. He was, however, in good company. Even Eliot, when overwhelmed by work at the bank, caring for Vivienne, and his editing chores and literary journalism, once wrote to Sydney that he was considering giving up writing altogether. He of course got over it, as did Sydney.

Sydney's next letter to Proust continued to reflect his odd blend of diffidence and arrogance, the poles of his personality. He wrote diffidently that Proust was right to feel closer to Violet than to him because her nature was "more instinctively noble" than his. He said he was working at improving himself, but that Violet "always has been and always will be what she is." He praised her wisdom and analytical abilities and observed that she never prejudged anything and was incapable of pettiness, all of which, in context, seemed to contrast with his view of himself. Perhaps most revealingly, though, he wrote with obvious approval that what Violet didn't say was often more significant than what she did, demonstrating that he had the intelligence to recognize that there were times when silence was the most appropriate form of communication. But he seemed emotionally incapable of acting on his insight. He showed once again that he either lacked a basic understanding of how his words might affect the person to whom they were addressed or believed he had an irrevocable moral obligation to express whatever he believed to be true even if there was no compelling reason to do so.

In the next paragraph, which initiated a discussion of how best to get *In Search of Lost Time* translated into English, he told Proust that the audience for good literature, especially good French literature, was very small in England and that the best-educated audience preferred to read the books in French. He strongly suggested that the likelihood of an English edition earning Proust any money was nonexistent. But then, having told Proust in effect that the effort would be wasted, he wrote that he knew of no one other than himself who could produce an acceptable translation. Eventually H. L. Scott Moncrieff was selected to do the English translation, which Sydney initially considered poor—probably because it wasn't his—but in the end came to admire. This translation in edited and updated versions is still the standard. Scott Moncrieff, however, died before finishing the job and Sydney translated the final volume, whose English title is *Time Regained*. His translation has long since been replaced by other versions, the most commonly used of which was done by Andreas Mayor.

In his next letter Proust again offered to get Sydney an appointment with a leading French physician he believed might be able to treat his deafness. But in his reply Sydney, who took Proust's well-meaning offer as an insult, said he wasn't really going deaf at all. He said his inability to hear was a function of his nerves and that no doctor could control or correct the problem. And he added with exaggerated politeness that bordered on mockery: "Therefore, dear sir, if in the future I will need recourse to your gracious intervention, it will be because I have grown deafer still and I dare to hope that this misfortune, if it has to happen, will happen with an indulgent slowness."

Sydney did not write again until November 15, at least in part because Violet had been ill and had undergone an operation. He described the surgery as painful but not serious and did not specify the reason for it. Violet, who had been bedridden for four weeks, also wrote to Proust. Although Sydney and Violet lived in a large house, during Violet's convalescence he slept at his mother-in-law's so that two nurses could sleep near her. He seemed to have enjoyed his stay and with a certain amount of pride described the Beddington milieu to Proust.

After noting that Zillah, whose husband, Samuel, had died in 1914 at eighty-five, lived in a spacious Victorian residence he wrote that two servants, one of whom had been with the family for thirty-five years and the other for about forty years, had retired. For most people this would have been an odd fact to emphasize, but it was Sydney's way of highlighting the stability, solidity, and social status of the Beddington family. He went on to describe Zillah as the best amateur pianist in existence and told Proust she knew all the great musicians. Then Sydney blissfully recounted for Proust the most emotionally charged experience of his stay at 21 Hyde Park Square:

"I had the good fortune to sleep in the same room my wife occupied for her entire life before we were married. . . . my eyes encountered the same prints on the walls, the same furniture and rug; from the window I saw the same branches dried by the wind in the old square."

Then, returning to the mundane, he wrote that the Beddingtons' old butler had taken good care of him and that he had enjoyed pleasant conversations with Zillah about concerts she had attended and musicians she had known. But rather than moving on and leaving well enough alone, Sydney could not resist sharply criticizing his mother-in-law. She was, he wrote, "egotistical in a way that was infantile and naïve" because she seemed more interested in her concerts than her daughter's illness. It seems almost as if the distinction between life and art had dissolved in his mind, as if the truth-telling injunction requiring full disclosure was in effect and he was treating her as a character in a novel. On the other hand, he knew to whom he was writing.

Much of the rest of this letter was devoted to Proust and his fiction, which Sydney discussed with voluptuous praise. "I taste your sentences," he emoted, "like I taste the flavor of an old Chambertin that one rolls in one's mouth, on the tongue before swallowing it. . . . No one but you can express the spirit of the times, the thoughts, moods and innate emotions of the most civilized people." Then, in comparing Proust to Henry James, he combined with the flattery a crystallization of one of his own primary concerns. "Before you," he wrote to Proust, "Henry James enlightened us and transported us to a Jamesian plane where Jamesian spirits lived. [But] he never succeeded in making us feel human beings mattered to him, he didn't know how to make one feel the skin and the blood and one descended from the heights disillusioned." In contrast, he wrote of Proust: "you take us by the hand, you lead us to the place you live where we find not only splendidly generous hospitality, but meet many people we know, precisely those you had wanted us to remember and meet again, and just like that your true friends are our friends. More than that, you give us yourself whom we love and keep in our hearts like a part of ourselves."

Sydney not only shared with Proust a reverence for truth and a strong conviction that it was the primary if not the sole object of literature, but apparently also similar beliefs about how best to tell the truth in fiction. In *A True Story*, like Proust in *In Search of Lost Time*, he assembled a large cast of characters, some of whom were introduced, then disappeared from the narrative only to turn up again and ultimately become well known to the novel's readers. And like Proust, who is present throughout his entire three-thousand-page work as a character and narrator named Marcel, Sydney as Richard Kurt is ubiquitous in his novel. It was also important to Sydney, like Proust, that his readers feel the flesh and blood of his characters and in this he largely succeeded.

Moreover, like Proust's, his novel concerns itself mainly with the inner lives of the people he considered most civilized, which reinforces the overly simplified notion that Sydney was a snob, an allegation often made about Proust. Yet when it came to their fiction both men were brutally honest about their characters, most of whom were identifiable as socially prominent real people. Proust, even more than Sydney, shredded the pretensions and moral enervation of the aristocratic class to which he was regularly accused of aspiring. And he wrote convincingly in his own defense that "a snobbish writer would never write that he would like to meet a duchess nor would he make fun of one." These similarities, of course, do not suggest that Sydney deserves a place in the history of literature anywhere near Proust, but they contribute to an assessment that he deserves some place in the history of literature.

At the end of his letter Sydney returned to everyday affairs, telling Proust he was taking Violet to Eastbourne in the hope that the fresh sea air would chase away what remained of her illness, and he noted in passing, without any expression of regret, that they would not stop in Paris on their way to the south of France in mid-

December. But he added that in the spring they hoped to realize their long-standing desire to spend several weeks there.

In a valetudinarian's version of one-upsmanship Proust replied to Sydney a few days later that while Violet was sick, he was at death's door. Then, perhaps to allay their concerns, he said he was feeling better. Toward the end of his letter, however, he reverted to his initial dolorous outlook, reporting that he was "a thousand times worse" than when they saw one another. He said he could not reply to both Sydney and Violet, which suggested he was not feeling well, but also that he had received a letter from Violet that subsequently was lost. He then proceeded to the main subject of his letter, which must have come as a pleasant surprise to Sydney. Proust wrote that some of Sydney's letters were so good they should be published and that the last one in particular was extraordinarily evocative: "the mother-in-law, the concerts, the tree, the marvelous servants, Henry James, all that," he elaborated, "is more remarkable than what one typically reads in books." He also went on fulsomely about the letter on the various Gautier-Vignals, emphasizing with obvious delight Sydney's "misanthropy" and the "tender contrast" he described between himself and Violet. Then at the end of the letter Proust acknowledged that he had come around to Sydney's way of thinking about Louis Gautier-Vignal. Some of this could have been mere flattery, but it seems likely that to some extent Proust's observations intimate a shared sensibility with Sydney, especially in their taste for the misanthropic. Whether he actually had changed his mind about Louis is harder to know.

Sydney's satisfaction with Proust's comments was evident in his swift response. "It is above all your delightful candor we like," he wrote, "your way of saying things as they are, not more, not less." Another recipient of a similar letter might have been more skeptical, but the temptation to uncritically accept Proust's praise must have been irresistible, even for a truth lover. Of course, Sydney might have been right. Proust could have meant what he said.

But then again, for both Sydney and Proust flattery was a notable exception to the rule of absolute truth telling.

Sydney, to his credit, did not dwell on the subject but rather launched into a curious discourse on snobbery. "To want to be noticed, to dissimulate, to pretend, these are the stigmata of snobbery," he wrote. "[But] there is no snobbism where there is candor." In other words, in life as in fiction, truth triumphs over all. He then provided a bizarre example of what he considered justifiable snobbism. The protagonist of his object lesson was his brother-in-law, the husband of his half sister Louise.

First he told Proust that Louise was "ugly, vulgar and a little (not too) nasty," information, even if accurate, that was irrelevant. Louise's husband was a physician who had benefited substantially from the largesse of his father. Alfred Schiff bought a provincial medical practice for his son-in-law and left the couple a generous inheritance. Soon thereafter Louise's husband became mayor of Faversham, the town in which they lived, and, in Sydney's words, "thanks to his decency and the relationships his money procured for him in important circles thereabouts, he obtained the title 'Sir,' which was the height of his ambition. So you see a man who was justified in his snobbery by the halo with which his career was crowned."

Then, in a glittering display of his own intellectual snobbery, Sydney wrote to Proust that "Setting aside all the rest, there are only three people in the world with whom we have any desire to have a commerce of ideas and thoughts and you are one of them. The two others, men about 35 years old, are a poet and critic, T.S. Eliot, and a writer [and] painter (perhaps the most noteworthy of our modern painters) Wyndham Lewis." Although Sydney appeared to put Eliot and Lewis on the same intellectual plane as Proust, he made a clear distinction between the relationships. With Proust it was a blend of intellect and love. "[It] is this mix of heart and head," he wrote to Proust in conclusion, "that we, my wife and I, have found reciprocally, that has been and will always be the insoluble cement of our life together." This, he told Proust, was the kind of relationship they shared with him. With Eliot and Lewis, he explained, while the friendship was genuine, its substance was purely intellectual.

It was not until eight months later, in July 1921, that the Schiffs received their next letter from Proust, in which he wrote he had sent them copies of the two latest volumes of his novel. He said he would have sent them sooner had he not been "just about moribund." The letter was relatively brief, but unusually revealing about Proust's attachment to Sydney and Violet. Proust wrote in a way that seems heartfelt that he wanted to know when the Schiffs would visit him again because, "as incredible as it might seem, I, who never miss anyone, constantly miss you." Then, almost plaintively, perhaps injecting a little guilt into the equation, he added, "now that you have so many villas everywhere I have little hope of your coming to Paris." At the time Sydney and Violet had houses in London, Roquebrune in the south of France, and at Eastbourne on the southern coast of England.

At this point there was either another hiatus in the correspondence or, as appears likely from Proust's next letter to the Schiffs, more missing letters. In a letter dated October 12, 1921, Proust wrote to express again his longing to see Sydney and Violet. "You and Madame Schiff," he said, "are the only two human beings I feel the desire to see every day." The letter also implied that once again Sydney and Violet had invited him to stay with them in England. He responded that such a visit was extremely unlikely, but that if it were to become possible he would rent an apartment and they could visit him. "But even that," he quickly added, "is undoable." He said he had suffered attacks of uremia and had been bedridden for four months, but on his doctor's advice he had begun going out once a week, usually to dine at the Ritz.

He lamented to Sydney, though, that even at the Ritz condi-

tions were difficult—the dining room was full of people he knew
who, seeing he was out, assumed he was better and invited him
to dinner at their homes, a prospect he could not face. There were
also breezes from the open windows he found unbearable. He said
he had rented private rooms for dinner, but that it was very expensive. He also said, perhaps tongue in cheek, that he wanted to avoid
being warned by the management that he would "be obliged to
leave before the end of dinner if an American arrives on the boat."
All of this complaining was to get Sydney to write on his behalf to
Henry Elles, the codirector of the Ritz, who he thought was ignorant of his eminence and therefore not sufficiently attentive to his
needs. Sydney, who knew Elles slightly, wrote a letter to him and
enclosed it in his next letter to Proust. But he wrote it in English, so
Proust sent it on without reading it. Whatever the letter said, and
whatever Elles made of it, Proust continued going to the Ritz, and
Odilon continued making midnight beer runs to the hotel almost
until the day Proust died.

Proust wrote to Sydney again on October 21, addressing him
for the first time as simply *"Cher ami."* But once again the content
of his letter made clear that at least one more of Sydney's letters
was missing. "Your letters," he enthused, "are as full of portraits
as a museum and as full of people as a town. I don't understand
why you don't take advantage of these astonishing gifts to write
books." Evidently, after almost two years and many letters, Proust
was still laboring under his original misconception that it was Violet who wrote books, that she was Stephen Hudson. He followed
up with a laundry list of the hardships he overcame daily just to be
able to write and exhorted Sydney, who he obviously thought had
far less to overcome, to show "a little courage [and] work!" Then, in
an abrupt change of tone, Proust lashed out at Sydney, apparently
in response to a recent letter, for not understanding the difficulties he had to overcome just to continue living, let alone writing.
He implied that Sydney expected too much from him and wrote

explicitly that the Schiffs didn't realize what a sacrifice it had been just to meet them at the Ritz sixteen months earlier.

But then Proust, who was often mercurial in his letters, shifted gears again and thanked Sydney, whose letter, he said, forced him to confront a reality he didn't want to face and that in the end he didn't regret because "the truth is always salutary." Before switching subjects, he asked Sydney and Violet to be sure not to tell anyone about his complaints because, he alleged, he never talked about himself. He went on to say he told people that "the only reason I never see anyone is my work" and that it would bother him if anyone thought otherwise. A commitment to truth telling, it seems, sometimes allows for an exception other than flattery.

In early November Proust wrote again, this time very briefly, to let Sydney and Violet know he had sent them a copy of a journal containing a fragment of the second volume of *Sodom and Gomorrah*, more commonly known in English as *Cities of the Plain*, a book which when finished he would dedicate to Sydney. And, in a phrase that suggested he had received another letter from Sydney, he wrote, "You and Madame Schiff impregnate even the simplest things with flavor and render them delicious. A banality from you seems impossible to me."

The next surviving letter from Sydney to Proust was dated Christmas Day, 1921. Hyperbole being of a piece with his conception of honesty, I think what he wrote was what he felt despite the excess. There is no reason to believe he ever attempted to hide who he was.

"Whether it is banal or not," his letter began, "I cannot let the New Year approach without telling you a little of what is in my heart and my mind for you. First I want to tell you that you are more than ever in our thoughts. Understand that our lives are lived in an atmosphere penetrated by you that is essentially yours. We are not ourselves when circumstances force us to leave you and our return to you is our return to ourselves. Therefore there is no question of a welcome. You are always alongside us, feeling what we feel, talking, listening, above all, laughing with us."

Sydney maintained that he and Violet knew Proust better than he knew them because as one of the world's great artists he had shared his soul with the world. Then, perhaps in response to Proust's mistake about Stephen Hudson's identity, he begged Proust to recognize him as a writer, by no means on a plane with himself, but as a writer nonetheless. He had recently sent him a copy of *Elinor Colhouse*, hoping Proust would help get it published in French and he assured Proust that if he read the book he would not think less of him. Then, switching from the serious to the frivolous, Sydney ended his letter with a preview of the Christmas dinner he and Violet were about to attend at the home of the poet Osbert Sitwell.

"His sister Edith and his brother Sacheverell are also poets," Sydney wrote, adding pointedly that "'Sachy' has a future." He described Osbert as a young patrician who was charming, fickle, and homosexual, and who belonged to an extreme left-wing set, "a way of thinking we've discerned among the elite and share to a small degree." He said it was all very amusing and went on to list the rest of the guests, including his sister-in-law, Ada Leverson (whom he described as a "novelist of the '90's and a friend of Oscar Wilde"), Wyndham Lewis, Aldous Huxley and his wife Maria Nys ("a not particularly intelligent Belgian"), and Michel de Zogheb, whom Sydney described as "a man of Italian-Syrian-Danish descent" who was charming and his friend. He said Violet had arranged the table so that the two of them wouldn't be far apart and to provoke a touch of wickedly humorous friction between Lewis and Osbert Sitwell, who didn't much like each other. Sydney then signed off, telling Proust he had to stop writing because it was time to dress for dinner. To surprise Osbert, "who loves fancy dress," he said he was going to wear a scarlet hunting coat.

CHAPTER 8

A FRIENDSHIP IN LETTERS II

⁓: ◯◯ :⁓

On April 7, 1922, in the hope that they might see Proust, the Schiffs traveled to Paris for an open-ended stay. Before trying to arrange a meeting with him, though, they paid a visit to Picasso. Sydney and Violet wrote separate letters to Wyndham Lewis about the visit, but Lewis responded only to Violet, with whom he kept up a regular correspondence during the Schiffs' Paris sojourn. He was, unsurprisingly, more interested in what he was or in some cases was not doing than in what they were doing. Among other things he bragged that Joyce thought he was the only prose writer in England worthy of notice.

The day the Schiffs arrived Proust, who knew they were coming, wrote a letter seeking a favor from Jacques Rivière, editor of the *Nouvelle Revue Française*, whose owners had started the publishing house Gallimard a decade earlier. Some time before, Proust had sent Rivière a copy of *Elinor Colhouse*. Rivière had not responded to Proust, who by then knew that Sydney was the writer, not Violet. He wanted Rivière to write immediately to Sydney about the book and forward the letter to him the same day so that he could pass it on.

Aware that he was asking a lot, Proust took no chances. Instead of leaving the contents of the letter to Rivière, he included what he modestly called a "little aide-memoire," but which in fact was the full text of the proposed letter. After making a few excuses, including illness and business travel, he had Rivière say he had sent Sydney's novel to a specialist in English literature to be translated into French and that when he finished reading the translation he would decide whether, in accord with Proust's wishes, he would be able to publish it in the *Nouvelle Revue Française*.

One might have thought that would have been quite enough, but Proust, acting in this instance a bit like Sydney, added a carefully couched request that Rivière consider a postscript saying that he knew Sydney was a friend of the *Nouvelle Revue Française* and inviting him cordially to visit the magazine's office. Proust also made sure to include a line in which Rivière made clear he was aware of Proust's considerable admiration for Sydney. And finally, Proust apologized for providing a ready-made text and for asking Rivière to respond instantly.

That night Proust, who was running a high fever, answered a letter from Sydney confirming that he and Violet had arrived in Paris. He agreed to meet them for dinner, but moaned, "You are about to see the total tragedy . . . of my situation." He immediately began injecting himself with adrenaline to have the energy to go out and reserved a room at the Ritz with the intent of spending the entire evening there and only going home to sleep. The Friday they were supposed to meet he arrived and asked a bellhop to find out for him what room Mr. and Mrs. Schiff were in. The boy left and didn't return for half an hour. When he finally reappeared he told Proust that Mr. Schiff was there, but without his wife. Proust, somewhat dismayed, sent him to check with the concierge, but another bellhop was filling in for the concierge and knew nothing. Proust was getting really worried at this point and exasperated about the service at the hotel. When the boy came back he told the by then anxiety-ridden Proust that "Mr. Schiff was definitely there, Mr. Mortimer Schiff." Sydney and Violet, it turns out, were at the Hotel Foyot near the Luxembourg Gardens, not at the Ritz. They either neglected to inform Proust or in his weakened state he failed to notice where they were staying and just assumed it was the Ritz.

Proust went home as soon as he discovered that the Schiff at the Ritz was not his Schiff. And when he wrote to tell Sydney about the foul-up he offered a detailed and mildly confusing explanation of the misunderstanding including the fact that he couldn't refer to their letter because his concierge's daughter, who handled the mail, had measles and whooping cough, as a result of which his mail was being sterilized and it was too soon to touch it. He then said he needed a minimum of eight days' rest before he could possibly go out again and asked Sydney for a time they might meet. Whatever times Sydney suggested, one of them worked. Proust's next letter, dated April 22, referred to their having been together. It was probably at the Ritz and late at night, but no account remains of the dinner.

Proust then told Sydney that he had taken advantage of his visit to Paris to try to get some action out of Rivière on *Elinor Colhouse* and that if it were not for his health he would come across to London often for twenty-four-hour visits.

Meanwhile, Rivière had sent Proust the letter to Sydney he had requested and followed up the next day with a report on the progress of the translator, a man named Charles Du Bos, who on first reading was unenthusiastic about *Elinor Colhouse*. But when he learned of Proust's interest he asked for an extension of three days to read the book again, which Rivière granted, and he said that if the *Nouvelle Revue* was unable to publish it he would try to find a French-language journal that would. Then, while Rivière was in the midst of writing to Proust, Du Bos phoned to say that he had finished rereading *Elinor Colhouse* but could not render a final judgment until he had read *Richard Kurt*. Rivière asked Proust if he had a copy Du Bos could borrow because Du Bos did not want to approach Stephen Hudson directly for fear that it might compromise him in his role as an independent reviewer. He also renewed his offer to see if it was possible to find the book another publisher in the event the *Nouvelle Revue Française* decided against it. Rivière then added parenthetically, and somewhat ironically, that he had given "quasi-exclusivity" for reports on English-language books to an Englishman, T. S. Eliot, "who seems rather difficult to influence."

In his letter of April 22, after referring to his recent meeting with Sydney and Violet, it is clear that Proust was again responding to something Sydney wrote in a letter that has been lost. "You were right," he told Sydney, that "we speak much too much of serious matters; serious conversations are made for people who have no inner life. Those who have an inner life, like the three of us, when they get outside of themselves and leave their hard interior labor behind, need some frivolity. We must as you said talk about all the little things in life and leave philosophy for our solitude." Proust also told Sydney he found it offensive that he thought Proust's opinion of him could be affected by the opinion of the *Nouvelle Revue Française*, whose staff he characterized as mediocre although allowing for one or two superior minds. Finally, he said, "If by chance you go to the Ritz before you leave, please let me know."

Sydney answered four days later from the Villa Majestic, where he and Violet were then staying. The letter was one of a series over the next three weeks in which he swung wildly from fawning over Proust to whining over trivia. Even though Sydney took the fawning to a new level, Proust, who had similar tendencies but a lighter touch, was reservedly receptive.

After extravagantly praising Proust's writing paper and asking where he might buy some, Sydney transcended the banality of stationery to deliver an encomium to the two loves of his life. "Violet and you represent my world," he wrote, "because you alone give me what I want, what I ask from life." Then, in a schizophrenic mood swing, he descended again, this time into a discursive complaint beginning with how tiring it was to get dressed for the day even though the pain was palliated by the tender attention of his servant, Ali, "who," he said, "little by little is becoming very helpful." But of course there were those annoying problems having to do with getting breakfast, the car, etc., after which came the travails of the restaurant Larue, which was "passable for breakfast, but foul in the evening." Then Sydney told Proust that the Ritz was acceptable, that they would meet him there anytime and, he implied, it wouldn't be an inconvenience because they went out for dinner anyway. But then, and it could only have been out of pigheadedness, he invited him to dine in their apartment, knowing that Proust only liked the Ritz and that the food was mediocre at the Villa Majestic.

And then, for no apparent reason, he served up a snide putdown of his sister Rose, whom he called "a big snob" who was never admitted to the set she sought to join, probably because she went out of her way to be disagreeable to everyone in it. Superficially, he wrote, "she seems to be intelligent because she is so emphatic," but actually "she is not reflective and never listens." He continued to disparage his sister with an account of their evening together at Larue, where they met some people Sydney knew, including a socially prominent woman named Mrs. Cohen. He wrote that Rose tried to get him to snub Mrs. Cohen, whom he had known all his life, because she was afraid it would look like she was running after her. The account continued with names dropped, references to wealth, and hints of Jewish backgrounds or connections. It's hard to tell whether Sydney was knowingly feeding Proust's gargantuan appetite for this sort of information or just being Sydney. Finally, he complained that they charged him champagne prices for beer and that his reserved table had been given away, which resulted in their party being served in a private room. This last bit of good news salved Sydney's wounds, but he just didn't have it in him to end on that note.

He couldn't resist getting in another dig at Louis Gautier-Vignal and, at the same time, his sister Edith. He had asked Edith if her stepson could recommend a young friend to act as a guide for him and Violet in Paris. She said she would ask but then reported to Sydney that Louis had told her he had "no such friend." Sydney allowed that this could have been true, but he was offended by what he took to be his sister's apparent pleasure in telling him so. "She was happy," he whined to Proust, "that I would have no one to help me and provide me with information." And to make matters worse, when Sydney complained to his sister that he was suffering a great deal because of his nerves, she blithely told him to take up golf and go dancing. He never did take up golf, but in later years he and Violet did go dancing.

Proust wrote again very briefly on April 29, enclosing a sheet of the paper he thought Sydney liked and requesting John Middleton Murry's address, which he asked to have left with the concierge, suggesting that he did not want Sydney or anyone else to disturb him. Sydney answered Proust the same afternoon. After noting that they had decided to remain in Paris until May 7 and that Violet was not feeling well and staying in bed, Sydney sought Proust's sympathy by saying that he had had lunch alone and would have dinner alone. He added that Violet was consoling herself by reading Proust's novel, but he, who was suffering only as much as he always suffered, had nothing with which to console himself. And then, in a fairly obvious attempt to lure Proust into joining him for dinner, he concluded wanly: "Think of me alone at the Ritz this evening as I will be thinking of you."

The next day, after having dined alone the night before, Sydney sent Proust one of his more peculiar letters. Out of nowhere he announced that because his valet, Ali, was a homosexual "everyone here must think I'm one, too." But "I'm just the opposite," he protested. "I'm excessively male, male to the point where I can't stand being shaved by a man, or having my hair cut by a man, or even having a man near me. Ali, who is like a young girl, is exactly right for me." And elaborating on his curiously made point, he told Proust he wanted Ali to cultivate "feline gestures and movements, smooth and sure, in contrast to the nervous, abrupt, uncertain canine movements of a dog." Sydney closed with a thinly veiled plea for Proust's company: "I'm going to lunch now at the Ritz—alone and I will dine there also—alone."

Proust wrote back the next day that he didn't know why Sydney would want to spend an evening with someone in his dreadful condition, of which as usual he provided a detailed account, but that if Sydney would make all the arrangements at the Ritz—and only the Ritz—and be sure that all the windows in the dining room would be closed, he would be ready to be picked up at eight. Sydney responded as soon as he received Proust's note. "Everything will be as you said," he told Proust, adding that his table was in the corner to the right of the entrance and that he would be at his door at eight. In fact, though, it was Violet who picked up Proust. Many years later she described him as "charming and gentle" that night but added, "He objected to my husband's drinking too much champagne, although he himself drank an enormous quantity of iced beer."

A day after their dinner together, Sydney intimated to Proust—by then addressed as *Mon très cher Marcel*—that each time they met his understanding of and feeling for Proust increased. But his primary point seemed to be that each time they met, Proust had an opportunity to learn more about Sydney. He was eager for Proust to appreciate his presence, habits, manner of speaking, and way of acting, in short, all of those superficialities a novelist needs to know to bring a character to life. And with a closely related and possibly more important goal in mind he told Proust that thanks to Jacques Rivière he had found a marvelous French translator for his short stories, which would allow Proust not only to read them and evaluate his work but also to understand "what I think and who I am when I withdraw into my secret garden." What he wanted was for Proust to feel the same kinship Sydney felt for him and to believe its reciprocation was justified. And most of all, he wanted Proust to know that their emotional experiences as children were similar because of a strong sense of inadequately expressed paternal love.

Proust wrote six days later, but his brief note was not responsive to Sydney's letter. Instead he reminded Sydney that he had suffered a painful attack before their dinner as a result of taking adrenaline and told him that after returning home from the Ritz he became violently ill with a high fever. As Violet recollected the evening, however, "No one could suspect that a few hours before he had nearly killed himself." Proust said he still wasn't able to get out of bed, but that as soon as he could they were the first people he wanted to see.

Sydney wrote again the next day, not to respond but to complain that his marvelous translator was turning out to be somewhat less adept than he had hoped. The work she was translating was written in his voice as a child (most likely an excerpt from *Prince Hempseed*), which she seemed to have great difficulty capturing. Sydney said he was reworking her translation but was having a hard time finding the right French idioms. He asked Proust's indulgence and said he would bring it to him the following day. Then, after praising *Sodom and Gomorrah*, Part 2, which he was reading, he outdid himself in praise of its author: "You are the most marvelous of men," he wrote. "With you the novel has reached its greatest height, after you it will go into decline because there is no more to do." And in what might have been an afterthought, but more likely was wishful thinking, he wrote the following:

"Thursday evening we are going to the premiere of a new Stravinsky ballet, and some old Russian ballets. Afterwards, we are having

Diaghilev and some members of the ballet to supper at the Hotel Majestic where I have taken a salon because Elles does not permit music [at the Ritz] after 12:30 a.m. There is no one worthy of meeting you except those you choose, but if, by a miracle, you decided to come, you would find us on the main floor around 12:30." Among the guests, he told Proust, would be "M. et Mme Picasso." He did not tell him that James Joyce, his leading competitor for the heavyweight championship of modernist novel writing, would be there too. *Ulysses* had been published in Paris just two months earlier. Nor did he tell him that Igor Stravinsky, modernism's music icon, would be there.

THE BIG FIVE

When Sydney and Violet Schiff awoke in their apartment at the Villa Majestic on the morning of May 18, 1922, the sun was shining and the forecast was for a clear, mild day with good weather expected throughout the evening and into the early hours of the next day. But Western Europe was on the cusp of a broiling heat wave that would give Paris its highest temperature in 116 years. Sydney and Violet however were too focused on the night to come to have noticed or cared. The evening was going to begin at the Palais Garnier, the vast and opulent Paris opera house named for its designer, Charles Garnier, a thirty-five-year-old architect who was picked from a field of 172 by Napoleon III. It was begun in 1861 and, slowed by a variety of geological and geopolitical problems including underground water on the site, war with Prussia, and the Paris Commune of 1871, completed only in 1875. Although it was of indeterminate style—Garnier told the Empress Eugénie that the extravagantly decorated building was pure Napoleon III—Claude Debussy described it as a railroad station on the outside and a Turkish bath on the inside. Nevertheless, it quickly became a Paris landmark and a favorite venue for the world's greatest composers, singers, conductors, dancers, and choreographers. It is hard to conceive of a better launching pad for the great Schiff gala.

In 1922 the Garnier was home to the Ballets Russes de Monte Carlo, one of the world's leading companies, under the direction of the imposing Russian impresario Serge Diaghilev. Its dancer-choreographers, especially Vaslav Nijinsky and Bronislava Nijinska, were among the world's best. Sets were designed by Picasso, Jean Cocteau, and Russia's finest avant-garde painters, such as Mikhail Larionov and Natalia Goncharova, and performances were staged by Michel Fokine. Diaghilev, who recognized talent early, commissioned new ballet music by young modernist composers—some of whom would achieve greatness, most notably Stravinsky, a Russian who became French and ultimately, in 1945, American. The Ballets Russes had performed his *Firebird* in 1910 when Stravinsky was just twenty-eight and he remembered the premiere for reasons other than the success of his music and the dancing. "The first night audience glittered indeed," Stravinsky wrote, "but the fact that it was heavily perfumed is more vivid in my memory. The . . . London audience . . . seemed almost deodorized by comparison." He also remembered meeting Proust. A year later his *Petrushka* was performed at the Garnier. Both ballets were fairly traditional and warmly received. But *The Rite of Spring*, which premiered in 1913, was something else altogether. It was dissonant, rhythmically radical, featured cumbersome choreography, and was both grisly and primitive in its subject matter. It provoked a full-scale riot. It also heralded the beginning of musical modernism.

The featured attraction on May 18, 1922, was a short, lighthearted Stravinsky ballet of a type sometimes called a burlesque. The music was originally commissioned in 1916 by a friend of Proust, the Princess Edmond de Polignac, formerly Winnaretta Singer, heiress to the Singer Sewing Machine fortune. Diaghilev's ballet version was called *Le Renard* and it portrayed the triumph of a cat, a cock, and a goat over a wily fox. It was only twenty minutes long. The choreographer was Nijinska, who also danced the fox, the conductor was Ernest Ansermet, and Larionov designed the production and costumes. The opening-night reception was mixed, tilting toward disapproval, but there is no indication that the lukewarm response dampened the enthusiasm of the Schiffs' guests, onstage, backstage, or in the audience. Toward midnight, this very select group—men in white ties and opera capes and women in long gowns—exited the opera house and made their way across town in taxis and private cars to the Hotel Majestic. The Princess de Polignac was among them.

The Schiffs' guests filed into the upstairs dining room; neither Proust nor Joyce had attended the performance and both arrived later. Dinner service had begun when Joyce appeared shortly after midnight. He did not own evening clothes so he came wrapped in an alcoholic fog to insulate him against any embarrassment resulting from lack of proper dress. Proust turned up an hour or two later wrapped as usual in a fur coat, that evening worn over a gray suit. The princess later complained that Proust had not worn evening clothes and that the collar on his fur coat looked ratty. Joyce thought Proust looked ten years younger than his age. The Bloomsbury art critic Clive Bell thought Proust looked "altogether too sleek and dank and plastered," although he described his eyes as "glorious." Stravinsky found Proust "as pale as a mid-afternoon moon" and said disapprovingly that "he spoke ecstatically about the late Beethoven quartets . . . an enthusiasm I would have shared if it had not been a commonplace among the *literati* of the time." Stravinsky learned afterwards that Joyce had been there but said that in his ignorance he had failed to recognize him.

Proust and Joyce were introduced, but they had little or nothing to say about each other's books or anything else. Joyce actually had read a bit of Proust and chose not to mention it, but Proust had not read a word of Joyce. Each made excuses for having read little or nothing of the other's work. Joyce's was his failing eyesight, which made it difficult to read Proust's long, dense sentences, and Proust's were his poor English, his failing health, and his almost fanatical focus on finishing his own novel.

In the absence of any written comments by Joyce or Proust about their meeting or the party, all that remains are three very slight firsthand accounts by Violet, Bell, and Stravinsky. There are also two similar but not identical versions of what happened when Joyce, uninvited, joined the Schiffs and Proust in Odilon's taxi at the end of the evening, one by Sydney and the other by Violet. And then there are two funny but totally unreliable secondhand accounts of the Joyce-Proust meeting by Joyce's friends Mary and Padraic Colum and Ford Madox Ford. The Colum and Ford versions are virtually identical in what they purport to describe, differ significantly in what they actually describe, and are both wrong about verifiable facts such as the venue and the hosts. I take both to be no more than entertainments. Here they are, the Colums' first:

> A certain hostess had thought she could create a historic occasion by bringing the two celebrated authors together in her salon, and Joyce told us about the event. He had arrived about ten o'clock. Eleven o'clock came and no Proust. Twelve o'clock came and still no Proust. At 1:00 a.m. Proust entered the salon, dressed, Joyce said, "like the hero of *The Sorrows of Satan*." The two authors were presented to each other, and the company arranged itself so as to not miss anything of the conversation. Here is what was said:
>
> PROUST: Ah, Monsieur Joyce . . . You know the princess . . .
> JOYCE: No, Monsieur.
> PROUST: Ah. You know the Countess . . .
> JOYCE: No, Monsieur.

And that terminated the Proust-Joyce meeting of minds.
It was probably characteristic of Proust. It was also
characteristic of Joyce: he was wont to be taciturn in
the presence of the featured great.

Ford Madox Ford's version is a bit longer and thus larded with
more errors. Here it is:

When he heard me say that I had read no Proust [Joyce]
confirmed for me a story that I had heard from the lips of the
lady in whose house it had happened. . . . The lady had asked
Joyce to a reception to meet Proust. Joyce, knowing nothing
of Proust's habits and no hour having been named, attended
at about eleven. Proust in those days rose at four in the
morning. But in honor of Mr. Joyce he had got up that night
at two and arrived about two-thirty. Mr. Joyce was then tired.

Two stiff chairs were obtained and placed, facing the one
the other, in the aperture of a folding doorway between two
rooms. The faithful of Mr. Joyce disposed themselves in a half
circle in one room; those of M. Proust completed the circle
in the other. Mr. Joyce and M. Proust sat upright, facing each
other and vertically parallel. They were incited to converse.
They did. "As I've said, Monsieur, in *Swann's Way*, which
without doubt you have read . . ."

Mr. Joyce gave a tiny vertical jump on his chair seat and
said: No, Monsieur. Then Mr. Joyce took up the conversation.
He said: "As Mr. Blum [*sic*] said in my *Ulysses*, which,
Monsieur, you have doubtless read . . ."

M. Proust gave a slightly higher vertical jump on his chair
seat. He said: "Of course not, Monsieur." Service fell again to
M. Proust. He apologized for the lateness of his arrival. He
said it was due to a malady of the liver. He detailed clearly
and with minuteness the symptoms of his illness.

". . . Well Monsieur," Joyce interrupted. "I have almost exactly the same symptoms. Only in my case, the analysis . . ."

So till eight the next morning, in perfect amity and enthusiasm, surrounded by the awed faithful, they discussed their maladies.

Whatever time in the morning it was, and although it wasn't planned that way, it does seem to be true that Proust and Joyce left the Majestic more or less together. Proust had invited Sydney and Violet to come home with him, and Joyce, unnoticed at first, stumbled after them. This is how Violet remembered it:

As soon as our guests had gone we followed Proust to his taxi and Joyce got in after us. Joyce's first gesture was to open the window and his second to light a cigarette. Sydney [a heavy smoker himself of cigarettes and one cigar a day] shut the window and asked Joyce to throw away the cigarette, knowing that Proust dreaded air and smoke on account of his asthma. Joyce watched Proust silently, while he [Proust] talked incessantly without addressing Joyce. When we arrived at the flat in Rue Hamelin, Proust said to Sydney: Please ask Monsieur Joyce to let my taxi driver take him home. Proust and I quickly entered the doorway, leaving Sydney and Joyce on the pavement.

Sydney's version is told in the voice of Proust's housekeeper, Céleste, and Sydney is represented as Richard Kurt:

Dawn was streaking the sky when the muffled bell at the entrance rang. My master entered on Madame Kurt's arm and both were laughing, because one of the guests, a famous English painter who was drunk, had come with them in the car, and as Monsieur did not want to bring him to the apartment, Monsieur Kurt had to keep him company until

Odilon, who had brought them up in the lift, could return and drive him home.

Sydney and Violet never saw Proust again. But they exchanged more letters during the six months before he died than at any other time in the three years they had been writing to each other. They expressed their love and devotion for each other often and in language that at times seems strained and extravagant to a postmodern ear, and occasionally were testy with one another.

On May 29, two days before the Schiffs left Paris, Proust wrote to Sydney that although he was "physically incapable of writing, he was morally forced to." The impetus for this superhuman effort was Sydney's apparent misapprehension that he was "running after" Proust whereas, Proust said, the truth was he was "running after" the Schiffs. Proust knew Sydney and Violet were about to return to London and told them he might be better in a day or two and if he were they shouldn't miss the opportunity to see each other one more time, perhaps thinking it would be the last. The next day Proust wrote again in response to a letter in which he apparently found Sydney too demanding and replied that although he was faithful and submissive, Sydney was tyrannical. But then he said Sydney was the man he loved the most and ended his letter with a paean of praise to Violet, whom he called more beautiful than Leonardo's women. To "the angel Violet, whom I have never seen in the same dress, but in whom I have always found the same character, the same comprehensive and inalterable sweetness," he sent his respectful homage, which, he said, he shared with Sydney. Just before the end of the letter, though, Proust made a rather abject apology to Sydney for having inflicted on him a visit to "the Turkish baths." This was apparently a guarded reference to his having taken Sydney to see Le Cuziat's brothel, where Proust went to gather information about clients and practices that he used to portray Jupien's homosexual brothel in his novel. This visit, judging from the apology, had not pleased Sydney.

Two weeks later Proust wrote a trivia-filled letter but concluded on a serious note. He expressed his concern that Sydney was drinking too much champagne and that if he didn't cut back on his consumption he would eventually damage his liver. He then advised him that if his blood pressure was too low and he suffered from fatigue a shot of adrenaline would do more good than a bottle of champagne. Sydney wrote back that he knew he sometimes drank too much champagne, but he hadn't had a drop since returning to London. He explained to Proust that he was nervous and unable to sleep well in Paris and that keeping Proust's late hours exhausted him. He did not respond to the suggestion that he switch to adrenaline. Sydney also advised Proust somewhat brazenly that the Schiffs' visits had made him feel better. His slightly tortured reasoning was that the effort Proust made on their behalf was the medicine that put him on his feet.

He then added that Wyndham Lewis was making drawings of Violet and himself and if they turned out well he would give them to Proust as a gift. "Wyndham Lewis is our Picasso," he told Proust, "but a difficult man, hard and without charm. He is very intelligent, perhaps the most intelligent man (after you) I know, but not at all wise, although intellectual. . . . I was afraid to introduce him to Violet, but they understood each other from the first moment they met. I don't like him, but he interests me enormously. As for the rest, I love no man but you and I don't want to love any other. Lewis's life force is as strong as Picasso's, but he hasn't reached the point where he paints as well as Picasso. Perhaps he never will. . . . Would you like me to ask Picasso to do a drawing of you . . . I have to write to P."

In his next letter to Proust, Sydney began modestly by professing that he lacked the "critical gift, the knowledge and the technique" to write a serious critique of Proust's work. But typically he qualified his self-deprecating observation by adding that no one else in England was capable of doing it either. When it came to the question of who was best qualified to translate Proust's novel into English, however, he was unrestrained by modesty and expressed his opinion without qualification. "I know I'm the only one who can do the translation," he wrote. "You won't believe it after having read and listened to my execrable French, but I know French better than it seems, and it really isn't a question of that, it's a matter of my sympathetic intuition, my literary taste and my mental faculties." His excessive self-confidence—especially given the colossal challenge of rendering Proust's French into English—was breathtaking, but there is little reason to think it wasn't genuine. It was consistent with his belief in his intellectual powers, his commitment to honesty, and his love of Proust. "I often think about it," he wrote. "Wouldn't it be better to set aside my work and undertake the complete translation of *La Recherche*?"

Sydney indirectly answered his rhetorical question by telling Proust he still had four books to write to complete his own multi-volume novel and other writing projects. He specified two, a collection of short stories and a book whose working title was *The Rock* but was almost certainly published as *Tony*. He told Proust it was based on the life of his uncle, Sir Ernest Schiff, his father's partner in A. G. Schiff. *Tony* does include an important character nicknamed "the Rock," who appears to be based on Sir Ernest. The title character and narrator was based on his brother, who was also named Ernest. Using his brother as the narrator was a device that allowed Sydney to say things about himself that would have sounded inappropriate coming from the mouth of Richard Kurt. *Tony*, as Sydney indicated it would be, was followed by two more novels, *Myrtle* and *Richard, Myrtle and I*. It turned out, though, that Sydney wasn't finished. After an eleven-year hiatus, at the age of sixty-eight, he published one more novel, *The Other Side*, which focused on some of the same deeply personal and painful issues raised in *Prince Hempseed* and *Richard Kurt*.

Although he appeared to have resolved the problem in favor of completing his own work, in a rather transparent attempt to have Proust beg him to do the translation, Sydney once again expressed ambivalence. After announcing that what he had set forth was the program for the rest of his life, which he was certain to accomplish because it was his destiny, he asked, with feigned reluctance: "Do I have to translate *La Recherche*?" How would he find the time? He said it wasn't about having the energy or anything like that, but rather it was about him being the only one who could do it "the way it had to be done." You can almost hear a plaintive "Oh Proust, dear Marcel, please ask me to do it" in his tone. In the end, though, Proust never asked and Scott Moncrieff was hired to do the translation.

Toward the end of this letter Sydney shared with Proust his belief that some in his British literary circle were, if not envious, then resentful of any success he might achieve with his writing. He named Eliot, Mansfield, and Murry but for some reason neglected to mention the gorilla in the room, Wyndham Lewis. The source of the resentment, he wrote, was that he was not a professional, by which they meant he did not have to earn his living by writing. "They also have a kind of idea . . . that what I do has real value, that my books don't die as quickly as they would hope, and that far from being discouraged by the small sale of my books, I go on with full confidence in my ideas, in my means and in my future without, nevertheless, the least ambition."

Sydney must have written again before Proust wrote to him around July 5, but his letter is missing. Judging from Proust's response, though, he complained bitterly that Proust was not paying enough attention to him. Proust, angry at having his loyalty questioned and his declining health unappreciated, found Sydney's letter "revolting" and wondered whether he should respond at all to what he felt was emotional "blackmail." "You know perfectly well that I see no one," he wrote to Sydney, and indeed with one exception, about which they already knew, he added, the Schiffs were the only people he had seen for many months. He also said that in his condition he could not even write letters and that the one to them was an exception written on scraps of paper he saved to light the powders he used to fumigate his room. He had to make do, he said, because his writing paper was out of reach and Céleste was asleep. He then launched a kind of counterattack against Sydney, accusing him of many things, but in at least one case—not reading his book—unfairly.

"You know that you yourself lead the kind of life that I don't, but that you reproach me for," he wrote. "If you read my book you will see the infatuations and bad tempers of this frivolous life from which I detached myself at the age of 20, but that didn't keep the *Nouvelle Revue Française* from rejecting *Swann* twenty years later as the work of a frivolous socialite. But you don't read my book because like all the socialites . . . in Paris you are too nervous, in London you are too busy and in the country you have too many guests." Obviously feeling sorry for himself, Proust said he wasn't sure Sydney even liked him, an allegation calculated to wound his devoted acolyte. And probably because of his state of despondency he told an irrelevant story with an opaque moral about the sad state of impoverished artists, which didn't apply to either the Schiffs or himself.

Whistler, he wrote, was accosted by bailiffs for nonpayment of debts while dining with several millionaires, any one of whom could have easily bought a picture or two and sent the bailiffs packing. But they didn't. Whistler said he didn't think this was because of avarice, or because they were bad people, but rather because of a lack of imagination. Then, recognizing the inapplicability of his story, Proust wrote, "the Whistler example has led us astray from the case I've unsuccessfully been building against you, but I'm too tired. I'm content to cite one example of my faithfulness," at which point Proust offered to show Sydney some fifty dinner invitations from Prince Antoine Bibesco, none of which he had accepted.

He seemed to think he was done when he wrote, "Place my respects at the feet of Madame Violet and believe in my profound affection, Marcel," but he wasn't. Despite his professed fatigue, he addressed several other simmering matters in a lengthy postscript.

Proust strenuously objected to Sydney's self-regarding supposition that he was feeling better after their last evening together. He was irritated at Sydney's inability to understand that the Schiffs' departure could only have caused him tears and emotional desolation. And on strictly physiological grounds Proust, whose father and brother were physicians, did not believe in mind over matter. He believed in and knew something about traditional medicine, as a result of which he repeated a series of recommendations he had given Sydney earlier about taking care of his health. These included quitting alcohol, not taking adrenaline if his blood pressure was low, and seeing a "serious" doctor about his "tension" and to examine his heart. Finally, he offered some fresh advice to Sydney that was not necessarily addressed to a specific complaint: "Take some Boissy laxative pills once every two weeks . . . and make sure to take them after eating and not to eat after taking them."

An increasingly touchy Proust, noting that their letters had crossed, wrote to Sydney about two weeks later to correct "many errors" in Sydney's letter. He asserted emphatically that he was "by no means cured" of his various ailments even though he had written to Sydney that his dizziness, the weakness in his legs, and his problems with language had almost entirely disappeared. He also alleged that Sydney had misunderstood his comments about Antoine Bibesco and praised Bibesco for having shown great enthusiasm for *Swann* in 1911 when he read extracts in manuscript. Then he took issue with a view of Sydney's that he most likely reaffirmed in the lost letter. Sydney took the position that if you really knew a person you didn't need to read his or her books, an attitude Proust thought was "absurd." Proust wrote that there was "a world" between what someone said in drawing-room conversation and the profound meditations they set down in their written work. He did allow that there were those who had things to say in conversation that were better than what they wrote in their books, but in those cases, he said, their books were not serious.

When he wrote only three days later Proust complained that their letters had crossed again and that it was "as bad as when one of us was left abandoned at the Ritz while the other was staying at the Foyot." He was so annoyed by it that he returned to the subject of crossing letters later, calling it "a form of epistolary hell." In a different vein, Proust played with the option of using *toi*, the familiar form of address, instead of the formal *vous*, which in those days in France indicated profound intimacy. But he did it in a way that left it open for Sydney to decide how to respond, although he must have known Sydney would be thrilled to have achieved that degree of closeness with him.

After explaining to Sydney in great detail and somewhat defensively his thoughts on the sale of his original manuscripts, he addressed the rest of this long letter to "Dear Madame Violet, hidden flower, fragrant and marvelous." He told her self-effacingly, but not credibly, that he was intimidated by her and therefore he would be brief. He thanked her for an apology she apparently had made for inviting his niece Suzy to visit Sydney and herself without asking his permission and generously added that it wasn't necessary to ask. Besides, he added, he knew nothing about it because his brother was too busy "cutting out tumors and resuscitating the dead" to give him any of his time. Suzy, however, offered another perspective. She said Proust was violently opposed to her going, which resulted in her never being invited again.

Proust asked Violet to tell Sydney he was going to be silent for a while because he needed to work and "hundreds" of letters had accumulated and he had to answer them. He also told her he had had lunch at the Ritz and had seen two men walking in the garden. He asked who they were and was told one was Mortimer Leo Schiff, the American banker who was staying at the Ritz the night he waited in vain for Sydney and Violet. The other was his son. He also said he had two stories to tell Sydney, but that it had taken him four days to write the letter she was reading and it had almost killed him.

Sydney wrote back to Proust the next day, July 30, and diametrically reversing his previously adamant position told him that not only did he not object to Proust selling his manuscripts, but if possible he would like to buy them. Indeed, he said, he had dreamed of possessing them for a long time, and the only thing that kept him from making an offer was his fear of getting involved in financial dealings with a friend. Perhaps he also was beginning to believe that Proust might really die soon. He said the only other writer whose manuscripts were of any interest to him was Wyndham Lewis. He distinguished between them, though, in that he wanted Proust's manuscripts because of the incredible achievement they represented while in Lewis's case it was because of his as-yet-unfulfilled promise. Sydney then evaluated Proust's work in a way that for almost any other writer would have seemed extravagant, but in Proust's case, arguably, was justified.

He began by saying Proust was on a level with the greatest writers of the past and that his works "have their permanent and definitive place in the history of European literature above everyone since Balzac." With respect to *In Search of Lost Time*, he wrote, "I think that with you we have arrived at the end of the novel form. There is nothing more one can do, everything of which the novel is capable you have done or will do." He said that he and Violet had read the best contemporary French literature and other European literature in translation and "without exception, it all fades, lacks reality, finesse, individuality, even intelligence, after you."

Having concluded that Proust had rendered novel writing "superfluous and vain" and having told him so, Sydney nonetheless tried to explain to him what he was after in his own work. "I am trying," he wrote, "in a very modest, simple and primitive way, to create a small chain of childhood memories, of brief scenes, each of which must show a phase of development of a person who is intelligent and sensitive, but rather middling in his intellectual attributes. I fully realize that the two badly translated little stories I have given you have not made a very favorable impression, but I think, first of all, if you knew the psychology of the English child, and above all, if you were able to read in English, you would say that I'm on the way to a new form of presentation that is worthwhile from the realist point of view." Once again Sydney's high regard for modesty was trumped by the vanity raging in his soul.

At the end of his long letter Sydney told Proust that he and Violet would come to Paris, and for the first time he used the familiar form of address, which Proust had implicitly encouraged him to do. But he did not do so without expressing his discomfort in a brief postscript. "'Tutoyer' doesn't come easy to me," he wrote. "As you know I've never spent more than ten weeks in France, with the exception of the Italian-French-English midi, which is not France." What he seemed to be saying, of course, was that he didn't know the French well enough to be sure he wasn't overstepping the bounds of propriety. By then, though, he and Proust were using first names in their salutations and freely expressing their devotion to one another, which suggests that Sydney's trepidations about using *tu* were overly fastidious.

Almost a month passed before Sydney received another letter, but this, Proust explained, was because a very long and important letter he had written was somehow lost, perhaps mistakenly thrown in the garbage, before it was mailed. "God knows what suffering it is for me to write," Proust complained, before addressing the *tutoyer* question in a complex, but comprehensible paragraph. He wrote: "My letter would no longer be altogether appropriate since I was reproaching you for things your new letter renders moot. Thus you were addressing me as 'tu,' while I was hesitant to do the same, but still had decided to do so. However, you answered me with a 'vous' letter, so I berated myself about my step forward causing me to make two steps backward. All the more so since you had said 'it is too difficult to say 'tu,' etc.' Nonetheless, the last letter annuls my self-berating since it is couched in 'tu'. All of this reminds me of Mallarmé's verses." Here Proust misquotes the first two lines of Mallarmé's poem "Placet futile," but his point and the point of the poem, which is dedicated to Mallarmé's mistress, Méry Laurent, is a slightly risqué switch from *vous* to *tu*.

The rest of the letter recounted a bit of gossip of the kind Proust believed interested Sydney. It concerned a report from Deauville in the *Figaro* that the daughter of one of Proust's friends, who according to Proust was married to a "detestable" Romanian, had entertained the shah of Persia at tea and the Prince of Greece for an afternoon snack. Proust questioned the difference between the two, asking himself wryly whether at tea there was nothing to eat and at a *goûter*, or snack, there was no tea. The letter was signed simply "Marcel."

A couple of days later Sydney wrote back to Proust from his country house at the time in East Sussex about thirty-five miles from London. He explained right off that his difficulty in using *tu* had nothing to do with his feelings for Proust, but rather with the fact that his lack of familiarity with using *tu* caused him to forget and lapse into the formal *vous* in the course of a letter. Indeed, he wrote, his feelings ran much deeper than the familiar personal pronouns could possibly express, an indication he was beginning to slip into one of his more excessive moods. He soon carried it to an extreme, one Proust hardly could find congenial. After declaring that Proust's letters were "the joy and the reward" of his life, he added bizarrely that "it would have been better if Céleste had thrown Odilon into the garbage [rather than the lost letter]," which, he said, "would have saved me undeserved suffering." Sydney was not beyond thinking this was a joke. Most of his efforts at humor were lame in this vein, and it is not always easy to tell if he meant something to be funny.

Sydney reported to Proust that Eliot had just spent a night with him and Violet in the country. Although Eliot did not admire Proust's work, his receipt of the Prix Goncourt had sent his reputation soaring, and Eliot had sought Sydney's help in getting a contribution for the *Criterion*. He had written directly to Proust, but Proust had not responded and Sydney took it upon himself to apologize on Proust's behalf, saying he hadn't answered because the appropriate persons at his French publisher were unavailable.

Sydney then returned, as he always seemed to at that time in his life, to his own work, reminding Proust of the sketches he had sent him. "I finished today my book that constitutes a chain of 28 of these stories," he wrote. "They are incidents or scenes in the life of a boy from the age of 3 until 18 written from his own point of view at the time of the incidents." He apologized for explaining the book's premise poorly, but said he was sure Proust would understand it. The book, although he didn't say so, was *Prince Hempseed*. He wrote that he hoped his friend the Belgian poet Jean de Bosschère would translate the volume and that nothing would make him happier than to be able to dedicate it to Proust. Rather than just ask Proust's permission to dedicate the book to him, though, Sydney, in his typically convoluted fashion, recited an argument against doing it before rather unsubtly trying to influence Proust to do it. The argument against was that he would be taking unfair advantage of Proust's immense literary prestige. The argument for was that he had poured his heart and soul into the book and it was the best thing he had done yet. So, he asked Proust, "What do you think?"

On September 9, Sydney wrote again to Proust, this time very briefly to let him know that the first announcement of the forthcoming publication of *Swann's Way* in English had appeared in the *Athenaeum* and to register his disapproval of the volume's title and also the general title, *Remembrance of Things Past*. With respect to *Swann's Way* Sydney favored something more like *In the Man-*

ner of Swann, but he had misunderstood Proust's meaning, which referred only to the physical path on which Swann's house was situated. His objection to the general title was better founded, however. Although Sydney had missed the fact that Scott Moncrieff had taken his title from the second line of Shakespeare's sonnet number 30, this was irrelevant because Scott Moncrieff, in choosing the line from Shakespeare, had missed Proust's larger purpose in the novel, which was to explore the nature of time. Although the phrase "remembrance of things past" can be read as an allusion to the recollections stimulated by the taste of a madeleine dipped in lime tea, it does a disservice to the complex treatment of time as a central theme of Proust's novel and loses the resonance between the general title and the title of the final volume, *Temps Retrouvé*, or *Time Regained*. Sydney said he would get a copy as soon as they became available and let Proust know what he thought of the translation.

On September 14, 1922, thirty-four days before his death, Proust wrote to Sydney. It was the last letter he sent to him that has survived. But on October 3 Sydney wrote in passing to Max Beerbohm that he had received a letter from Proust that morning. Sydney, who was deeply concerned about Proust's failing health, told Beerbohm Proust's handwriting seemed distressingly feeble. He apologized in his letter to Beerbohm for not having sent him *Swann's Way* as promised and said he would send him the Scott Moncrieff translation immediately and that he was eager to have his opinion of it. And if Beerbohm shared the Schiffs' love for the book, Sydney added, it would give him great satisfaction to be able to tell Proust. But there was no time to waste.

Proust's September 14 letter to Sydney was also distressing, in this case for its lack of warmth and its testiness, both reflecting Proust's rapidly declining health and the desperate urgency he felt to finish correcting his novel. He told Sydney he was ill again, possibly because a broken fireplace was leaking carbon dioxide into his room and asphyxiating him, which was unlikely because the fireplaces at 44 rue Hamelin smoked so badly they were never used. "Whatever the cause," Proust wrote, "the effect is a despair worse than death. I am obliged to work under these conditions without a day of respite." He said he didn't like to complain, but Sydney in his last letter had asked [more or less begged] for a response, although just a few lines. Proust then flatly rejected Sydney's suggestion that the English title of *Swann's Way* be changed to *In the Manner of Swann* or *In the Fashion of Swann*, as Sydney had suggested. And after describing some commercial transactions involving the sale of his manuscripts he called Sydney "a torturer" for "demanding" a letter from him. He concluded with "My respectful admiration to the angel Violet" and signed himself Marcel Proust, with no word of respect or affection for Sydney. It turned out, though, that he was not quite done. He added a postscript.

"Read the praise—setting aside the absurdity of its exaggeration—for me by Léon Daudet in *L'Action Française*. We do not agree politically, which adds to its merit." Proust then called Sydney "odious" (the same word Katherine Mansfield once used to describe the Schiffs) for not having answered various questions he had asked in previous letters, and in what appeared to be a way of telling Sydney that he was far from the first to appreciate Proust's talent, he wrote: "When I was twenty years old Antoine Bibesco already had said to me, 'Little Marcel, you are the most (but it is too flattering, I cannot finish the sentence).'" Proust then said that in his next letter he would respond to a comment Sydney had made about his friend Sir Philip Sassoon, adding that "it will perhaps be a long time because I have a crazy amount of work to do—unless death comes for me first."

Sydney's last letter to Proust was written exactly a month later. But in it he referred to two unanswered letters he had written since receiving Proust's letter of September 14. The tone of Proust's last letter had upset him greatly, but there was no indication in his reply that he sensed Proust would actually die within weeks. He wrote to Proust that he was profoundly saddened by his letter, felt separated from him, and no longer knew how much Proust liked [or perhaps he meant loved] him. He wallowed a bit more in the depression Proust's letter had caused him before shifting almost seamlessly to a more mundane matter, namely the reception of the English translation of Proust's novel. He wrote that the reviews were more or less banal and not very intelligent, which didn't seem to surprise him. But he was so irritated by the favorable impression Scott Moncrieff's translation was making on the English reviewers that he wrote: "Each time I read the effusive praise for your translator I feel like vomiting." Then he told Proust he was in the midst of correcting the proofs of *Prince Hempseed* and needed to know as soon as possible whether Proust objected to the book being dedicated to him.

Sydney then wrote what would be his last words to his dear Marcel, the only person in the world other than Violet he had loved and admired unconditionally: "I have thought many times of going to Paris for two days just to see you for a moment. You have no idea how I have spent these last days—with what despair. A letter from you would have been for me the prayer my lips would not let escape, the tears my eyes did not want to release. But it didn't come and I don't know if you are better or worse, if you think of me or not, if I must continue to say to myself: he is there, he is there, or if, like all the rest except one he has disappeared into thin air and the earth is naked. I send you all my affection, Your Sydney."

Proust died four days later on Saturday, November 18, at fifty-one. It seems unlikely that he read Sydney's last letter. On December 12 his niece Suzy wrote to Violet that before he died her uncle had asked that the waistcoat he wore the last time he was with the Schiffs be given to Sydney.

CHAPTER 9

A FALLING-OUT

No record survives of the emotional impact Proust's death had on Sydney and Violet, but their letters leave no doubt of the profound attachment they felt for him and the extent to which his presence dominated their lives. During the few years they knew him they continued working on Sydney's multivolume novel, visiting friends, giving lunches, dinners, and game-playing parties, and traveling to their country houses in England and the south of France. But in retrospect all these things seem peripheral to their love affair with the great French novelist. No one knows how they mourned him, but Sydney did all he could to promote *In Search of Lost Time* and to keep Proust's memory vividly alive in England. He helped Eliot get a selection for the *Criterion*. He wrote a short story for the *Criterion* based on Céleste Albaret's devoted service to Proust. He published an essay in a volume titled *Marcel Proust: An English Tribute*. When Scott Moncrieff died Sydney translated *Time Regained*, the final volume of Proust's novel. And when *Prince Hempseed*, the third volume of his own autobiographical novel, was published several months later he dedicated it "To the memory of my beloved friend, Marcel Proust."

But by the spring of 1923, however deeply they felt the loss of Proust, the Schiffs had moved on to what was in effect the next stage of their lives. They began working, together as usual, on *Tony*, which was intended to be the third volume in *A True Story* but was not included in any of the three published versions of the work. They entertained their friends frequently at 18 Cambridge Square and at a country house they bought at Lye Green, Chesham, in Buckinghamshire near London instead of the one they previously had occupied at Eastbourne on the southern coast. The change of vacation houses came as an unpleasant surprise to the Eliots, who had rented a cottage near Eastbourne especially to be near the Schiffs, but it didn't seem to cause a rift. In fact Sydney became more involved with the *Criterion* than at any time since he brought Eliot and Lady Rothermere together. And as Vivienne's health, both physical and mental, declined, her attachment to Violet, who could be comforting and compassionate when she sensed the need and cared for the person, grew even closer.

Eliot complained to both Schiffs that he was totally worn down by his work at the bank and by putting out the magazine and caring for Vivienne, all of which left him no time for poetry or serious criticism. Undoubtedly counting on Sydney's sympathy and possibly hoping for more, perhaps in the form of financial support or at least an idea or two about how to improve his situation, Eliot sent him a drawn-out sigh of a letter on March 12. "Ever since I saw you last," he wrote, "I have been in a state of worry to the point of paralysis. . . . I must now either give up the Criterion . . . or I must give up the bank and find some work that I can fit in with the Criterion." He wrote that he had been offered the literary editorship of another journal, apparently with the help of Virginia Woolf, but it paid only half of what he was making at the bank and was too insecure. He was considering the offer nonetheless and was forced to turn down a dinner invitation from the Schiffs because he needed to be available to meet the owners of the journal at their convenience. He said, however, that he would come after dinner and was looking forward to seeing John Middleton Murry, who was also invited.

There is no indication Sydney responded to Eliot's plaintive missive, but two weeks later Eliot wrote to tell Sydney he had decided to stay at the bank. Meanwhile, Violet wrote to Eliot inviting him and Vivienne to lunch to meet Max Beerbohm, who was the author of the charming Oxford-based novel *Zuleika Dobson* and an uproariously funny essay called "A Defense of Cosmetics," also known as "The Pervasion of Rouge." Beerbohm, who would be knighted in 1939 for his contribution to art and letters, was also a brilliant caricaturist. He and his wife, Florence, an American actress, who were living in Rapallo when World War II broke out, would accept the Schiffs' invitation to stay in a cottage on their property at Abinger in Surrey during the war.

Eliot wrote back that he would have "liked very much to meet Beerbohm" but begged off partly because of Vivienne's health— among other things she was having a bad reaction to colonic irrigation—and their general weariness. "Sunday is now our one day of real rest," Eliot wrote. "We shut ourselves up and don't have our servant come . . . you will understand that we are just keeping *alive* and no more . . . but I *do* want to see you both soon." The letter is signed, "With love from both, Tom."

The tone and content of Eliot's letters to the Schiffs and theirs to him certainly suggested intimacy. But how sincere was he when he wrote "love" and what if anything did he expect from the Schiffs besides friendship? The handful of scholars and writers who have paid more than passing attention to the Schiffs, such as Eliot's biographer Lyndall Gordon and Richard Davenport-Hines, have reached different conclusions about their relationships with Eliot and, of course, Proust. In Proust's case, for example, Davenport-Hines saw the Schiffs as little more than fawning acolytes. My reading of the letters suggests a relationship that while petulant and irritating at times was much warmer and more substantive. As far as Eliot was concerned, I see no evidence that Sydney had anything more than a marginal influence, if that, on Eliot's poetry or criticism. He was supportive, made profitable introductions, and helped Eliot solicit work for the *Criterion*, all useful forms of assistance, none of which, however, supports Gordon's opinion that Sydney became Eliot's mentor.

There were rough patches in the Eliot-Schiff relationship, usually owing to Sydney's petulance or lack of tact and Eliot's touchiness. As for the use of the phrase "with love," I think it was sincere. Although Eliot was quite capable when the situation required it of holding his nose and behaving graciously toward someone he disliked but found useful, it would have been out of character for him to use the word "love" without meaning it.

The Schiffs' admiration for Eliot as a poet, critic, and all-around man of letters was enshrined when Sydney told Proust he considered Eliot and Lewis the only writers in England worthy of inclusion in his intellectual realm. Coming from him there could be no higher praise. The existing evidence also suggests Eliot held Sydney and Violet in considerable intellectual esteem. Eliot admired much of what Sydney had done in reviving *Art and Letters*. Both Eliot and Vivienne commented seriously—often positively, but not always—on Sydney's novels. Eliot published fiction and translations by Sydney in the *Criterion*. When he was soliciting a short story from Rebecca West, among the *Criterion* fiction writers he cited to attract her interest were Virginia Woolf, Luigi Pirandello, and Stephen Hudson. And Eliot once said the Schiffs were among the very few persons in London with whom one could have a real conversation.

By the middle of 1923, however, even though the Eliots and Schiffs did not live far apart, their close personal relationship had turned into an epistolary one. This was mainly because of Vivienne's health and Eliot's workload. There is a sense of regret, even

guilt, in Eliot's frequent and often histrionic letters explaining why
they were mostly inaccessible to the Schiffs. Eliot wrote to Sydney
at one point that "when we do get to the country we shall simply
have to bury ourselves completely in order to save our lives, otherwise we could die with less effort in London." He told them that
Vivienne's doctor, "who never exaggerates," had warned her that
if she didn't take care of herself she would *certainly die* [emphasis
Eliot's]." Was the prognosis really that dire? Perhaps, but while the
modernists in general and Eliot in particular prided themselves on
embodying the spirit of classicism, with which they infused their
work, their manner of expressing private concerns was often melo-
dramatic.

Eliot nonetheless ended his letter in a way that suggested Vivienne might be getting reasonably good medical advice for the times,
that his own understanding of medicine was fairly advanced, and
that he was passing on information about Vivienne's condition
because he thought Sydney was sophisticated enough to understand it. "I know that you are one of the exceptional people who are
intelligently interested in health and disease, medicine and hygiene,"
he wrote. "Nearly everybody is ignorant of everything but measles,
appendicitis and 'nerves' as they call them. Nobody has ever heard
of *malnutrition*—the root and core of Vivienne's illness—of which
colitis is only a symptom."

Eliot's description of colitis as a symptom of malnutrition was
the accepted theory of the day, but we now know that there are
various kinds of colitis, each of which has a different cause, none of
them malnutrition. Medical minutiae were a preoccupation of the
modernists and infused their correspondence. But Violet's empathy was especially strong because she often suffered from similar
if less acute symptoms than Vivienne. It was a bond that provided
comfort to both Eliots.

After a couple of months during which no letters were exchanged, Eliot wrote again to Sydney in mid-July to solicit a story

or sketch for the *Criterion*. He said he had delayed writing only because he knew how hard Sydney was working, but now that *Prince Hempseed* was finished he was eager for a contribution and even had something specific in mind. "I think that you could do a very amusing satirical sketch of present times and manners; you know the sort of thing I mean. Yours is a very satirical and observant mind and you might write some very caustic sketches of the sort of people who are typical of our time. This is a sort of thing that the Criterion needs. Can you do something for us *now*?"

What Eliot seemed to be asking for was a slicing and dicing of Bayswater, Bloomsbury, and Garsington, possibly with a lighter touch than Lewis's. It suggests Eliot believed Sydney could be both funny and scathing. There are hints in his fiction and evidence in his letters of the latter, but none anywhere of the former. On the other hand modernist satire is remarkably short on what most people would recognize as humor today. In a brief postscript Eliot apologized to Sydney for the tone of his letter, which he apparently thought was too businesslike and which he attributed to the difficulties of dictating to a new secretary. To correct his perceived breach of etiquette, he wrote rather cloyingly: "I could have said simply that Vol. II *must* have something from you! There are *only* half a dozen writers of fiction and I *depend* on you." Sydney fulfilled Eliot's request for a contribution, but not with the caustic put-down of modernism's finest that Eliot had in mind. What he eventually submitted in February 1924 was *Celeste*.

Sydney and Violet worked at an unusually fast pace during the summer and fall of 1923. Before the end of the year *Tony* was finished and they had sent a manuscript copy to the Eliots. Although *Tony* was initially conceived as part of the series that would eventually be published as *A True Story*, it represented a significant departure from the preceding volumes because it was not told in the voice of Richard Kurt (i.e., Sydney), but rather in the voice of Richard's brother Tony (Ernest in real life). The point was to portray Richard critically in a way that would have been impossible in his own voice. Using a character based on his brother provided the necessary distance. The extent to which Tony resembled Ernest is impossible to say because almost nothing is known about Ernest except that he met his end in the same way Tony did.

Vivienne's response to the book was ambivalent in that she limited her praise to a relatively short section at the end and a single characterization. "What has struck me *most* forcibly in the book," she wrote, "is an extraordinary change of key in the writing. . . . it seems to me you have achieved a *most moving and serious* piece of work, an important document in the history of that period and a fine piece of character work. I think 'the Rock' is very cleverly done, and with such economy." In a separate letter Eliot wrote that he thought "the Rock is extremely real and alive." The "Rock" is portrayed as hard-hearted, but with a preference for Richard over Tony and with pro-German sentiments during World War I. There is no evidence for or against this characterization, but if the real Rock, Sydney's uncle Ernest, had been pro-German he would hardly have been exceptional among his class in the Britain of 1914 to 1918, although very likely in a minority among his Jewish coreligionists.

In late February 1924 Eliot received *Celeste*, for which he thanked Sydney profusely, calling it "a brilliant piece of work." Judging from Céleste's own book called *Monsieur Proust*, which was written many years later, Sydney captured her voice with remarkable accuracy. A week or so later Eliot wrote again to thank Sydney for an inscribed copy of *Tony*. Sydney also must have enclosed a copy of an explanatory letter he had written to his publisher about the book because Eliot said he and Vivienne were "very much struck" by his "exposition of the fundamental idea of *Tony*" as expressed in the letter. Eliot then not too subtly commented that he wished the letter had appeared as a preface because "not many readers, no matter how much they appreciate the skill of the story," would be able to draw the right conclusion. The implicit message would seem to have been that neither he nor Vivienne was able to figure it out on their own either. Unfortunately the explanatory letter is missing, so exactly what Sydney had to say about the "fundamental idea of *Tony*" is lost. But he did say years later that his goal in *Tony* was to introduce a character whose view of Richard, that is himself, was "antithetic" to his own view.

As late as April 1924 the Schiffs and Eliots were still communicating mostly through letters, many of which were devoted to health and the tiresome business of daily life, but a few letters have been preserved that deal with weightier matters. Eliot wrote to Sydney, "As you know, I have read very little Proust, but I am so far as I am qualified to speak, of the opinion that he is not a 'classical' writer. . . . Reconstructions of a past period and investigations of the unconscious do not appear to me relevant: they might be attributes of either classic or romantic. Proust appears to me, from what little I know of him, to be far too much a sensationalist. It is I am sure a wonderful commentary on the world that exists and has existed, not the discovery of a new one." Earlier, Eliot had written to Pound that Proust was "not to my taste, merely a necessary sensation . . . he is not part of the program." Perhaps Proust's novel did not fit neatly inside the Bayswater branch's modernist box and therefore seemed irrelevant. As for Wyndham Lewis, as usual his taste for excess trumped his intellect. "In Proust," he wrote in *Time and Western Man*, "we have in a sense a new type of historical practitioner. Proust embalmed himself alive. He died as a sensational creature in order that he should live as an historian of his dead sensational self."

The Schiffs, of course, were not limiting their social and intellectual life to correspondence with the Eliots. They continued to run a salon at 18 Cambridge Square and to buy contemporary art— Picasso, Matisse, Gauguin, van Gogh, and Chirico, among others, including English artists such as John Nash and Jacob Epstein. And right about then they met the Scottish poet, critic, and translator

Edwin Muir and his wife, Willa, who, as with Sydney and Violet, was a full partner in the Muirs' intellectual enterprises.

Edwin Muir was born into a tenant-farming family in the Orkney Islands. They moved to Glasgow to try to improve their economic situation, and at the age of fourteen he began a series of soul-killing jobs in offices and factories, including one that turned animal bones into charcoal. He was hired as a bookkeeper, but his white-collar job did not protect him from the stench. Years later he described in his autobiography how "the thick, oily smoke hung around in stagnant coils," adding that "sometimes by mischance, a human bone, white and dry, an arm or a skull, would be found" in the mix, but "the animals' bones were always juicy and soft, though the fat had gone sour on them, and the marrow inside was beginning to rot." During these years in Glasgow there was nothing to suggest that his future would be anything but grim, yet by force of will, intellect, and good luck he overcame his circumstances and lack of formal education.

He managed to find a group of sensitive, intelligent friends who helped put him on the path to an autodidact's education. Over the next few years his circle of friends grew to include the Scottish songwriter Francis George Scott and Denis Saurat, who taught French at the University of Glasgow. Then, while working as a clerk in a shipbuilding firm in the winter of 1918, he met Willa Anderson, a teacher and linguist with a first-class honors degree in educational psychology from the University of St. Andrews, Scotland's premier university. They were married the following summer and if by then he was still in need of salvation, he had found it.

The friendship between the Muirs and the Schiffs began with a book review and a letter. Sydney read Edwin Muir's review of *Prince Hempseed* in an American magazine called the *Freeman*, which was modeled on the *Spectator*, promoted the economics of Henry George, and was respected for its high literary standards. In a letter to Muir, whom he did not know, he expressed delight with the review overall and especially with Muir's having detected a flaw in the novel and identified its cause. Sydney acknowledged that Muir was right to conclude he had trouble figuring out how to end the book. Without explaining why, he said he worried that if he carried Richard beyond the point to which he had brought him, the character "would become self-conscious." The "voyage to America," he added, "marked the end of that stage of Richard's life. He was never the same afterwards, and the influence of his experience in America on his future was decisive." It seems fair to say that this judgment reflected Sydney's actual experience in America, which even apart from his marriage to Marion influenced his life in ways he never could have contemplated. At the end of his letter, which was filled with flattery, Sydney said he would send Muir copies of *Elinor Colhouse* and *Tony*, which he did.

Less than two weeks later Sydney received a reply more satisfying than any he could have hoped for. "The most striking thing in both these novels," Muir wrote, "seems to me the success with which you have imparted a sort of *weight* to narratives which are limpid and on the surface simple and ordinary . . . it makes the reader feel that in this way things happened, and only in this way could they have happened. It is a very rare and high gift and very few writers have had it, and I can think of nobody else who has it at present but yourself." Such praise was obviously more than welcome, but what followed was even more so. Muir wrote that if *Tony* was published in the near future he would review it in the *New York Literary Review*, where he had a connection.

While the Schiffs were in the process of forming a new and satisfying friendship with the Muirs, their relationship with the irascible Wyndham Lewis, which might have been irreparably damaged by his bad behavior toward Katherine Mansfield, seemed to be flourishing. Lewis must have been feeling unusually warm toward Sydney and Violet, who at the time were providing him with relatively modest but fairly regular financial support, because he took the rare step of reading to them some passages from a novel in progress. Judging from their effusive reaction, they considered it something of a masterpiece. The work was "astounding," Violet wrote to Lewis afterwards, and Sydney scrawled "I quite agree" across the page. Violet also added that she wished "a bit of it could appear in the Criterion" and lo and behold six days later Eliot wrote to Sydney that indeed he had offered to publish excerpts in the magazine. Eliot seemed surprised that while Lewis had taken the Schiffs into his confidence by reading to them from the working manuscript, he had failed to tell them that he, Eliot, had offered to publish a selection. Lewis initially turned down the opportunity because he thought the book would do better if all of it first appeared between hard covers. But it didn't take long for him to change his mind, perhaps because he realized the book would take years to finish and no doubt because as always he needed the money.

The first excerpt appeared in February 1924 under the title "Mr. Zagreus and the Split Man" below a brief preface in which Lewis wrote that he hoped to complete the book "by next autumn." The second selection appeared in the April issue and was titled "Extract from Encyclical Addressed to Daniel Boleyn by Mr. Zagreus." The finished work was called *The Apes of God*, but it did not finally emerge in book form until 1930, one year before Lewis published *Hitler*, his most infamous book, arguing that the benighted Austrian painter of insipid landscapes, the venomous anti-Semite who would become Germany's fuehrer three years later, was that country's incipient savior and should be lionized, not vilified.

There is no record of what Lewis read to Sydney and Violet, but it probably wasn't from *Hitler* or "Chez Lionel Kein," the chapter in *The Apes of God* in which they would be wickedly and anti-Semitically skewered. Doubtless, though, it was from a chapter in *The Apes* that caricatured and metaphorically disemboweled one or more of their friends—the Sitwells, possibly—a fact that did not seem to enter into their resoundingly positive reaction to whatever selection Lewis read to them. When "Extract from Encyclical," which contained a snide reference to Sydney, appeared in the *Criterion*, however, the Schiffs began to have second thoughts.

Evidence of this appeared in early May when Eliot, who was feeling massively put upon by his editorial responsibilities and was under siege from the multiple targets of Lewis's sulfurous excerpts in the *Criterion*, wrote a rather whiney and short-tempered letter to Virginia Woolf. He complained somewhat hyperbolically that he had already "been 'warned' . . . by our venerable and august friend Mr. Sydney Schiff, that I may be met on my return at Victoria Station by a mass meeting of protestants against my careless editing—in not having had time to read and expurgate Wyndham Lewis's article before publication, there being only twenty-four hours in a day." He went on to say, "This armed and menacing meeting of all those who feel that 'the cap fits' (I expect to recognize many friendly faces) will presumably be led by Mr. Sydney Schiff himself in the costume and headpiece of a pseudo-Proust."

Eliot was referring to a specific slur by Zagreus in the April *Criterion* excerpt—"In a little artificial world of carefully fostered self-esteem I will show you a pseudo-Proust"—which everyone in Bayswater recognized instantly as a reference to Sydney. But Bloomsbury was not as clued in about the Schiffs. Woolf wrote to Eliot a few days later that she and her husband, Leonard, thought the Proust reference was to Katherine Mansfield's husband, John Middleton Murry. She added with a trace of glee: "Everyone, Lytton [Strachey], Osbert Sitwell, Mary Hutchinson is claiming to be an Ape of God and identifying the rest of the pack." Although "*Apes* ID" was the hottest parlor game in her set, the overall reception of the excerpts was not quite so benign. Eliot wrote to his friend Harold Monro that there had been "a torrent of abuse."

As typically happened, though, the *Apes* episode blew over and was only minimally damaging to the Schiffs' relationships with Eliot and Lewis. Six months later, though, Sydney suffered one of his periodic lapses in tact, which compromised both relationships much more significantly. He made the egregious mistake of writing two agitated letters to Eliot complaining about Lewis badgering him for money. Sydney had lent Lewis money to tide him over during a particularly difficult time, but Lewis kept pressing him for more, and in ever greater amounts. Fed up and not knowing what else to do, he asked Eliot to intervene. Eliot found the request presumptuous but nevertheless agreed to meet Sydney, who to his dismay presented him with a typed list of all the money he had lent Lewis. The total was 120 pounds. Things had come to a head when Lewis asked for still more, no doubt in his usual self-deprecating, gracious, and undemanding way, and Sydney, exasperated and pushed to his emotional if not financial limit, told him, "I cannot go on giving you money at this rate."

Eliot, who was thoroughly incensed at Sydney's clumsy attempt to entangle him in the matter, reacted by sending Lewis a detailed account of the meeting, which he said he attended absolutely against his will and which caused him "infinite annoyance." He said he refused to interfere, in response to which Sydney lost his temper and "some disagreeable words" passed between them. Eliot then warned Lewis that Sydney might attempt "to make mischief" between Lewis and himself, but that Lewis should keep his letter confidential and do nothing. Soon thereafter, Sydney, eager to smooth things over with Lewis and unaware of Eliot's letter to him, wrote to Lewis asking where their relationship stood. Lewis, who had spent Sydney's money and had no interest in paying it back or making up, wrote cryptically to Sydney that he had "put him in a fix" and he was still dealing with its unpleasant consequences. It was not the first nor would it be the last breach in their relations. What Sydney might not have known, though, was that a patronage fund from which Lewis had been receiving sixteen pounds a month had also dried up, leaving him even more destitute than usual.

There is no indication that Sydney and Violet saw, spoke to, or wrote to the Eliots again until mid-April 1925. The Schiffs' letter resuming the correspondence is missing, but it is evident from Eliot's response that Sydney and Violet had invited the Eliots to visit them. Eliot said they couldn't come without explaining why and added that "it is hopeless to try to explain what things have been and what they are, until we meet," suggesting that a lot of time had passed since they had been in touch and that there was a lot to talk about.

During the five months since the fiasco over Lewis's debts, Sydney and Violet had kept busy finishing still another volume of his ever-expanding fictional autobiography. This one was called *Myrtle* and was mostly about Violet, not Sydney, although Richard Kurt appears as a character. Each chapter portrays Violet in the context of her relationship with a person who was or might have been important in her life. Although the Eliot-Schiff relationship had cooled considerably, Sydney had sent Eliot a copy, probably hoping it would be reviewed in the *Criterion*. Eliot noted that he had received the book but had not had a chance to read it and then displayed his not inconsiderable capacity for disingenuousness: "I don't know *when* I shall be able to read *Myrtle*—but Vivienne has told me something about it, and anything she says in praise of a book is worthwhile, because it is always definite—the only kind of praise worth having, in my opinion."

It is impossible to tell from the way Eliot constructed his sentence whether Vivienne had anything at all to say in praise of the book, but it would be unfair to Eliot to think the sentence had been haphazardly constructed. There is no doubt, however, that Eliot did not tell Sydney that Vivienne's less-than-flattering review of *Myrtle* was about to appear in the April issue of the *Criterion*. The review, signed "F.M.," the initials of Feiron Morris—one of several pseudonyms Vivienne used when writing for the journal so that Lady Rothermere would pay her for the reviews—began with praise for Sydney's ability to saturate the reader in a particular atmosphere. But she quickly homed in and elaborated on what she saw as a glaring and, judging from her tone, fatal flaw in the book. The problem with *Myrtle*, she wrote in a gently mocking voice, "is that one cannot find Myrtle, and one is worried by looking for her all the time. . . . The result is a collection of character studies of somewhat uninteresting and unsavory persons. But, as one peers between the figures, hoping to catch sight of the supremely interesting figure of Myrtle, around which this odd assemblage is hung, one is perpetually baffled. Where is Myrtle?"

There is no record of how Sydney felt about Vivienne's review at the time, or whether he responded to it, but years later in his essay for *Ten Contemporaries* he explained that *Myrtle* was a failed effort to portray the woman Richard loved through the consciousness of nine different individuals. He said that as a result of his faulty technique Myrtle's vitality failed to emerge. His ego having been reconstituted by Violet, Sydney was rarely if ever defensive about his writing. In the same essay he disparaged *Tony*, calling it an unsuccessful experiment in technique. He said he was without ambition (for literary recognition presumably) and wrote only to understand himself. And should there be any doubt that *A True Story* was autobiographical, he wrote, "I have for long been living that novel and I am still living it." His work was narrowly conceived, he almost always knew when he had failed to meet his goals, and he had few if any inhibitions about acknowledging his shortcomings, so it seems unlikely he would have resented or perhaps even disagreed with Vivienne's review.

Eliot wrote again two days later, this time to Violet, making two things clear: that he was increasingly preoccupied with Vivienne's health, which together with work at the bank and on the *Criterion* was exhausting him, and that he was eager to repair relations with the Schiffs. How much of the latter had to do with Vivienne's health and her wishes to see them was unexpressed, but implicit—a lot. After another catalog of her most recent ailments, Eliot took note of a warm letter from Violet to Vivienne and said, "We *must* meet (tell S.) when <*as soon as*> you come back. I think of you often." After signing off as "Yrs affectionately, Tom," Eliot asked, more as a wish than a question, "Should we have more charades next winter?" This was still another indication that Vivienne, who enjoyed the games at the Schiffs', and was better at them than her husband, was his current priority. He knew Sydney and Violet were favorites of Vivienne's and probably believed that bringing her together with them could ease his life as well as hers.

During much of the next two months the Schiffs appear to have been away from London, either at Lye Green in Buckinghamshire or at their house in Roquebrune. For whatever reason, they did not write to the Eliots during this period, which led to a terse letter, not to Sydney but to Violet, that could only have been designed to induce guilt. "My dear Violet," Eliot wrote, "why do V and I never hear from either of you? How are you? V's new treatment continues, but will be very hard and very long. She was just on the verge of paralysis of the intestine and some terrible functional liver trouble. The doctor said he had never seen so bad a liver on a woman, or an intestine so nearly dead. I am sure she would like to hear from you. Ever aff, Tom." Given Eliot's sensitivity to social forms, it is unlikely his failure to say that he too would like to hear from Violet or Sydney was an oversight.

The Schiffs' correspondence with the Eliots was now petering out, but the last letters exchanged during this period were poignant and revealing. Violet wrote to Eliot sometime between June 17 and September 8, 1925. The letter is lost, but it prompted a long, sensitive response from Eliot on Vivienne's gifts and her grit. However difficult their marriage had been, she had qualities he admired and in his way he cared for her and about her. He also cared for and admired Violet and believed the two women were "professional," that they had much more in common than their at times similar medical complaints. He wrote that Vivienne had three means of artistic expression, all of which came more naturally to her than writing—painting, music, and dance—and all of which were thwarted by physical disabilities. This was background to his main point, which was that by "pure force of character" she had made herself a writer. Then he addressed himself to Violet, whom he pronounced definitively was "essentially a singer." She apparently was giving singing lessons at the time because Eliot asked her forgiveness for saying that training others was not enough for someone of her ability. "You will," he wrote, "I hope and believe, find some other direct means of expressing yourself—like Vivienne—in some other art or profession."

Finally, perhaps feeling he might have come across as condescending, Eliot addressed his own career self-deprecatingly by saying, "I am not sure . . . that I have not been *forced* into poetry by my weakness in other directions—that there is not something else that I want. . . . The admission of this fact may help you to admit that I understand in part the tragedy of others."

During 1925 the Schiff-Eliot correspondence continued to dwindle, but the couples were still meeting socially at the Schiffs', once again together with Lewis. "I was often with Mr. Eliot at the Schiffs" during that period, Lewis wrote in a rare unmannered, unaffected comment, "in . . . a household where we were very much spoiled by our hosts, for my part for the last time I saw Mr. Eliot in a mood that was very young. There he would read his latest work." This was the only mention of the Schiffs by name in either of Lewis's two autobiographies.

Although they had heard nothing from Eliot for some time, on December 16 the Schiffs received a desperate-sounding letter from Vivienne from the Stansborough Park Sanitarium, a so-called "hydrotherapeutic health institution" in Watford, Hertfordshire, about twenty miles from central London. In late October Eliot, who said he had reached his outer limit in trying to cope with her illness, had deposited her there. He then went off for a little rest and recreation at La Turbie, not far from the Schiffs' house in Roquebrune, but perhaps more relevantly near Monte Carlo, where his friends from the Ballets Russes were in summer residence. Before leaving he had made various efforts to find someone who could help Vivienne but apparently got nothing but bad advice. Leonard Woolf had recommended a doctor named Sir Henry Head but probably hadn't told Eliot that Virginia had tried to commit suicide after a session with Head in 1913. Eliot rejected Head on grounds that his treatments were not up to date and he didn't like his manner.

Vivienne, who was obviously distraught, first wrote to Ezra Pound pleading for him to ask Eliot to "rescue" her, but Pound demurred. Eliot joined Pound in Rapallo soon thereafter and Vivienne remained incarcerated. Finally she wrote to Sydney and Violet: "I have always looked upon you as friends. Am I right? I am in very great difficulty, and in a most lonely and precarious situation. I do not know what to do, and I can think of no people who could advise me better than yourselves." She begged them to come by car to visit her and to ask the matron "if you may take me out for a short drive and then return me." She warned them not to be upset by her looks. "I look worse than I am," she said. "This is chiefly worry and fear and torment. . . . I am going quite gray. Do help me. Do write and then do *come.*"

Sydney and Violet responded promptly to Vivienne's plea for help, and after seeing her they sent Eliot a copy of her letter and told him they found her less agitated than the letter indicated. By the end of their visit, they wrote, she "became perfectly reasonable." The Schiffs said Vivienne attributed most of her troubles to years of taking chloral hydrate, a popular sedative and hypnotic drug that was overused and often misprescribed at the time. The exact nature of her illness, though, was never adequately diagnosed. Whatever the reasons for Vivienne's state of mind, her stay at the Stansborough might accurately be called the beginning of the end of a marriage that was doomed from the start. Her life with Eliot was certainly no easier than his was with her. Very likely it was more difficult because of her mental fragility. Over the next seven years she had affairs, contemplated leaving Eliot, and was in and out of sanitariums, sometimes with him and sometimes without him, until finally, in 1933, he left her. In 1937, after being found wandering the streets at 5 a.m. in an incoherent state, she was committed to a mental institution. She died there on January 22, 1947.

CHAPTER 10

NEW FRIENDS

~:ʘʘ:~

Sometime in 1923—it might have been when the Schiffs moved from Eastbourne to Lye Green, disappointing the Eliots—a potentially unsettling transformation in their lives slowly began unfolding. There is no telling when they noticed it or how much they were discomfited by it. But by the end of 1925 the friends around whom their social life had revolved were gone, almost as if they'd never existed. Proust was dead and the Eliots and Lewis might as well have been. They neither saw nor talked nor wrote to one another. Eliot no longer asked Sydney to contribute to the *Criterion*, and the *Criterion* no longer reviewed his books. And Vivienne no longer sought Violet's companionship or empathy.

Exactly why this came to pass is unclear. Perhaps Sydney's behavior in the episode of Lewis's finances, or the way he acted over the publication of the second *Apes of God* excerpt, never stopped irritating Eliot. Irritation exacerbated by a debilitating combination of work and taking care of Vivienne easily could have turned to ire. Eliot had nothing to say about it, though, and what Sydney had to say was not illuminating. He told his friend Edwin Muir, "Of Eliot I have seen nothing. Our intercourse came abruptly to an end as

a result of certain happenings about which I prefer not to write."
As for Lewis, the money incident almost certainly enraged him at
first and grated on him afterwards. He might also have correctly
concluded that Sydney was no longer a reliable and inexhaustible
source of cash. Sydney, however, was no more enlightening about
this breakup: "Of Lewis too I hear nothing," he told Muir. "I see
nobody who sees him and cannot imagine who his associates are."

As disconcerting as it might have been, though, this turn of
events hardly left the Schiffs bereft of friends. In the years between
1925 and 1930 social life in Cambridge Square and Lye Green continued to flourish. Some old friends like the painter John Nash,
whose work they collected, continued to come, formerly infrequent
visitors came more often, and some new names were added to the
guest list. Nash helped them when they were looking for a new
house to buy in the country, and when they settled on the one in
Lye Green he took charge of relandscaping the property, a well-
intended gesture that led to a certain amount of acrimony. Sydney,
it seems, nagged Nash and asked more of him than he thought
proper, which annoyed him considerably, but not enough to sever
the relationship. Nash was fully aware that Sydney was his benefactor as well as the beneficiary of his gardening services. He continued to visit the Schiffs often, kept up a correspondence when they
were apart, and executed a series of wood engravings for *Celeste and
Other Sketches*, a book published in 1930.

Sydney and Violet's intellectually satisfying friendship with
Sydney Waterlow, a diplomat, university lecturer, and literary critic
well known in Bayswater circles, also ripened toward the beginning
of 1925. Waterlow was a counselor in the Foreign Office and later
served as British ambassador to Thailand, Ethiopia, Bulgaria, and
Greece. He reviewed books in respected journals and published
articles under the name John Franklin, and if T. S. Eliot is to be
believed, he subsisted entirely on fruit and omelets. He wrote to
Sydney Schiff on October 3, 1924, to thank him for his favorable

comments on an article he had written about D. H. Lawrence. He also asked him to please not disclose that he was John Franklin. Waterlow suggested that he and the Schiffs meet for dinner soon, which they did at the Schiffs' four days later. And judging from a remarkably self-revelatory letter Sydney wrote to Waterlow the next day, they must have discussed *A True Story* ad nauseam that evening.

Sydney was afraid that Waterlow might not have understood what he was trying to get across and offered an odd, but very Sydney-like explanation:

> In reviewing in my mind our talk of last night I told you
> that unless my novel (I include in the word novel all the six
> books, including the last one which is not yet published) is
> the most significant one known to me, published in England
> in the last 25 years, it has failed. But I omitted to tell you that
> I spoke with such boldness and confidence about it because I
> do not feel that I am myself entitled to any self-complacency
> on that account. . . . I feel, and have always felt in the course
> of writing these books, that I have been merely an instrument
> in the writing of them. . . . Repeatedly in the course of writing
> these six books I have had the experience that ideas present
> themselves to me without conscious volition on my part and
> even whole sentences came into my mind already formed
> and ready to be written down. You will therefore, understand
> that in assessing the book as highly as I do I am moved by no
> personal vanity whatever.

It is hard to imagine that Sydney thought the creative success or failure of his book should rest solely on a comparison with other books published in England over the preceding twenty-five years. This would have been inconsistent with his conception of truth as his sole criterion for success. And he must have been aware that quite apart from the "spiritual" phenomenon called automatic writing, evocative sentences, stunning images, and rhapsodic phrases sometimes materialized fully formed in the imagination of creative artists. It also seems unlikely that he believed responsibility for the book belonged to a spectral third party. That would, of course, dispose of any doubts about his personal vanity, or rather his lack of it. But it might also make one wonder whether he was playing with a full deck.

Waterlow wrote to Sydney again a month later and enclosed the copies of reviews and articles by Edwin Muir he had borrowed. These almost certainly included Muir's very positive review of *Prince Hempseed* that ran in the *Freeman*. Around that time Sydney and Muir, who was destined to become one of the most respected critics of the era, began a regular correspondence and exchanged copies of their work. Sydney sent Muir copies of *Tony*, *Elinor Colhouse*, and *Richard Kurt*, and Muir sent Sydney copies of his poems and asked for his critical opinion. He also hinted that he would appreciate any help Sydney could give him in getting them published.

Muir was always flattering in his letters. He wrote to Sydney that "in all your books you avoid exploiting *every* possibility of your subject matter, that you strive to select what is typical, and this is a virtue, for it gives your narrative its weight, its authority, and makes it organic as no other writing of the present day is." But he could be critical as well. In May 1924 he wrote bluntly that as "pure writing" *Prince Hempseed* and *Tony* delighted him, but *Richard Kurt* "did not." He did, however, take out the sting by adding that "by its truth and seriousness the book is a magnificent one." The rest of the letter was devoted to complaints about health, finances, and other distractions. Like Eliot, Muir needed to work in an office to eat, which drained his energy and cut into his writing time.

Muir wrote again on June 17, and that letter suggested the relationship Sydney was beginning to form with him would be satisfying in a totally different way from the ones he once had with Proust, Eliot, and Lewis. Muir noted that at thirty-seven he was about twenty years younger than Sydney, which, he said, made him feel better about his relatively small literary output and lack of success. In other words, for the first time, Sydney—who was also much older than the better-known Eliot and Lewis—was the recognized writer eagerly sought after by an admiring tyro. That would have further pumped up his ego, which apparently was already on steroids from Violet's injections, and which might have been enough to sustain a relationship for a while. But eventually there would have to be more, and there was. Muir was intelligent, genuinely liked Sydney's work, and was beginning to make a name for himself as a critic and poet, all of which indicated good prospects for an intellectually rewarding, relatively trouble-free, and mutually profitable friendship.

In early July of 1924 the Muirs passed through London on their way to Scotland. They went to the French Institute to see their old friend Denis Saurat, who ran it, and found an invitation from the Schiffs waiting for them. Muir wrote to say he and Willa could visit the Schiffs at Lye Green for a couple of days beginning on July 15 or 16. He added that he was glad "there will be no ceremony because we are both rather shy people." After accepting the Schiffs' invitation Muir returned to the subject that dominated their correspondence, books. Perhaps in response to Sydney's suggestion that the Muirs read the German novelist and playwright Fritz von Unruh, Muir recommended that the Schiffs read the great German Romantic poet Johann Christian Friedrich Hölderlin, whose work the Muirs introduced to the English-speaking public through their translations, as they did the works of Franz Kafka.

From the moment they arrived the Muirs were charmed by the older Schiffs, who received them warmly. And as the visit progressed they were dazzled by their sophistication and especially by talk of their circle of eminent literary friends and acquaintances past and present. Willa Muir thought she and Edwin must have seemed "very unfinished" to the Schiffs, but Sydney and Violet quickly made both Muirs feel comfortable. Willa was particularly pleased at the way Edwin and Sydney got along. They "lit each other up," she said. "I marveled at the passion driving each of them as they discussed the making of works of art. . . . They were both agreed on the need to detach oneself from emotion, and here I could not follow them, for I could never detach myself from my emotions. . . . But I was exhilarated by the invisible fireworks they were setting off."

Willa found Violet a calming and steadying influence. She thought she was poised and beautiful, a woman with far-seeing eyes. She told Edwin that Sydney's eyes "looked as if they feared to be hurt, so that I felt I had to be kind to him, but Violet's eyes made me nurse the hope that she would be kind to me." Willa, who admired Violet greatly, was also like her in important ways, a similarity exemplified by what she read in both their eyes. She instantly recognized Sydney's vulnerability and defensiveness as Violet had and Violet's toughness and unassertive self-confidence, which she shared.

After the Muirs left Lye Green, Edwin had a plethora of ideas, which he attributed partly to his conversations with Sydney, about the volume of literary essays he was beginning to write. It would be a series of studies of contemporary writers in relation to the transitional age in which they were living.

From mid-July through late September letters were exchanged frequently and most of the content was literary. In a letter from Scotland, for example, Muir discoursed on the importance of clarity in literature, noting dryly that he didn't think Joyce had "succeeded perfectly" in achieving it. In another letter Muir suggested with neither noticeable resentment nor gratitude that Sydney had completely rewritten an article he had sent him on Hugo von Hofmannsthal, the Viennese poet and playwright who also wrote librettos for several Richard Strauss operas, including *Der Rosenkavalier*.

Muir's letters until then, as well as Sydney's, had grown progressively warmer and more open, but in Muir's next one it became obvious that the relationship had attained real intimacy. He thanked the Schiffs for their efforts in trying to find a cottage for Willa and him somewhere near them. He also alluded to a book of criticism he was working on. This was a clear reference to the volume that would eventually be called *Transition*, a series of nine essays on living writers whose work Muir believed would still be read generations later. He told Sydney he would include Stephen Hudson in the book, which he did, along with Joyce, Eliot, Pound, D. H. Lawrence, and Virginia Woolf, among others. The most interesting thing about this letter, however, was the way Muir ended it: "All good wishes for the novel from us both, as well as our love to its joint creators." With very few exceptions only those who knew the Schiffs well knew that Sydney was Stephen Hudson, and only those few who knew them very well were aware that Violet was his collaborator. The Muirs and the Schiffs had become close friends by then, and as with the Schiffs' relationship with the Eliots it was a true couples friendship.

The link between Sydney and Edwin was close, but the one between Violet and Willa was even closer. They both were formidably intelligent women, but they also were temperamentally in tune with one another. Willa was described by those who knew her as "gay, caustic, brave, forthright, intellectual and fun to be with," a description that in the main applied to Violet as well and that suggests their bond transcended the purely intellectual. Perhaps the most persuasive indication of how close Willa felt to Violet emerged early on from a prescient manuscript she sent her for criticism sometime late in 1924. It was a long essay scheduled to be issued the following year in a distinguished series published by Leonard and Virginia Woolf's Hogarth Press. Other authors in the series included Eliot, Herbert Read, Robert Graves, Roger Fry, Edith Sitwell, and both Woolfs. The essay was titled *Women: An Inquiry*. It was a groundbreaking work and it was dedicated to Violet, who read it carefully and sent her comments to Willa.

After absorbing Violet's response, which she found positive and constructive except for her objection to Willa's calling housewifery "relatively unimportant," Willa wrote to express her appreciation. She characterized Violet as "a woman with a genius for woman-hood" and then surprisingly asserted that the essay was not only dedicated to her but was largely modeled on her. Despite their rela-tively short acquaintance, Muir must have thought she knew Violet well enough to draw inferences from her about the essential nature of women in general. Alternatively, she might have found in Violet confirmation of her previously held views on the essential nature of women. In either case important parts of the forty-page essay seem consistent enough with what is known about Violet to make Muir's claim credible. The deeper value of her essay, though, is that it is replete with insights on a lingering and conflicted issue, many of which are as relevant today as they were in her day.

Women: An Inquiry is not a traditional feminist work. It is, as its title indicates, a series of questions, the subject of which is the difference—or differences—between men and women. Muir defined its scope as an effort to find out if dividing the human race into men and women implies a division of spiritual as well as sexual func-tions. She was mainly interested in whether creativity in women differed from creativity in men. She began by asserting that many reputed differences between men and women were not essential but were socially constructed. To support her contention she made the following claim:

"In a State where men are dominant, as in most of our civilized States for the past 2000 years, certain attributes are considered to be characteristic of women which are equally characteristic of men in a State where women are dominant, as it is said they were for some time in ancient Egypt." She went on to say that in each case, "The subordinate sex . . . is excluded from complete development, and is considered to be less intelligent, less courageous, and more domesticated," but both men and women "are capable of courage, fear, cruelty, tenderness, intelligence and stupidity. When exhilarated by power and responsibility they display the more dominating qualities, and in subordinate positions they manifest a 'slave psychology.'"

She quickly departed from this sociological line of argument, however, and got to the heart of the matter. The fundamental difference between men and women, she argued, is that men are principally intellectual systematizers and organizers of life whereas women are intuitive creators and nurturers of life. What this leads men to do is substitute for life's vicissitudes a behavioral model. "Religion becomes a creed, morality a code of law, government a party machine . . . The financial machine in our own day," she contended, "is an excellent example of masculine activity pushed to extremes: it has been successfully detached from human values so that it exists for the production of money and not for the production of goods and services to humanity."

From an early-twenty-first-century perspective one would have to say this is not bad for someone writing in the early twentieth. At the same time, one can't help wondering what Muir would make of today's women who run corporations and work in the City (London) and on Wall Street.

In the section of the essay most obviously influenced by Violet, Muir wrote that people are what most interest women. "Almost from the cradle a girl studies the people around her more attentively than a boy does, and is quicker in imitating their tricks of speech and behavior. . . . She is inquisitive about human relationships of every kind . . . she values things for their associations, or the power they give her over other people. . . . Their interest [in life] is not that of mere spectators . . . they are ready to play important parts in it; and they test at every point their influence over others."

The essay and the letters exchanged until then suggest a deeper, richer friendship between the two women than between the two men. Sydney and Edwin Muir's correspondence, with a couple of notable exceptions, exemplifies a relationship more intensely focused on the intellectual and practical—the "you scratch my back and I'll scratch yours"—aspects of literature. Through the years there were occasional forays into politics, religion, and morality, but the dialogue almost always returned to books. While the two men seemed to have similar literary taste and generally liked each other's work, they disagreed about the work of some of their contemporaries, including Wyndham Lewis. At a time when Sydney admired Lewis's work greatly, Muir thought he had come nowhere near fulfilling his promise, which he did, however, think was considerable. Muir wrote to Sydney that he thought Lewis's first novel, *Tarr,* was "as a work of art . . . almost completely a failure." He went on to say that "I can hardly include Lewis in my book of criticisms."

Sometime in mid-1925, after they had moved into the cottage the Schiffs had found for them on the outskirts of the village of Penn, Sydney arranged for the Muirs to meet Lewis for tea in London. But, as in the case of Katherine Mansfield, it did not go well. Lewis watched both Muirs suspiciously the whole time and barely spoke to Willa. She felt he resented her for being there at all and thought Edwin was a coward who had brought her along as protective cover.

Later, in a letter to Sydney, Muir returned to the subject of Lewis. "About Lewis I have never come to any satisfactory conclusions," he wrote, "except unconsciously, where I know I dislike him . . . I find him interesting—there are very few evil, positively evil figures in our literature at present, and positive evil has an inspiring quality." But he added that Lewis's evil struck him as a limitation because he did not seem to recognize it himself and because he was so self-righteous, always thinking he was right and everyone else was wrong.

Meanwhile, *Richard, Myrtle and I* had become a source of friction between the Muirs, who found its meaning obscure, and Sydney, who apparently took their criticism personally. His letter complaining about their criticism is missing, but Edwin Muir's response makes clear that it was full of resentment. Muir wrote that he was pained by Sydney's letter, but although his affection for Sydney made it difficult, he wrote in perfect honesty, which was what he would expect from a friend criticizing his work. He softened the blow as best he could by saying he thought "the whole conception of the book more profound than that of any other written by any living writer," then added candidly, "but, there it is, for me the presentation is not adequate to the conception."

Letters continued after that, but less frequently. In the spring of 1927 Sydney wrote to Muir that he and Violet had decided to stay in Switzerland. They were spending their time in Caux enjoying their "bourgeois" activities and the spectacular view of Lake Geneva from the thousand-meter elevation of the village. The hotel had a dancing instructor who taught them the Charleston, which Sydney said was "the most damnably difficult dance I have ever been up against." They were also spending time on the lakeshore in Montreux, and in Paris. There is no indication Sydney was writing during this period.

In the same letter Muir also had some things to say about Lewis and Joyce. At the time Lewis was editing another of his short-lived journals, this one called the *Enemy*, in which he published an essay of his own on Joyce. Muir called it "a brilliant and decisive piece of work" that "cleared up a number of things" for him about *Ulysses*. He said Lewis's article showed him that much of the book was "atrociously written . . . and that it is packed with sentimentality." But, he added, "I think that Lewis is altogether wrong about Bloom, who I still think is the greatest character in contemporary fiction. Lewis takes him as a Jew, but I never think of Bloom particularly as a Jew, but as a human being, like Shylock, who is much more human than Jewish."

After this 1927 letter from Muir the correspondence between the couples tapered off, and although the relationship was not obviously strained they probably saw little or nothing of each other.

Most likely this was because of the Muirs' peripatetic existence. After a stretch in Italy and Austria they settled in England, but this was while the Schiffs were still living in Caux, and then, in this order, Edwin and Willa moved to France, Scotland, Czechoslovakia, and Italy.

It seems that this on-again, off-again kind of relationship was not unusual for the Schiffs and their footloose friends. From the letters between Sydney and Aldous Huxley, for example, it would be easy to assume—correctly or otherwise—a degree of intimacy that the actual time they spent together would not justify. The Schiffs and Huxleys probably met sometime in 1920 and saw each other socially even though the Huxleys were Bloomsbury hangers-on and Garsington habitués. They often spent weekends at Ottoline Morrell's country estate, where it appears the Bayswater Schiffs were never invited.

Edith Sitwell, with whom the Schiffs were also quite friendly and who was consistently enthusiastic about Sydney's writing, described Huxley in her autobiography in words that are hard to improve on: "Aldous Huxley was extremely tall, had full lips and a rather ripe, full, but not at all loud voice. His hair was of the brown, living color of the earth on garden beds. As a young man, though he was always friendly, his silences seemed to stretch for miles, extinguishing life, when they occurred, as a snuffer extinguishes a candle. On the other hand, he was (when uninterrupted) one of the most accomplished talkers I have ever known, and his monologues on every conceivable subject were astonishingly floriated variations of an amazing brilliance, and, occasionally, of a most deliberate absurdity." In an age renowned for its brilliant talkers and replete with connoisseurs of absurdity, this had to be the Everest of encomium.

On May 1, 1925, Huxley wrote to Sydney from Florence to thank him for generously praising his novel *Those Barren Leaves*, in which, as he had done in *Crome Yellow*, he eviscerated his Garsington hostess and her guests. Sydney apparently also passed on "praise" for the book from Stella Benson, a writer living in China with whom he had been corresponding. He had sent her *Those Barren Leaves* along with four volumes of Proust in French. Huxley, who knew of but hadn't met Benson, called her words "charming." But what he didn't know, because Sydney hadn't told him, was that she detested his novel. She trashed it for pages, calling it unworthy, savage to women, wicked, and dishonest before weakening and tacking on, rather unpersuasively, "The book is witty and brilliant and perhaps it is leaden-minded of me to feel so much shaken up by it." It's more than likely that all Sydney quoted to Huxley were the first six words in Benson's final sentence, which would demonstrate still again that despite his sworn attachment to truth, like most if not all of his illustrious literary contemporaries, at times Sydney approached veracity with flexibility.

Huxley invited the Schiffs to visit in Florence, which he diffidently belittled as provincial, but added that "the sun atones for much," inexplicably ignoring the Uffizi, the Pitti Palace, the Accademia, the Medici Chapel, and the Bargello. He said he would knock on the Schiffs' door when he arrived in London in July. His next letter to them, in November from Lahore, described his travels with his wife, Maria, in Kashmir and northern India.

"This place is rather a disappointment," he wrote, with the condescension typical of his nationality, class, and time. "One has seen the same thing before in Europe. It is Switzerland and the Italian lakes on a larger and coarser scale. . . . The palaces and gardens of the Moguls are very inferior to anything of the kind in Europe. . . . Kashmir is a small and very corrupt despotism; there are courtiers and intriguers; plots and counterminings; Judas-like betrayals, monstrous prostitutions and panderings." He found similarly descriptive language for relations between the English and their "educated" Indian subjects, especially when a mixed marriage was involved. "The cruelties," he wrote, "the humiliations, the pompous make-believes, the snobberies . . . Proust should have lived here for a few years." But he did allow with refreshing objectivity that in these relationships the English were as bad as "their darker brothers." He summed up the entire scene as "an Arabian Nights entertainment." And finally, with an odd mix of concern and detachment, he wrote: "I look on with a horrified amusement at this farce which is always potentially a tragedy and which is obviously destined to work up, within a few years, to some unheard-of and appalling denouement. One day, I think you ought to persuade your wife to come and have a look at it all. It would amuse you both."

The Schiffs and Huxleys stayed in touch and grew closer. The salutation, which was "Dear Schiff" in 1925, had become "My dear Sydney" by 1930. Also, by then Huxley referred to Violet by her given name, not as "your wife." However, he never signed his letters anything other than "Yours" or "Ever yours." When Huxley wrote on March 28, 1930, it was to tell the Schiffs that he had been in the south of France with D. H. Lawrence, whom he knew well from Garsington, during the week he died—"a very painful thing to see an indomitable spirit finally broken and put out." Huxley also apologized to the Schiffs for having been in London for three weeks without trying to contact them. And the last but not the least important thing Huxley told the Schiffs was that he and Maria had bought "a little house in the Midi" two hundred yards from the sea "with a very nicely planted vineyard and fruit garden" and that they would be welcome guests, especially around Easter.

Huxley had visited the Schiffs at 37 Porchester Terrace in London, a house they bought after deciding against living in Switzerland, in early May of 1930, and on May 6 he wrote from the Athenaeum Club to thank Sydney for returning his waistcoat, which he had left at their house the night before. He also thanked him for a copy of Kafka's *The Castle*, most likely the edition translated by the Muirs, and enclosed the first three acts of a play he was writing called *The World of Light*. He apologized for staying late, which, he said, "was in a sense your fault for not having allowed me to be for a moment bored and so preventing me from realizing the passage of time." He concluded with regrets that they had not talked about *A True Story*, which had just been published in a single volume comprising *Prince Hempseed, Richard Kurt, Elinor Colhouse*, and a section of *Myrtle*. Huxley said he had already read it "with great pleasure and admiration of the very subtle way [Sydney] had made the consciousness of the hero expand through the first half of the book, as he grows up—so that everything grows up including the style, the words, the thoughts." Huxley found Virginia "a fascinating character" and his one regret was that Sydney's method, "which entails only looking thro' Kurt's eyes, shouldn't have allowed [him] to get inside her skin and give her vision of the curious events. But as a piece of observed, strictly 'behaviorist' psychology, her character is masterly."

Sydney and Violet studied Huxley's play and sent him suggestions, which he apparently followed. "I have re-modeled the end of my play," he wrote in mid-June, "omitting the scene on the island altogether—for you and Violet were quite right: it was complete as it stood, complete, but improvable." He said he had also read the two books in German the Schiffs had sent him, Hermann Hesse's *Steppenwolf* and Kafka's *The Castle*. He thought *Steppenwolf* was "good, but not so very good." *The Castle*, on the other hand, was "a different story: it's so exceedingly queer and incalculable in its realistically nightmare-like way that it's quite unlike anything. One would have to have a very special sort of mind to write it; it's something new, something one couldn't do oneself." He admitted to uncertainty about the allegorical meaning of the book, but found it "strangely significant" nevertheless. He also said that he'd been absorbed mostly in historical and philosophical works, but for a diversion—"and a most hair-raising diversion"—he had been reading Michelet's *L'Amour*. "It's one of the most extraordinary and appalling works I ever set eyes on," he said, urging both Schiffs to read it. "You feel that the whole of its four hundred pages were written in a continuous state of erection—erection, moreover, provoked by the most extraordinary stimuli, such as tender broodings on the anatomy of the matrix, or the menstrual flow."

Huxley wrote again in December asking Sydney how long he and Violet intended to stay in their chalet, which suggests that they were in Switzerland again, although not at the Grand Hotel, and noting that except for painting, the work on the Huxleys' cottage in the south of France was finished. He said the place was lovely and he hoped the Schiffs would visit them. Sydney must have answered Huxley's letter almost immediately. In responding, on January 5, 1931, Huxley wrote, "I reply at once at [sic] your letter with its Proustian enigma." Sydney was working on his translation of Proust's final volume, *Time Regained*, and asked Huxley's help in resolving a knotty linguistic problem involving whales, protozoa, the perfection of animal and physical life, and the organization of spiritual life. In a translator's note he acknowledged Huxley's help and attributed the difficulty to a misreading of Proust's manuscript or a printer's error.

Huxley wrote again on May 7. He said he was writing a novel about the future "and the absolute horror of it" and described the project as "amusing, but difficult" because he wanted "to make a comprehensible picture of a psychology based on quite different first principles from ours." The book, of course, was *Brave New World*, the best known and most popular of Huxley's novels. He also told Sydney he had seen a London production of *The World of Light*, which he liked, and he said most of the critics liked it too, "at least all those who matter intellectually, tho' not those who matter box-officially: for the public remains conspicuous by its absence." Finally he asked Sydney how he was getting on with his translation of *Time Regained*.

Sydney, who was nearly done, sent Huxley a copy at the end of June. When he wrote back, Huxley said he had read enough to know he liked the translation, adding that it "seems to me to walk along Proust's devious tight rope of stretched words with all the grace and nimbleness that can be put into that all but impossible proceeding." But not everyone agreed with Huxley about the quality of the translation. By 1934 Andreas Mayor's version had replaced it in most English-language editions. Huxley then told the Schiffs he was struggling with revisions of early chapters of *Brave New World* while long sections remained to be written. He said he hoped Sydney's shingles were better and asked him if he had tried Delbiase, a French remedy composed of magnesium chloride and bromide that was relatively new at the time. Its inventor, Pierre Delbet, believed it would increase the ability of white blood cells to protect against infection. Huxley for some reason was under the impression it would work wonders with "anything wrong with the skin." It is still available today as a dietary supplement, but there is no evidence it prevents infection or does anything for the skin. Coincidentally, one of the first sites that pops up on Google when you enter "Delbiase" is a pharmacy almost directly across the street from where the Huxleys lived in Suresnes before moving to their cottage in La Gorguette. Anyone interested can order it from them.

The letters exchanged during the thirties were warm and similar in content and tone to those written earlier. One interesting if minor item that emerges from one written in 1932 is that despite their falling-out Sydney was still reading Wyndham Lewis, apparently with pleasure. He sent Huxley a copy of *Snooty Baronet*, which Huxley referred to in a 1933 letter from Kingston, Jamaica. Like his letter from Lahore, it is richly redolent of the mood there, but also the condescension the modernists so eloquently expressed toward those they considered their inferiors:

> Our voyage was pleasant; for we called at curious and
> amusing places—Barbados, Trinidad (a lovely island and
> we met some really charming people); La Guayra, the port

for Caracas, capital of Venezuela—most picturesque and exceedingly odd in its Spanishness: Panama, where the mixture of races is even more extraordinary than in the rest of the West Indies—for on top of the usual negroes, Hindus and Chinese, there are many Japs, local Indians (Red Men), Arabs, and representatives of all the white races—the whole quietly simmering in the tropical heat: queer and profoundly depressing (as indeed most of these hot countries are *au fond*—such a sense of hopelessness).

The last letter from Huxley to Sydney and possibly the last contact between the Huxleys and the Schiffs was dated March 17, 1937; it was only two brief paragraphs long, but its sense and sensibility are of a piece with all of the others. There is no hint there had been a four-year break in the correspondence, nor that this very likely was the last letter that ever passed between them. Huxley was in London and wrote to thank Sydney for sending him an inscribed copy of his novel *The Other Side*, which had just been published. He said he read it with "a great deal of pleasure" and said he was "specially delighted with the extraordinary freshness and youthfulness you manage to express." To have "captured and held throughout a whole book the spirit of adolescence is a most remarkable achievement." The last paragraph, which is just five lines long, includes hopes the Schiffs are well, a report on the extraction of Lewis's impacted wisdom teeth in Paris, a few words about their impending trip to America, a wish that they might meet before they leave for the States, and, in a break with past practice, "Our love to you both."

CHAPTER 11

THE APES OF GOD AND MODERNIST SATIRE

<W>yndham Lewis, a man with a capacious intellect, had a diminutive idea that he transmogrified into a monstrous, ramshackle literary blunderbuss. He called it *The Apes of God*. It was published in 1930 and was almost immediately forgotten because most of it is hopelessly obscure unless you are intimately familiar with the lives of the real people who were its hapless targets. It was also forgotten because it is pretentious in its display of frequently irrelevant erudition that would distract from the narrative if there were one. And it was forgotten because its argument, much but not all of which is banal, is too often encrusted in deliberately baroque language spoken by puppets, not people. Lewis's prose envelops you like quicksand; you feel you will suffocate if you don't extract yourself from it. And for good measure it is plotless, packed with prejudices, gratuitously mean-spirited, practically humorless, and 623 pages long. At bottom *The Apes of God* was a self-serving vehicle for Lewis to express his towering rage driven by envy and resentment toward putative friends, especially those who were better off than he was, more especially if they had artistic aspirations and most especially if they also had fed, clothed, and housed him.

On the other hand, the great William Butler Yeats seemed to think the book, which was so radical that to this day there is nothing comparable to it, was a worthy successor to the works of Swift. What's more, Lewis, whose forte was not consistency, never deviated in this work from his passionately held and explicitly stated belief that "True satire must be vicious." And, as one might suspect, it was an almost bottomless source of scintillating gossip among the precious elite for whom it was intended.

So why bother with any of this here? The easy answer is that second only to the Sitwells, Sydney and Violet were the most obviously and viciously attacked. As we know, Lewis was not always antagonistic to the Schiffs. They were what passed for friends and for a time he actually seemed to like them, enjoy their company, and even respect—or at least not be contemptuous of—their intellects. He praised *Prince Hempseed* when it first appeared and published a fragment from it in his journal the *Tyro* (which Sydney supported financially). But their quarrel over money, which ultimately led to the disintegration of their relationship, most likely motivated his strikingly disproportionate if not totally unwarranted assault. On the other hand, Lewis was not a man who would let friendship keep him from shooting a pair of sitting ducks. He couldn't help cutting the Schiffs down and carving them up. It satisfied his insatiable need to feed the rage and insecurity at the core of his arrogance and bluster. They were wealthy, had literary aspirations, and were Lewis's financial benefactors, which made them delectably fat targets. They were in Lewis's mind the essence of "Apedom."

The Apes of God is the most notorious—or, for the Lewis scholars, the most glorious—work in the tradition of modernist satire. It was certainly the most ambitious and the cruelest, which, considering the highly competitive environment in which it was composed, was a considerable achievement. Moreover, its large cast of characters features a pantheon of modernists, not all of whom were "apes." These include James Joyce, who was conflated with the Jewish poet,

editor, and publisher John Rodker to create James Julius Ratner; a
young Stephen Spender as Dan Boleyn, a species of idiot who was
passed off as a genius; Edwin Muir as Keith, a fawning critic; and
T. S. Eliot in a cameo role as Mr. Horty.

In most ways *The Apes of God* was a thing unto itself, but in one
respect it was typical. The satirical novel was the weapon of choice
for settling scores among the modernists. Unsurprisingly, sometimes the victims took revenge on their tormentors. Edith Sitwell
responded to *Apes* with *I Live Under a Black Sun*, in which Lewis
appears as the villainous sculptor Henry Debingham who lives in
a studio "situated in a piece of waste ground haunted by pallid
hens." He was capable, Sitwell wrote, of transforming instantly
from "the simple-minded artist sunk in an abstruse meditation"
into "a rather sinister, piratic, formidable dago." And he practiced
his art, she added, "in those moments which he could spare from
thinking about himself, and from making plans to confute his ene-
mies." It is clearly printed in the front of her book that all of the
characters are fictitious, but Lewis is as easily identifiable as are the
Schiffs and Sitwells in *The Apes of God*.

Lewis denied that he had modeled his characters on real people.
But just like Aldous Huxley, who caricatured Lewis as well as many
of his Bloomsbury/Garsington friends, D. H. Lawrence, Sitwell,
and many others, he lied. His long chapter in *The Apes of God* titled
"Chez Lionel Kein, Esq." is transparently about the Schiffs. No one
in London literary circles at the time would have had the slightest trouble identifying Lionel and Elizabeth Kein as Sydney and
Violet. Their double portrait, like all satire, was exaggerated and
unflattering, like much satire it was unfair, and like some satire it
was needlessly cruel. But it also necessarily contained a few easily
identifiable truths and half-truths. Sydney and Violet's relationship with Proust, for example, characterized by Lewis in the exaggerated form appropriate to satire, really was uncritical, more like
worship than admiration.

To put Lewis's assault on the Schiffs in context, it helps to consider the gentler satirical tradition from which he, more than any of his contemporaries, radically departed, a tradition that includes the novels of Violet's sister Ada Leverson. Ada, who, like Sydney and Violet, was ridiculed in *The Apes of God*, was thirteen years older than Violet. She was more Victorian in her tastes and temperament than her younger sister, which clearly influenced her articles, theater reviews, and, most notably, a series of six lighthearted and mildly satirical novels that are no better remembered than Stephen Hudson's or Wyndham Lewis's. For those few who do remember Ada, it is most likely for an act of courage and kindness she and her husband performed in May of 1895.

Like Sydney and Violet, Ada cultivated relationships with famous writers and artists including the Sitwells, Aubrey Beardsley, Max Beerbohm, and George Moore. Her most notable friendship, however, was with Oscar Wilde, who called her "the Sphinx," apparently because she had written a flattering sketch in *Punch* about his poem "The Sphinx," titling it "The Minx." After reading it Wilde wrote her a note saying, "I am afraid she really was a minx after all. You are the only Sphinx," which was how he referred to her ever after. It was not until three years later, though, when Ada and her husband Ernest supported Wilde in his time of greatest need—a time when virtually all of England viewed him as a pariah—that their friendship was forged forever.

Just four days after Wilde's most famous play, *The Importance of Being Earnest*, opened triumphantly in London, a seemingly trivial event occurred that marked the beginning of an abrupt descent in his fortunes. John Sholto Douglas, the eighth Marquess of Queensberry, whose son, Lord Alfred Douglas, was intimately involved with Wilde, left his card with the doorman of the Albemarle Club bearing this murky, spelling-challenged message: "To Oscar Wilde posing as a somdomite." Wilde, presumably to his ever-lasting regret, was sufficiently offended by Queensberry's note to make the biggest mistake of his life. He sued the rich and powerful marquess for libel. He denied to his lawyer that there was any substance to Queensberry's allegation, which was a lie, and then he lied again, this time under oath, when asked the same question in court.

It soon became clear that Wilde's case was doomed, and his lawyer convinced him to withdraw the suit, but it was too late. The marquess's lawyer had already sent the public prosecutor copies of statements by several witnesses who were prepared to testify that they had had sexual encounters with Wilde. That same afternoon, under a recently enacted law that had been interpreted to mean homosexuality was a criminal offense, a warrant was issued for Wilde's arrest. His friends Robbie Ross and Reggie Turner urged him to catch the last boat train to France, but instead he sat in a bar at the Cadogan Hotel too traumatized to act, drinking hock and seltzer until he was arrested. He was denied bail and held in Holloway Prison until his criminal trial began on April 26.

Wilde was confronted on the first day with one young male witness after another who testified that they had had sexual contact with him. When he finally took the stand after listening to four days of their testimony he quietly denied that he was guilty of any indecent behavior. And when the prosecutor asked him, "What is 'the love that dare not speak its name'?" a line from a poem by Douglas, Wilde responded confidently and eloquently:

> The love that dare not speak its name in this century is such
> a great affection of an elder for a younger man as there was
> between David and Jonathan, such as Plato made the very
> basis of his philosophy, and such as you find in the sonnets
> of Michelangelo and Shakespeare. It is that deep, spiritual
> affection that is as pure as it is perfect. It dictates and
> pervades great works of art like those of Shakespeare and
> Michelangelo, and those two letters of mine, such as they are.
> It is in this century misunderstood, so much misunderstood

that it may be described as 'The love that dare not speak its
name,' and on account of it I am placed where I am now.
It is beautiful, it is fine, it is the noblest form of affection.
There is nothing unnatural about it. It is intellectual, and it
repeatedly exists between an elder and a younger man, when
the elder man has an intellect, and the younger man has all
the joy, hope and glamour of life before him. That it should
be so the world does not understand. The world mocks it and
sometimes puts one in the pillory for it.

What effect these words had on the jury is unknown, but they
acquitted Wilde on one count and were unable to reach verdicts on
the others. A new trial was scheduled for three weeks later and this
time Wilde was released on bail. He spent those three weeks with
Ada and her husband, Ernest, who took him in when he was unwel-
come elsewhere. Ernest also advanced him five hundred pounds to
pay his lawyers.

All of the hotels and clubs in London and even his friends refused
to take in Wilde between the trials. He had the option of staying
with his family but chose to stay with Ada and Ernest. Before he
came to their house the Leversons called the servants together, told
them Wilde was coming, and offered them a month's wages if they
wanted to leave. The affair was now a major scandal and the papers
were full of it. According to Leverson, "America, Germany, all the
Continent joined in the controversy, the [Europeans] saying, 'This
is how you behave to your poets,' while the Americans said, 'This is
how your poets behave.'" The servants all stayed, but the Leversons
sent their coachman away because they were worried he might talk
in the pubs.

Ada went to pick up Wilde in a carriage and installed him in an
apartment on the nursery floor of their house. She asked him if
he would like her to take away the toys, but he asked her to please
leave them. As a result, his conversations with his lawyer about the

upcoming second trial were held "in the presence of a rocking-horse, golliwogs [and] a blue and white nursery dado with rabbits and other animals on it." A considerable effort was made to keep Wilde's whereabouts secret, although his hairdresser visited him daily to shave him and wave his hair. Ada said his "ambition was always to look like a Roman bust." He never left the nursery floor during the day but came down each night, dressed for dinner with a flower in his buttonhole—probably a green carnation. He ate with the Leversons, then stayed on a bit to talk and chain-smoke in the drawing room. However, in an exquisite display of delicacy, he never mentioned his troubles. Otherwise his conversation ranged widely, including a disquisition one evening on the effects of absinthe. "After the first glass," he said, "you see things as you wish they were. After the second, you see them as they are not. Finally you see things as they really are, and that is the most horrible thing in the world."

Wilde's wife, Constance, came to visit him with a message from her lawyer urging him to leave the country immediately because the next trial would surely land him in prison. But again, he would not go. His mother had told him that to leave would be dishonorable, and, according to Ada, "he never expected anything in his life to turn out badly." On the morning the second trial was due to begin Wilde stopped on his way out of the house and asked Ada to please write to him if things ended badly. Then he left for the Old Bailey in a brougham the Leversons had hired for him. Later that day Ada received a telegram telling her that he had been convicted and sentenced to two years in prison. While he was in prison Wilde's mother and brother died, and less than a year after he was released Constance died. She had changed her name and the children's to Holland and forced Wilde to give up his parental rights.

The day of his release the Leversons rose early to meet Wilde at the Bloomsbury house of the Reverend Stuart Headlam. Ada was dressed all in black and wore a floppy wide-brimmed hat. Wilde, with a flower in his buttonhole and smoking a cigarette, said to Ada with his usual aplomb, "Sphinx, how marvelous of you to know exactly the right hat to wear at seven o-clock in the morning to meet a friend who has been away." She continued to dress that way for the rest of her life. Wilde spent the remaining three years of his life abroad. Ada visited him only once, in Paris. He died on November 30, 1900, and is buried in Père Lachaise Cemetery under a monumental sculpture by Jacob Epstein paid for by Wilde's friends and admirers and put in place ten years after his death.

Ada did not begin her cycle of six novels until several years after Wilde died. The first one, *The Twelfth Hour*, was published in 1907 and the last, *Love at Second Sight*, in 1916. The satire in all six is nontoxic, mostly of types rather than individuals, and relies on paradox for most of its humor, such as it is. On the first page of *The Twelfth Hour*, for example, a sixteen-year-old boy knocks on his sister's door: "'I say, Felicity, can I come in?' he asks. 'Who's there? Don't come in,' she says. Upon which invitation he entered the room with a firm step." If you think this eventually becomes tiresome, you are right.

Nevertheless, Leverson's books are not without their rewards. She was especially good at both physical description and sketching relationships. The novels are all quite similar and some are sequels. Their territory is the confluence of the haute bourgeoisie and the bottom tier of the aristocracy, beer barons and baronets. New money mixes with old money, a cultural icon or two is displayed, and there are affairs, lots of affairs, all of which are treated lightly. Occasionally a character reminiscent of a real person turns up, for example, Sir Tito Landi, the Italian composer in *Love at Second Sight*, who always speaks in French, just like Sir Paolo Tosti. These books have more in common with Jane Austen and Trollope—although they are very slight by comparison—than they do with Wyndham Lewis. But many of Lewis's readers read Leverson's novels before reading Lewis's satirical bombshell.

The Apes of God broke sharply with the gently satirical tradition of Leverson and the Grossmith brothers' *Diary of a Nobody*, the story of a lower-middle-class man with outsized pretensions, and Robert Hichens's *The Green Carnation*, which parodied Wilde and his crowd. And compared to Lewis even writers like Huxley, Lawrence, Richard Aldington, and the Sitwells were pussycats. Aldington parodied Eliot in his novel *Stepping Heavenward*, but denied that his Eliot-like character Jeremy Cibber was modeled on a living person. However, in making the transparently false claim that his satire aimed at "something beyond the personal by attacking intellectual vices and emotional defects common to the highbrow 'aristocracy' and, especially, the dangerous fad of Anglo-Catholicism," he made it obvious to all of Bloomsbury and Bayswater that he was talking about Eliot, a highbrow aristocrat closely identified with Anglo-Catholicism.

Sometimes the writers were trying to get even, as in Huxley's parodies of Lewis and Nancy Cunard in *Antic Hay*, and sometimes they satirized friends and benefactors for no obvious reason except that they were vulnerable, which seemed to have been the case with poor Lady Ottoline, whom dear friends Lawrence and Huxley subjected to ridicule. Huxley especially upset her because apart from herself and her husband, virtually the whole Garsington ensemble—Bertrand Russell, Dora Carrington, and Mark Gertler among them—were made to look foolish in *Crome Yellow*. She must have been an especially appealing target, though, because she was also satirized by Osbert Sitwell, her friend Gilbert Cannan, and Walter Turner, another friend, at least by the standards of the day. Their satire was broad and often cruel, but it differed from Lewis's, which was grotesque.

Lewis, on the other hand, was hard to parody because he was a living, breathing caricature of himself. This is perhaps best illustrated by Osbert Sitwell's 1938 work of fiction, *Those Were the Days, Panorama with Figures*, in which Sitwell's character Stanley Esor is so much like the real Lewis that no one who knew anything about him could have possibly mistaken Esor for anyone else, or have thought Sitwell was being anything other than faithful to Lewis's irrepressible self. Those who knew nothing about him surely would have concluded that the characterization was meant to be satirical or more likely that Esor was a fantastic invention. With the exception of one low blow—the fictional Esor was rejected for military service in World War I, while Lewis served as an artilleryman and later an officer and war artist—Sitwell's portrait is spot on, as this brief but typical example of his misogynistic behavior demonstrates:

> Nevertheless, wherever he lived—and he moved his abode at very frequent intervals, so as to add to the aura of romance and secrecy with which he liked to invest himself or often, perhaps, for other, more practical reasons—his slaves, at a distance, would accompany him; dim, gaunt, tall, sturdy, freckled, faded females, who, after the manner of the vague, sandy-haired goddesses of northern countries, always seemed to inhabit some cloud, suspended above him, at the back of his studio. Yet these Amazons, plainly of an altogether formidable strength and character, existed, it appeared, only to serve him. Thus no one was ever able to discover their names, the positions they occupied, or what professions they followed; apart from him they seemed to have no being; but, at the least sign of trouble for their master, at once they would materialize out of the void, sure and inalienable . . . How did they know; why did they care? Their mothering of him, he may have felt, ill matched the superman vision of himself which he was trying to fix in the eye of the world; that vision of a strong man, self-willed, a solitary being of unique grandeur, defying the past and saluting the future.

Apart from its arch tone, this description could easily have come from either of the admirable and generally admiring Lewis biographies cited in this book. It is quite simply an accurate rendering of the man as he was.

The Apes of God appeared to mixed, strongly partisan reviews. It is not the kind of book that reviewers, or anyone for that matter, would be wishy-washy about. Among those in the pro-*Apes* camp was Lewis's friend the poet Roy Campbell, whose review was rejected by the *New Statesman* for being excessively laudatory. Campbell was asked to revise it but refused. Richard Aldington also wrote a rave review, which was published in the *Sunday Referee*. After noting that Lewis's satire was cruel, he wrote ecstatically that *Apes* was "one of the most tremendous farces ever conceived in the mind of man. For comparison one must fall back on Rabelais and Aristophanes." He concluded by anointing it "the greatest piece of writing since *Ulysses*." A year later, however, a letter he wrote to Sydney reflected a radically different point of view:

> My objections to the satire of Lewis I imagine are similar to your own. This satire almost invariably springs from deep personal rancor, at the expense of persons who are either insignificant or quite innocent. It is labored to the point of being intolerable through its damned iteration. It becomes grotesque and inhuman, because all proportion is lost; gigantic puppets are hewn into pieces without the slightest danger to the swordsman, who nevertheless pretends to be in imminent peril from his own harmless monsters. It is butchery, not artistry. And it is fundamentally inhuman. Nevertheless, one must recognize the energy and the remarkable gift of vituperation.

Aldington, a well-respected poet, novelist, and critic, seems to have been struck by a bolt of intellectual lightning sometime between June 1930, when *Apes* first appeared, and June 1931, when he wrote to Sydney. Or he was just being two-faced, a mode of behavior as common then as it is now. Sydney certainly would have read or at least heard about Aldington's review in the *Sunday Referee*, and Aldington would almost certainly have assumed he had read it. If this is correct it would have been shameless of Aldington to write as he did without at least explaining his dramatic turnabout. On the other hand it was taken for granted in those days that writers would lie about the obvious, as when they denied they had modeled their characters on their friends and acquaintances. The only firm conclusion I can draw from any of this is that Aldington was a lot closer to the critical bull's-eye the second time than he was the first.

Lewis was so angered by the *New Statesman*'s rejection of Campbell's review of *Apes* that he was moved to publish a sixty-three-page pamphlet defending the book, for which he solicited letters in praise of it from friends. Two of the more interesting ones are from H. G. Wells and W. B. Yeats. Wells's brief missive is notable for three reasons: It is addressed to the Arthur Press, Lewis's self-publishing entity, not Lewis himself; the praise is conditional; and the letter contains unexplained ellipses. Yeats's letter is descriptive and favorable in spirit, but it is ambiguous and avoids direct praise of *Apes*. It also chides Lewis for satirizing Edith Sitwell, whose book *Gold Coast Customs* he praises.

A trio of characters animates the action in *The Apes of God*. Horace Zagreus is a kind of agitator whose primary role is to provoke the *Apes* into revealing their true selves. His secondary role is to act as a mouthpiece for a shadowy figure known only as Pierpoint, whom everyone considers a genius but who never actually appears in the book. Zagreus "broadcasts" Pierpoint's "wisdom" to the *Apes*, sometimes at great length, revealing an outlook on life remarkably similar to Lewis's and in effect providing instructions on what to make of an otherwise opaque work. The third character is Dan Boleyn, the dull-witted young man ironically labeled a genius by Zagreus. Although the scholar Robert T. Chapman refers to him as a kind of "medium" for channeling the satire, to me on the whole he seems superfluous.

CHEZ LIONEL KEIN, ESQ.

Compared to the gentle jabs of Leverson, the Grossmiths, and Hichens, Lewis was launching grenades in *The Apes of God*. The portrait of the Schiffs in the chapter devoted to them is spiked with crude anti-Semitism, innuendoes of homosexuality, and obvious allusions to social and intellectual pretension and naive hero worship. The critic John Gawsworth, who shared some of Lewis's prejudices as well as his spectacular misjudgment of Hitler, wrote generally and approvingly: "Conscience never makes a coward of Lewis. He feeds it no sops. Jews, homosexuals, Lyon's tea shops, he blasts them all, soundly and impersonally, for the good, if not of his soul, at least for the improvement of the present and the hope of the future." We can stipulate here that Lewis's anti-Semitic references in *The Apes of God* were ad hominem attacks not deserving a response and that despite several references in *A True Story* to homosexuality and one in his letters to Proust, there is no evidence that Sydney was homosexual. His pretension and hero worship of Proust were fair game.

Part Nine, like every segment of *The Apes of God*, begins with a Lewis drawing. It is an unmistakable likeness of Sydney in the Vorticist style.

A group of distinguished persons have gathered for dinner at the elegant London residence of Lionel and Isabel Kein. Mr. Zagreus and Dan Boleyn are among the guests. Zagreus wastes no time. From the moment he arrives he sets out in workmanlike fashion to provoke and antagonize both Keins. He begins with gratuitous references to Lionel's deafness and his servant Hassan's effeminate affect. Then, after overhearing Isabel singing German lieder, he asks her in German, "On which Jew street did you get that accent, dear

Isabel?" And just in case any reader might still have failed to figure out that the Keins are the Schiffs, Lewis introduces a multitude of Schiff-related allusions to music, painting, Proust, and Sydney's novel *Myrtle*, which he has transparently renamed *Primrose*.

After this bombardment of obvious references, Lewis takes aim at Lionel's love affair with Proust, goading him with an irritating question designed to elicit an unconsidered response. "Would I like to be one of Proust's characters," Kein repeated, "do I understand you Zagreus, that is your question? I should consider it *well worth the privilege* . . . of having known Proust, to be treated in *any* way by him that he thought fit!" Zagreus, or Lewis, must have licked his lips thinking he had succeeded brilliantly. Lionel, on the other hand, being Sydney, knew full well that Proust's characters, with few exceptions, ranged from disagreeable to repulsive. But it didn't matter. He had unlimited faith in Proust's literary integrity. And his own commitment to honesty in art was unshakable, which he had demonstrated by the dispassionate way he treated himself in *A True Story*. So it seems only natural that he would put himself in the hands of his literary god, who he was certain would tell the truth, which he welcomed rather than feared. It would have been a rational choice, an opportunity to be grasped, not a pitfall to be avoided.

Lewis pursued the theme more directly. Most people when looking at the world saw everything but themselves, Zagreus argued. But then if they did see themselves, captured unsentimentally and accurately as Proust would have done, they wouldn't have been able to bear it. There is nothing wrong with that fairly commonplace observation except its source: Self-awareness was not among Zagreus/Lewis's conspicuous virtues. Lionel/Sydney was not a paragon of self-awareness either—he seemed unaware, for example, that his compulsive honesty might offend other people—but compared to Zagreus/Lewis he looks like Mr. Introspection, a superhero of self-awareness.

In keeping with his concept of himself as a great artist, Lewis set up a contrast between Wyndham "the great" and Sydney and Violet "the little." He wrote that "the atmosphere of the salon," which he characterized as organized pettiness, "has been adapted always to provide a place where the little can revenge themselves upon the great." It seems highly unlikely that Sydney and Violet, who were appropriately categorized as salon keepers, ever had the slightest desire to impose anything "upon the great," a category in which they came close to including Lewis, other than their admiration and hospitality. But the idea of revenge would have been completely out of character for them. Lewis exhibited the same fault here that he did in the Proust reference above. Satire, if it is to inflict even a minor wound, must have a reference point in reality.

After another long lecture by Zagreus/Pierpoint the action, such as it is, moves to the dining room. The scene opens with a description of Isabel: "The herd ate and drank beneath the eyes of Mrs. Kein, who drank water and ate a little toast. Such restraint in public as regards nourishment was god-like and enhanced her arrogant detachment towards her guests. Her brilliant handsome profile was like a large ornate knife at the head of the table. A certain taint of craft was suggested, in her face, by the massive receding expanse of white forehead, from which the hair was pulled back—by the vivacity of the great, too-conspicuously knowing eyes—the long well-shaped piscine nose, like a metal fish."

Setting aside the unflattering physical description, it is at first hard to know exactly what to make of this paragraph: godlike restraint; arrogant detachment; a taint of craft; too-conspicuously knowing eyes, and (physical, but too good to leave out) a nose like a metal fish. But with a little reflection it is not impossible, if you cut Lewis a little slack. Violet suffered from a variety of ailments that might have accounted for her Spartan eating habits and, given her perennial equanimity, it is not too much of a stretch to accept that her demeanor could legitimately have been satirized as godlike. As far as arrogant detachment is concerned, she did not suffer fools and might well have come across as detached in certain company. The detachment probably wasn't arrogant, but the adjective seems permissible in satire. Did she have a taint of craft, or more than a taint? Of course she did. And what about those too-conspicuously knowing eyes? I'm prepared to concede, since there is no evidence to the contrary, that Violet had knowing eyes and that Lewis did not exceed the reasonable bounds of satire when he labeled them too conspicuous. I have no idea, however, what to make of Lewis's description of her nose looking like a metal fish.

In another self-regarding instance a little further on, Lewis casts a cynical light on Sydney's ability to retain a certain loyalty and even fondness for someone who has shown a lack of gratitude for his generosity and maligned him unfairly. Lewis the puppet master has the puppet Lionel express his feelings for and about the genius Pierpoint, who, we must remember, is Lewis:

> Well as you know I've stuck to Pierpoint through thick and thin. Isabel and I will never change in our regard for him—our deep regard. Once we give that we never take it back! But there are things about Pierpoint which even his most devoted friend would find it difficult to defend—that it is impossible to deny. I am sorry to say. I wish I could! Poor Pierpoint! I wish I could have helped him to—to, not to lay himself open to so much hostile criticism. What he will do now I really do not know—Isabel and I often ask each other that! We often wonder—. We talk a lot about it. . . . He has no money. What I'm terribly afraid of is that he may—well really *go under*—a man like that depends so much on the support of a few friends—*good friends*!

Lewis must have planted a bug at 18 Cambridge Square. Sydney could have spoken Lionel's lines exactly as they were written and he would have meant every word of it. Lewis reconstructed his feelings precisely and came close to re-creating his voice. At first it seemed as if he wanted Pierpoint to come across as pitiful and Lionel as compassionate. But that was a setup. As the conversation developed, what Lewis, who depended on patrons but hated feeling patronized, was actually getting at became clear. Lionel was shamelessly promoting his own benevolence and lying to boot. Zagreus explained to Dan Boleyn that "It's all fantastically untrue . . . they never utter anything but a pack of lachrymose lies."

A bit later Lewis introduces a Scottish journalist named Keith who was based on Edwin Muir. He then attempts to slay Keith and Lionel with a single thrust. He declares that Lionel had "vamped up" a "little book" that he immediately sent off to Keith for review. The book itself he characterized as "Li-ing self-portraiture," punning on the English nickname for Lionel, which is pronounced "lie." It was "about Li's school days (. . . resorted to in order to reach a vein of homosexual episodes. . . .)." Setting aside Lewis's belittling comments about the book and his innuendoes about Lionel's sexuality, his main point was that Lionel had sent his book off to his friend Keith in the hope, or perhaps the certainty, that it would get a good review. But this tactic was as common then as it is now, Lewis indulged in it as much as anyone, and anyone likely to have read *The Apes of God* would have known about it and in many cases used it, so what exactly was Lewis's point?

By the end of the episode Lewis, apparently so enraged that he was no longer capable of satire, was reduced to pure invective: "Kein at last has 'an admirer'! Oh ho! A something-for-nothing, a boob in the flesh—an authentic *unpaid* supporter! Demented curiosity in the Kein household! *Who is the unknown idiot?* Who can this unmatched moron be. . . ." Et cetera.

Lewis had still more to say about Sydney's literary efforts, which he denigrated on the one hand and attributed to Violet on the other. He also mocked Sydney's love for Violet, referring to her extravagantly as "that astonishing jewel," language that once again would have seemed perfectly natural and hardly risible coming from Sydney's lips. And then Lewis returned to one of his pet prejudices, pederasty. "Lionel, as you know," he wrote, "since Proust's imposition of the pederastic motif upon post-war society, has not of course become a practitioner—his years preclude that: but as far as possible he has worked into his scheme of things the pederastic pattern. Nothing if not in the swim, old Li: so he immediately on realizing the way the wind was blowing, secures a pederastic major-domo (our friend the butler), who is encouraged to ogle all his male guests in the hall, valse away with their coats and hats and so on—as you have seen." And as if that were not enough, Lewis manipulated his puppets Li and Keithie in a way that intimated Sydney had made a play for Muir, "from the purist pederastic position," whatever that means.

Lewis, the frequently and vociferously self-proclaimed artist/satirist, who never seemed to know when enough was enough, next launched another assault on Violet's (or Isabel's, if anyone is still inclined to think she's not Violet) personal appearance. It is worth reproducing here not so much to provide another example of Lewis's unpleasantness, but rather to demonstrate that certain techniques of cosmetic enhancement that we tend to think of as typical of our own era have a long history: "I do not at all mind Isabel. Her face has been lifted they say nineteen times—gathered behind the ear, you know, and laterally adjusted—she has had paraffin injections beneath the skin—she cannot see clearly more than a foot and a half: in spite of the fact that she eats nothing, Isabel is fat."

With heavy-handed irony Lewis attributed Isabel's beauty aids, and here it has to be Isabel, because there is no evidence that Violet had either face-lifts or paraffin (the Botox of its day) injections, to her "perfect good-sense." He then went on, redundantly once again, to insist that Violet was the true author, "the all pervasive editor," of Sydney's books. While there is no doubt that she played an editorial role, and probably a significant one, nobody knows how significant and no one else, to my knowledge, has suggested that it was a larger role than is played by good editors everywhere. Zagreus continued mockingly about the book Lewis called *Primrose* and was actually *Myrtle* until Isabel finally lost her temper and hissed, "That's enough Zagreus! Take your latest boy somewhere else if you wish to slander people!" Lionel, who had some difficulty following what was going on because of his deafness, finally caught up and told Zagreus, "My wife wishes you to leave. . . . Will you please do so as you have annoyed everybody." Isabel, however, was not satisfied. "He has not annoyed everybody," she cried out. "He has insulted *me*—deliberately. Tell him to go—at once!"

Zagreus was not willing to be ejected quite so easily, however. He asked Mr. Horty, Lewis's surrogate for T. S. Eliot, whether he had done anything to warrant his being turned out, but Horty did not wish to become involved. " 'You leave me out of it,' he said, wriggling his lean bottom, and pulling down tightly his mirthless upper lip as though dryly to sip a little tea." When Zagreus was finally departing, Lionel stood at the top of the stairs shooing him away "with gestures to hasten the departure of an animal. Kein's batrachian muzzle stuck over with its bristling military mustache— the toffee eyes behind the spectacles—stared solemnly down—the black loosely-hanging frustrum of the cranky trunk above the rail, and, beneath the ascending animated soffit, the shining linen—the cigar held in the hand remained a moment as though commanded to stand still by some super-natural agency—immobilized to gaze inscrutably down into the twilit well of the hall." (Although it does nothing to help clarify Lewis's tortured syntax and the eccentric language of the quotation above, here are three definitions for those readers who are semi-illiterate like me: "batrachian" means froglike, a soffit is the underside of a beam or other architectural element, and a frustrum is the part of a conical solid left after cutting off part of the top portion, leaving a plane parallel to the base.)

Aside from offering another angle of vision on Sydney and Violet, Lewis's magnum opus, *The Apes of God*, exemplifies the outer limit of modernist satire. It is more ambitious, more malicious, more eccentric, more radical, more repetitive, more irritating, and much longer than the relatively puny satirical works of Lawrence, Huxley, Aldington, and the Sitwells. In its way, it was the appropriate culmination of a mostly trivial trend in English literature. But in another sense it was, for better or for worse, sui generis, a class unto itself, bearing little resemblance to the satire that preceded or followed it. It wasn't, however, if I can be so bold as to vigorously disagree with the great Yeats, worthy of comparison, favorable or otherwise, with the works of Jonathan Swift. Lewis's mess of a novel bears no resemblance whatsoever to the superbly crafted and bitingly effective works of Swift, whether brief but singularly devastating like *A Modest Proposal* or extended and unceasingly brilliant like *Gulliver's Travels*.

Sydney's work on the other hand was about as far as you could get from Lewis's sardonic, static satire. He captured the inner lives of his characters through meticulous observation of their evolving behavior. Unlike Lewis's iconoclastic work, for the time in which it was written Sydney's was more conventional than radical—a few critics even compared *A True Story* to nineteenth-century realist masters such as Stendhal and Thackeray. Lewis's writings mirror the anger and turmoil that tortured him his whole life, while Sydney's novel reflects the journey of his soul from extreme misery as a young child, a schoolboy, and an unhappily married man to eventual exquisite happiness with Violet and in his life as a writer.

After the publication of Lewis's magnum opus, which was not a commercial success, his economic situation and his health deteriorated to a point where he had to swallow his pride once again and appeal to his old benefactors, whom he had so recently and publicly maligned, for support. In February of 1933 he wrote to Sydney to thank him for a fifty-pound check, and in March he wrote twice to Violet, first telling her he was sorry to hear about her ice-skating accident and that he hoped her wrist was better and then to say he was sorry illness had taken her and Joyce to Zurich at the same time. And in May he wrote to Sydney with a pathetic plea. He thanked him for an additional twenty-five pounds and said he had been ill for six months and could not work, otherwise he would not have asked for money. He complained about his inability to afford the meanest studio or, for that matter, even an easel, and then asked Sydney to help him mount a retrospective exhibition of his paintings. "Is it really out of the question," he wrote, "for you, one of the few people who care for pictures in London, to do something to facilitate this?" Finally, he told Sydney how grateful he was for his help. I don't know whether Sydney made an effort on his behalf, but no such exhibition ever took place.

CHAPTER 12

VIOLET ALONE

Sydney and Violet had owned and rented houses in the country before, but none really became their home until Abinger Manor did. Perhaps it had to do with their age, with a desire for a quieter life. They bought it when Sydney was sixty-five and Violet was fifty-nine. By then Sydney had been diagnosed with coronary artery disease, for which the only treatment at the time was rest and digitalis. Or it could have been the war. Before the German invasion of Poland they divided their time between London and Surrey. But when the fighting began they moved to the country full-time except for occasional brief excursions to London. They probably thought it would be safer.

The large multilevel seventeenth-century stone dwelling with sharply pitched roofs and a portico at the back was comfortable and of historic interest, but architecturally undistinguished. It was beautifully situated on a hilltop surrounded by rolling countryside. The house was built by John Evelyn, a diarist whose works are now mostly forgotten because he had the misfortune of being a contemporary of Samuel Pepys. Edward Beddington-Behrens invited the distinguished archaeologist Louis Leakey to examine the surrounding area and Leakey thought it could have been the site of the oldest settlement in Britain, but more recent scholarship has cast some doubt on that assessment. Sydney, who had learned something about landscaping from John Nash, and might have been inspired by the Italian gardens of his friend Arthur Kitson, designed the garden with the help of the Schiffs' secretary, Freda Almond (Gardner after she married), whose father was a horticulturist.

There was a small cottage on the property, where at Sydney and Violet's invitation Max Beerbohm and his American wife, Florence, lived from early in 1939 until the end of the war. The Schiffs had few visitors during those years and infrequently socialized with the Beerbohms. In fact the two couples were so concerned about their privacy that they agreed never to talk to each other in person unless a formal arrangement had been made beforehand by letter. If either couple had anything to communicate they wrote a letter, which they did frequently, or if it was more or less urgent they used the telephone or left a note in the other's mailbox or under the door. This agreement, however, was sometimes honored in the breach. The two houses were only about fifty yards apart and they were separated by a hedge and a low wall. On a summer's day Sydney and Max would often stroll along together on their respective sides of these barriers, "dressed in the light gray or lavender suits they both loved," deep in conversation. Apart from the constraint on communications, the only restriction placed on the Beerbohms was a ban on cats imposed by Violet.

Years later Violet told Julian Fane, the young writer she befriended after Sydney died, that the Beerbohms had lived in their cottage, but she said nothing about the code of silence. She told him Max and Florence had been living in Italy and had to return to England because of the war and were homeless. "We were . . . friends of theirs," she said, "we had a big house in the country, and we offered them a refuge." Beerbohm apparently never completely adapted to country living. Whenever he went out, even if it was only to put a letter in the mailbox at the end of the driveway, he dressed in one of his elegant suits, wore a gray homburg, and carried a walking stick.

Newspapers were hard to get during the war, but the Schiffs had a subscription to the *Times*. They passed on their copy to Beerbohm, who regularly and mischievously altered it, using pencils exactly the color of the *Times*'s type, before passing it on to the local schoolmistress. On one occasion he modified an insurance company advertisement showing an elderly couple sitting in armchairs on either side of a snug fire. The picture was captioned, "Mr. and Mrs. Smith have nothing to fear . . ." Beerbohm drew a diabolical face rising from the flames. His specialty, however, was turning pictures of British dignitaries such as the Lord Mayor of London and the Commissioner of the Metropolitan Police into likenesses of Goering and Himmler. Whatever the schoolmistress thought of these alterations, she never said a word, which left Beerbohm bemused.

The letters Sydney and Max wrote to one another often consisted of gossip and other trivia about mutual friends, but they also reported on every bout with "the wretched influenza" and other infirmities, from time to time extravagantly praised a book of the other's they had just read, and passed on literary opinions and recommendations. Also, Max wrote numerous times with great sincerity to express his and Florence's gratitude to the Schiffs for taking them in. After receiving a gracious note from Max expressing the Beerbohms' appreciation for the Schiffs' generosity, which included periodic gifts of wine and cigarettes, Sydney replied that he wished he had Max's gift for saying the right thing at the right time. He added, rather too self-deprecatingly, that the best he could do was "to try in my lame way to say what I think and feel," which was: "Your and Florence's presence near us enriches our lives; every time we catch a glimpse of one of you, she running nimbly up the church yard path, you strolling down the lane or standing at your cottage door, we bless the hand of Destiny for guiding you in our direction."

Soon afterwards Sydney and Violet sent one of their relatively few explicit invitations to the Beerbohms to join them in celebrating their thirty-first wedding anniversary. For the Schiffs—and perhaps for the Beerbohms—it would appear that despite the unfailing warmth of their letters, those chance glimpses, with intermittent exceptions, constituted just the right amount of enrichment.

Although most of their correspondence was ephemeral, occasionally the two men exchanged views on more consequential matters. During March and May of 1939 the subject was the collapse of the social order they were born into. They bemoaned the fading of the aristocracy, which they both believed was the great guarantor of social stability and even civilization itself. Beerbohm noted with just a soupçon of irony that "there can't be any sort of aristocracy without slavery . . . and now it is ceasing to exist, alas!" But he added in his typically wry fashion that in "a rather remote corner" of his heart he was "pleased that the lives of the majority of my fellow-creatures are happier than they were." Sydney, who had no gift for wryness nor irony, responded earnestly that "it gratifies me deeply that we feel alike about many things." Warming to the subject, he said, "The very gentle knight of chivalry was the realization of the highest ideal of mankind" and grumbled that "the new order professes to despise gentlemanhood because its leaders, the so-called intelligentsia, envy and hate their moral and social superiors." He continued what was fast becoming a screed—although not without a modicum of truth to it—with a blast about self-righteous Russian revolutionary types who advocated proletarian rights but who in reality were just promoting their own selfish interests. Finally, recognizing that he was sounding rather shrill, he asked Beerbohm's forgiveness for boring him by "letting off this steam."

The most extensive exchange of letters, though, was between

Max and Violet, whose correspondence began in 1925 and continued well into the 1950s. Many of the letters were written during the war, when the Schiffs and Beerbohms were living within shouting distance of each other, and while most of them were mundane, some lapsed into silly rhyme and others were revealing. One written by Max on November 14, 1939, for example, thanked Violet for the portraits she had drawn of him and Florence. "You have made me look just as I would most like to look," he wrote. "Will R[othenstein] had flattered me and you have carried the flattery further, you have canonized me." There is no record that Violet drew portraits or anything else, before then, but a few years later Beerbohm makes another reference to a drawing by Violet. All three, regrettably, have vanished. Beerbohm's appraisal of her sketches could have been flattering or slyly disparaging. We'll never know.

Early in the war the Schiffs also took in an eight-and-a-half-year-old Austrian refugee named Stella Jadwabuik. Violet thought she was intelligent and musically gifted. It seems likely she taught her to play the piano while she was living with them and stimulated her interest in literature. Violet's maid, "Cam" (Lily Cameron), liked her and took her out from time to time. In the spring of 1945, when she was thirteen, Violet sent her to her parents, who by then were in Palestine. In June Max wrote to her, "We do so hope Stella will be happy . . . but we wish she were not going for of course you will miss her and, after you had done so much for her, would have liked to see her becoming a young woman." Although they were not in touch regularly, at one point Violet heard Stella was working as a secretary, which disappointed her. She concluded that her parents were "uneducated and unimaginative people" who were either not capable of or not interested in providing her with the means to develop her mind and talents. Sydney included her in his will with a bequest of three hundred pounds.

Sometime in 1940 a bomb damaged the London house of a niece of Sydney's; by then a half dozen or more of their circle of friends had been made homeless by German bombs. But for the most part the war years passed quietly at Abinger. Sydney was no longer writing and the Schiffs' correspondence dwindled as well. They had their paintings, books, and music to amuse them and their servants to look after them. The war itself must have been little more than a dull murmur in their tranquil corner of Surrey, that is, until August 3, 1944, the tenth anniversary of their purchase of Abinger Manor. At 8 a.m. that morning a German rocket, probably a relatively slow-moving V-1 carrying a ton of high explosives, smashed into the nearby St. James's Church, which was unoccupied. The blast destroyed the belfry and seriously damaged the roof of the nave and the walls. It also caused extensive damage to the manor. Part of the roof was blown off, all of the windows were broken, and fallen plaster was everywhere. The cottage was barely damaged and neither Beerbohm was hurt. The servants hadn't arrived yet, and Stella ran out of the house and avoided injury. Sydney was not injured, but Violet was.

Edward Beddington-Behrens arrived an hour after the rocket attack and found the whole village milling around. Violet was lying on a mattress outside the house. The blast had blown the bedroom door off its hinges and flung it across the room, where it hit her in the back and arm. She had taken a couple of aspirin and was feeling no pain, but one of her vertebrae had been broken. Beddington-Behrens quickly arranged for a room for them at the Sackville Court Hotel in nearby Hove, where they had often stayed. He wanted to leave immediately, but Sydney, with the help of Cam, was still picking through the rubble. He finally found what he was looking for, a light-gray flannel suit and the perfect tie to go with it for the short trip. A number of local friends gathered around the car to say good-bye, and as they drove away Max Beerbohm cried. Violet wrote to Richard Aldington in 1949 that "they were [all] quite gay and cheerful and enjoyed the journey." They stayed in the hotel for three weeks with Violet in bed the whole time. But she did not get proper medical care, her back never fully healed, and her mobility was impaired for the rest of her life. As uncomfortable and inconvenient as that was, though, it did not unduly disrupt Violet's normal routine. She had long been accustomed to spending days or even weeks at a time in bed or lying on a couch getting over one ailment or another.

Sydney, too, had been feeling ill for some time after the bombing. On October 27 Max Beerbohm wrote to Violet that he and Florence hoped Sydney would "soon be better and stronger," adding, "It must be a frightfully sad and anxious time for you." Two days later, on Saturday, October 29, Sydney died in the Sackville Court Hotel. He was just over six weeks short of his seventy-sixth birthday. According to the death certificate he died of myocardial degeneration, atheroma, and emphysema or, more simply, heart failure.

On November 1 Violet wrote to the Beerbohms that Sydney had left a note with his lawyer asking to be cremated. He wanted "no flowers, no mourning, no service." She told them his ashes would be scattered on "the garden that he loved." Violet had never seen a dead person and dreaded having to look at Sydney's body, but when she finally did she thought he looked "incredibly noble (and strangely young)." Those who were there, she wrote, "were moved and impressed as by a great work of art." This idealized vision of her beloved life partner led her, oddly and unpredictably, to find someone to photograph the body before the coffin slid into the flames. Her last words, before signing the letter with "Much love," were "I am inutterably [sic] miserable and broken down."

In December, although they had been out of touch for many years, Eliot wrote a condolence letter to Violet in which he said, "You were among my oldest friends: I had not seen you for a long time, but I was hoping to come see you at Abinger when conditions became more favorable. This is a grievous loss and I send you, however belatedly, my warmest sympathy and personal sorrow."

After thirty-three years during which she had almost never been separated from the love of her life, Violet was alone. Brokenhearted and desolated, but not defeated, she waited out the war at Abinger Manor. When it was over she returned to their London house at 1A Ilchester Place in Kensington.

❦

Alone with her memories: Sydney was gone, her parents were gone, and so were all of her brothers: George, who died of typhoid when he was twenty-two; Charles, who played a role in the writing of *Charley's Aunt* and became a successful divorce lawyer; Frank, who made the semifinals of the Diamond Sculls twenty years apart; and Arthur, who had a mental breakdown as a young man, lived under a doctor's care in Brussels, and believed he was far ahead of Einstein in his understanding of the physical universe. Her sisters were dead, too. Evelyn, her favorite, died in Paris when her twin sons were still children. Ada, the author of gentle satires and friend and benefactor of Oscar Wilde, lost her hearing, but not her sense of humor before dying at seventy. And Sybil, who was small and sweet-natured and had a fine singing voice of unusual power for her diminutive size, died in 1936 at sixty-seven.

It was perhaps Sybil she thought of most because without Sybil she would not have met Sydney that night at Covent Garden. The opera, as we know, was *La Bohème* and Sybil would not have missed it for the world, no matter how many times she had already seen it, because her very special friend was its composer. Sybil, who was married to the American banker David Seligman, had a twenty-year relationship with Giacomo Puccini, who was also married. There is to this day doubt about the precise nature of the relationship, but Violet, in whom her older sister confided, was convinced that at least in the early years they were lovers. What is certain is that Violet told Mosco Carner, one of Puccini's many biographers, that "Sybil's relationship with Puccini was at first by no means platonic." Why she told Carner this, whether it was true or not, remains a mystery. In the years that followed, Sybil was Puccini's closest confidante, with whom he discussed his health, marital problems, and much more. She was also a source of ideas, although mostly bad ones in his opinion, for new librettos.

But alone as she was—the last of her generation of Beddingtons and without her beloved Sydney—Violet was not about to spend the rest of her life mourning. Sydney had often told her that if she survived him he wanted her to live "in the same way and in the same spirit" as she had with him. Three days after his death she wrote to her friend Joan Countess Drogheda, wife of the Earl of Drogheda: "I can't talk to you on the telephone because I'd only cry. I long to see you, but today I'm in bed—I can't sleep or eat yet. I shall never get over it of course. But I am not a miserable person, I believe in love and happiness and goodness because I have known them. Also I refuse to be a widow—I am not one somehow—I am still darling Sydney's wife as I always have been."

She was in the best sense of the word pragmatic. She believed consciousness and meaning ended with death and that those who still had some life left in them should not willingly waste it in mourning or otherwise. She also had a mission—to promote *A True Story*, her late husband's life work. Without that, perhaps, she would have given in sooner to her physical disabilities—primarily chronic back pain and increasing deafness—and her self-described valetudinarianism. She was looked after by a doctor named Leo Rau in whom she seemed to have a great deal of confidence.

Violet went out rarely, according to Julian Fane, the young writer who befriended her around 1950 when he was in his twenties and she was in her seventies. During a ten- or eleven-year period, he remembered her leaving the house only three times—to visit her friend Countess Drogheda, to attend a matinee of a Cocteau film, and to see Danny Kaye at the Palladium.

An accident she had right around the time she met Fane contributed to her preference for staying at home. She tripped in her bedroom at Abinger cottage, broke her femur, and injured her leg below the knee as well. She was taken to the London Clinic, where a minor operation was performed and her lower leg was put in a cast. Four days later she was taken back to the cottage, where Fane first met her, for three months of bed rest. She saw friends and occasionally other interesting visitors at home in the country and at Ilchester Place. Her nephew Frederick Beddington recalled inviting her to see Charlie Chaplin's recently released 1952 film *Limelight* with him. She told him she really couldn't bear the idea of going out to the movies and that "in any case he's coming to tea with me tomorrow and will tell me all about it." In December 1953, in a departure from the house that Fane apparently missed, she went out for the second time that year to have her eyes checked. But when Dr. Rau offered in 1954 to take her to visit Max Beerbohm in Rapallo, where he had returned after the war, she did not accept.

In 1957 Violet renewed her friendship with T. S. Eliot and warmly welcomed his new wife, Valerie, into her small but devoted circle of friends. Violet also kept up an active correspondence with a few other friends, including the Beerbohms. Florence died in 1951 and from then on Max's secretary, Elisabeth Jungmann, cared for him like a wife. She also wrote to Violet, looked after her briefly when she was ill, and visited her several times without Max. Beerbohm married her in 1956, a few weeks before he died.

Fane was introduced to Violet by a woman he identified in his brief book *Memoir in the Middle of the Journey* as Ellen C., but who actually was Countess Drogheda. Fane, the second son of the fourteenth Earl of Westmoreland was, among other things, one of Princess Margaret's escorts when she was young and single. Almost half of his *Memoir in the Middle of the Journey*, which came out in 1971, is devoted to his recollections of Violet. There is a section on his nanny, Anne Harvey, and about a third of the book is about Joyce

Cary. He read Cary's great novel *The Horse's Mouth*, whose protagonist, Gulley Jimson, may be the finest characterization of an artist
in all of literature, about three years after he met Violet. The lessons he learned from it, apart from the pleasure it gave him, go a
long way toward explaining what Violet eventually would mean to
him although he was still too young to realize it.

Gulley Jimson was a poor, old recently released convict who
was supposed to be a great artist but couldn't sell his work. Yet
he took life as it came and didn't complain. He knew who he was.
Young Fane saw himself as a beginner, which of course he was,
who "had no right to expect success and feared [he] could not get
along without it." While he was experiencing these feelings of inad-
equacy, although he probably didn't know it, Violet was already in
the process of doing for him what she had done so successfully
for Sydney: nurturing his talent and building his confidence, laying the groundwork for self-respect. If she had lived long enough
she would have been gratified to know just how successful he was.
Shortly after Fane died in December 2009, his fiftieth book was
published.

Countess Drogheda took Fane to tea with Violet at the cottage
in Surrey where the Beerbohms had lived during the war. Edward
Beddington-Behrens was living in the manor house, which he
would inherit on Violet's death, with his son Serge, who was about
five at the time. Fane remembered entering into a combined living
and dining room that was painted white and that there were many
windows, the furniture was "expensively austere," and a painting
by Stanley Spencer hung over the fireplace.

Violet was reclining "against pillows in white linen pillow-cases
as well as the cushions on the sofa, her feet up, a rug covering her
legs." Evelyn Richardson, Violet's grandniece, saw her between
twenty and thirty times during the fifties. She always found her
lying on a sofa elegantly dressed in dark flowing robes, her white
hair piled high on her head, and wearing a long strand of pearls.

Violet was losing her hearing and used a large contraption in a leather case with two receivers and wires leading to an earpiece to amplify sound. In her eagerness not to miss anything she shifted back and forth between them, which tangled the wires. Fane, who couldn't take his eyes off her, thought "her Jewish origins showed" in profile and that she looked like "the feminine equivalent of some beautiful statue of Moses." It was an odd image, but well meant. Obviously Fane was not thinking of the famous horned Moses in the church of San Pietro in Vincoli in Rome, which Serge Beddington-Behrens's bitter childhood memory of Violet conjures up. Beddington-Behrens's image, like Michelangelo's sculpture, is powerful and forbidding. He called her "a ghastly old heartless bag . . . who held some kind of a perverse hold [over my father] connecting him to his artistic Jewish side."

Violet would have been seventy-four or seventy-five when Fane met her and there is no doubt that she remained intellectually formidable, held strong opinions about the things that mattered to her—literature, music, human character and motivation—that she would not suffer fools and could be intimidating, and that she was not particularly child-friendly. Evelyn Richardson came to visit when she was between ten and fifteen years old and Violet would always say, "Come here Duckams," in her rather posh manner of speaking and command her to play the piano and then would be deep in conversation with someone else before the first note was struck. Young Evelyn, as one might expect, found this rather irritating. Violet also often asked Evelyn's mother, Irene, and her stepfather, Edward Beddington-Behrens, to sing and Joan, a talented musician, to play the piano. She inherited the instrument when Violet died. The one time they ate lunch together Violet instructed Evelyn to hold her fork like a pencil and apart from that said nothing to her.

As a young girl Violet would not spend her time with anyone she thought would waste it and she was even less likely to do so as a septuagenarian. Fane took to her immediately nonetheless, not only because of "her wit, imagination [and] subtlety," but also because of the intimacy of her conversation, her ability to make the universal themes she was articulating directly relevant to whomever she was with.

She wasn't necessarily looking for a project. There was still work to be done with *A True Story*. But right from the beginning she must have sensed something in him—his budding intellect, his embryonic talent—and before long she surely felt genuine affection for him. Perhaps in time Fane became the son Violet never had. Like Sydney he was an aspiring writer who needed encouragement and was more than grateful for her support, for her editorial assistance, and for her friendship. She also did whatever she could over the next decade to help him publish and get his books reviewed where it counted. He returned her loving friendship with deep affection of his own and with his adoring memoir.

Sometime during the summer Fane met Violet she became ill and returned to 1A Ilchester Place, the last of the three houses she and Sydney had shared in London, and never stayed overnight at the cottage in Surrey or anywhere else again. It was a large, pink brick house in West Kensington that looks much the same today. The interior reflected Violet's eccentricity as she grew older and also conveyed something of the surroundings in which she had lived with Sydney. Fane believed, I think correctly, that the art and the black and gold Biedermeier furniture with orange upholstery and black cushions reflected Sydney's taste, but the security measures, the piano, and the phonograph probably owed more to Violet's concerns and interests than his:

The front door was fitted with an assortment of anti-burglar devices, locks, bolts, chains and a barred peephole. On the ground floor were the usual offices, a dark hall and an ugly angular staircase, a dining-room and a sitting-room. The sitting-room had five big windows, two marble and stainless steel fireplaces with mirrors over them, sofas at each end and chairs to match, a circular table with piles of books round the edge, a grand piano, a gramophone and bookshelves. . . . The curtains were . . . brown. There were several pictures painted in the twenties and thirties hanging on the dun-colored walls, a sculpted figure of a girl dancing in the nude by Gaudier-Brzeska and a couple of heads by Epstein.

A portrait of Violet as a young woman hung in the dining-room. She was leaning on a parasol, "wasp-waisted, soft-eyed and a little florid."

The mood inside the house was somber. The windows were shaded and closed. Violet hated sunlight and had a morbid fear of fresh air. She disliked the outdoors and avoided all exercise, including walking. Everything she needed was delivered by tradesmen or picked up by Cam, who continued to look after her needs just as she had when Violet was a young girl. Freda Almond, the Schiffs' longtime secretary, managed the affairs of the house. Even her dentist treated her at home. But none of this was new to Violet. She had always lived that way.

She missed Sydney terribly, but she gradually rebuilt her life and somehow managed to keep him in it. "After the first frightful year," she wrote to Countess Drogheda in 1948, "when I nearly read myself to death (mercifully I was able to do that) I managed to restore some sort of equilibrium to my inner life. I was not forced into an alien atmosphere, and could live on in the same mental world which Sydney and I had shared."

One of the ways Violet did this was to throw herself yet again into what must have seemed like a never-ending task, the editing of *A True Story*, and in trying to find a new publisher for it. She wrote to Thornton Wilder, whom she barely knew, asking for his help. He answered her letter on June 27, 1947, saying that in the past he had helped various unknown writers and some difficult known writers such as Gertrude Stein and Jean-Paul Sartre win audiences. But he said he did not think Stephen Hudson's novels fit either category because they "have been long before the public and have had many readers as appreciative as myself." Therefore he respectfully declined to help.

In April or May of 1948, while going through some papers of Sydney's, she came across a brief essay he had written that she thought would make a perfect epilogue to his novel. On May 3 she wrote to Peter Baker, who owned the Falcon Press, which was preparing to publish her newly edited edition of *A True Story*, to tell him about her discovery. Sydney's essay was an undisguised love letter to Myrtle, which is to say to Violet, which makes abundantly clear why she was so eager to have it used. But if there is any lingering doubt, this brief passage from the epilogue should lay it to rest:

> Morning after morning as we lie side by side, from the moment of opening my eyes the working consciousness struggles with the memory of dreams and reveals your presence there in the flesh and the ever-fresh wonder that all this is mine to take and hold during our time together here within the brittle shell of numbered days, each one made memorable by your magic. . . . And you wonder why I touch your hands and lean over to kiss you.

Her commitment to Sydney's memory and his legacy was formidable and she did succeed, but with a caveat. The Falcon edition of *A True Story* was published later in 1948 with the epilogue. But unfortunately, soon after it appeared, Baker was convicted of defrauding Barclay's Bank of about forty thousand pounds. He went to prison for seven years, and *A True Story* for all practical purposes disappeared until it was republished in 1965. Violet sent Eliot a copy of the Falcon edition. In his letter of thanks he wrote that he considered it "a document of its age (and I think a well written one) which ought to last." But promoting Sydney's novel was not Violet's sole occupation. Despite her bad back, her deafness, and a variety of other ailments real and imagined, she also found time to translate several books from French into English.

Fane admired her greatly, but he was not blind to the strategies she used to accomplish as much as she did despite her apparent physical weakness. He believed she had realized long before that to meet her highly focused goals she had to set clear priorities, which meant avoiding certain responsibilities. And in a not-unrelated summing up of her realistic attitude toward the things she cared most about in life, he wrote: "Violet never forgot that the preliminary condition of her atmosphere, her moral and aesthetic elevation, the quality of her friendship, the happiness of her marriage, love itself as she saw it, and the creation of ninety per cent of the masterpieces of art she preferred, was financial independence." So there you have her philosophy of life in a nutshell: Don't waste energy on things that are not important and make sure you have enough money to enjoy those that are.

From an early age it seems Violet felt self-confident and secure. For one thing, money was never a problem. It was simply there, and there was never any fear that it wouldn't be. Her parents were happily married. She grew up seeing that her mother was completely free to pursue her music, which meant six or seven hours a day at the piano, and the female children were treated as equals to their brothers. In other ways Samuel and Zillah provided a stable and very comfortable Victorian environment for their large brood of children. Violet, as the youngest and her father's favorite, might have been pampered a bit more than the others, but if she was, it did not keep her from being tough-minded. She knew what mattered to her long before she met Sydney, and when it came to her values and principles she was uncompromising. She demonstrated her steadfastness often and in diverse circumstances, but never as convincingly as when she bluntly told Sydney, to whom she was deeply attracted, that until he made a clean break from Marion she would not see him again. Her moral certainty and her unwillingness to compromise on matters of principle was what attracted to her a certain breed of person that included Sydney Schiff, Julian Fane, Eliot, and Proust and alienated others, like most of Bloomsbury.

Edward Beddington-Behrens, who spent summers with the Schiffs as a boy after the death of his mother, Violet's sister Evelyn, felt deeply indebted to and affectionate toward them, regarding them almost as a second set of parents. But there were times when he felt their love and attention were suffocating. Once when he was short of money because of bad investments he decided to explore business opportunities in the United States, partly because he wanted to be away from their dominating personalities. He knew he might make mistakes, but he wanted to make them on his own. He also resented their opposition to his marrying Irene Ash, his first and greatest love, who eventually became his third wife. But almost everything he had to say about them was positive and affectionate. They clearly felt close to him because they left him Abinger and most of their art collection.

Beddington-Behrens's son Serge, however, who holds an English literature degree from Oxford and a PhD in holistic psychology, first met Violet in 1950 when he was five years old, and saw her on and off until her death twelve years later, took an immediate and violent dislike to her. Time has not dulled his animus. He has expressed his feelings about Violet in writing several times and the basic sentiment never varies. "I found 'Aunt Violet' malevolent and sinister. Not a loving presence. Full of a certain kind of Jewish intellectuality which was wholly devoid of heart. I felt this when I was a lot older than five. I can't remember when she died, but I was born in 1945, and my feelings go up to that time." Serge felt Violet had been a very bad influence on his father. He believes that because his father's mother died young and his father was never there for him, and because he suffered from "shell shock" during World War I, his father was vulnerable and fell under Violet's spell.

Reflecting the not entirely satisfactory relationship he had with his own father, Serge wrote:

> I would feel that many of the less than human traits, which he showed in his life, had much to do with her influence. . . . I personally felt that [Sydney and Violet's] world was an essentially artificial one full of name dropping and pretension. . . . I don't think that either one of them had much humanity and compassion despite all that drooling over Proust. . . . I would imagine that most of the "Violet gushers" are people who either belonged to, or were at the periphery of, that world, which I think, deep down, was a cold and superficial one, despite pretensions of intellectual depths. And depth, we remember, is something of the heart and soul. It is not about cleverness. Yes, they were both clever, but not deep genuine human beings.

Some of what Beddington-Behrens had to say will almost certainly resonate with anyone who knows enough about Sydney and Violet to have formed an opinion of them. It is easy to think, for example, that they were name-dropping snobs. And there is no doubt that the world in which they moved in some respects really was cold, superficial, and inhumane. There also is no doubt that they sought out persons of intellectual distinction, entertained them well, and talked about them freely, which could be seen as instances of snobbery, social climbing, and name-dropping. But a careful reading of their correspondence with people like Eliot, Proust, Lewis, Huxley, and Mansfield suggests otherwise. It suggests instead relationships of equality, with benefits flowing in both directions. And where there was fawning or gushing, that too seems to have flowed both ways.

Moreover, anyone who has read Sydney's body of work with an understanding of Violet's contribution to it would be hard pressed to say they were no more than shallow name-droppers. Beddington-Behrens said he had not read the books and had no interest in reading them. Other factors to consider in judging them might be their support of artists such as Isaac Rosenberg and Wyndham Lewis, and their giving "refuge," to use Violet's word, to the Beerbohms during the war, as well as taking in the young refugee Stella Jadwabuik. These acts, I think, imply more humanity than Beddington-Behrens gives them credit for.

Apart from her letters and a diary that has been lost or destroyed, Violet wrote almost nothing of her own. And although we know she was an incisive editor and critic, no manuscripts of Sydney's books have been preserved, so there is no way to fully evaluate her contribution to his writings. The best remaining evidence of her critical and editorial method and style consists of thirteen type-written pages of suggestions for works in progress by Julian Fane stored in an archive in Lewes, England. These pages reveal a great deal about her taste and acuity, but also about her respect for the integrity of authorship. She wrote the following explicit comment on authorial autonomy after recommending brutal cuts in a work titled *Leo's Birthday*:

> I do not wish you to make such a drastic cut on my advice, but for the sake of the book itself as a work of art I cannot help saying what I think and believe. There is no reason why you should be guided by my taste in the matter as it is *your book*. There is no criterion about a work of art and it is not a matter of being right or wrong. If after another point of view (mine) has been exposed to you, you prefer your own, then *you are right*. (Italics are Violet's in both cases.)

In the paragraph above she expressed an obligation to the work of art itself, almost as if it were completely autonomous. But she also acknowledged the absolute right of its creator to mold it as he saw fit. She offered advice to the creator as one should—if one feels one must—to a parent, in language that made clear she understood that the work of art under consideration was his child, not hers. And finally she specified that if he rejected her advice, not only would she recognize his right to reject it, but she would defer to his judgment. She was taking a position that was appropriately respectful of the artist and the work of art and was anything but arrogant.

There is only one other record of Violet's editing. Not long before she died Theophilus Boll sent her his biographical note and critical essay on Stephen Hudson, both of which appeared in his 1962 edition of *Richard, Myrtle and I*, for fact checking. She was displeased to the point of annoyance with the biographical note and responded in a tone that was demanding and disrespectful. Her comments typically ranged from blunt to acerbic: "Your account of the artistic, intellectual atmosphere of the Schiff home is completely false"; "Uncle Charles and his wife did not in the least understand Sydney's temperament"; "Will you please delete this, which is quite untrue and would have been an impossibility." Time and again she asked Boll to delete paragraphs and sometimes whole pages, and she directed him to fix grammar and usage. Boll, however, refused to be intimidated. The only changes he made were to correct factual errors, which were minor and few, and, where he agreed, errors in grammar and usage.

It is probably fair to assume that Violet grew testier as she grew older; nevertheless Fane's characterization of her in her mid-seventies was totally consistent with many contemporary accounts of the thirty-four-year-old woman Sydney fell in love with and married two years later.

"When I knew her she was impressed by erudition," Fane wrote, "but for her own part recoiled from anything academic—it was life that claimed her attention. And she had a positive genius for getting her way and for self-protection. She must have been born unusual, perhaps more child-like than childish, not fond of nature or animals, serious and wise and able to dominate her environment, willful and sweet-tempered, and dedicated to the proposition that she existed to help everyone to be happy. The branch of life she specialized in was human relations, and art in its more romantic aspect became nearly her religion."

Fane's layered portrait accurately captured Violet's defining qualities and contradictions, her standards and her spirit. She could be manipulative, willful, and domineering, but also wise, sweet-natured, and altruistic. Proust thought she was formidably intelligent and angelically sweet. Yet to Serge Beddington-Behrens she was sinister and shallow. Of course Proust knew her mainly through her letters, which were suffused with admiration for him and his work, which, to be fair, might have influenced his views. We don't know for sure how she perceived or treated Beddington-Behrens when he was between the ages of five and seventeen. There is, however, nothing in her life story to suggest that she ever had the slightest affinity for children. And finally, if Fane was correct that Violet believed she existed to make others happy, it is probably also true that she thought she knew better than they did what would make them happy.

Violet Schiff died on July 2, 1962. She was eighty-six years old. Her obituary appeared in the *Times* of London on July 9 under the headline: "All Embracing Interest in the Arts." The following letter from T. S. Eliot was appended to it:

The death of Violet Schiff, after a long illness, will cause great grief to relatives and to many friends, among whom I and my wife are proud to be numbered. I write, however, not only to express a personal sorrow but because of my memories of Violet and her husband the late Sydney Schiff in the world of art and letters 40 years ago. In the 1920s the

Schiffs' hospitality, generosity and encouragement meant much to a number of young artists and writers of whom I was one. The Schiffs' acquaintance was cosmopolitan, and their interests embraced all the arts. At their house I met for example, [Frederick] Delius and Arthur Symons, and the first Viscountess Rothermere, who founded *The Criterion* under my editorship. [John] Middleton Murry and Katherine Mansfield knew their house, and Wyndham Lewis and Charles Scott-Moncrieff, and many others.

When I married in 1957, Violet Schiff welcomed me and my wife, whom she took to her heart at once. She was already an invalid and could not be persuaded to pay visits, but was always happy to receive her friends. Her mind was as active as ever, and her interest in people and in the arts was undiminished. It was, indeed, in her last years when she was house-bound and, I suspect, often in pain, that her qualities impressed me most deeply: the vigor of her speech, the animation of her face, and the warmth of her sympathy. Hers was a sympathy which made one feel that she understood much more than had been, or could be, put into words: that she was aware of, and responded to, that which could not be spoken. In consequence of this sensitiveness she could regard people with a gentle, clear-sighted charity.

I write primarily to pay homage to a beloved friend, but also in the hope that some future chronicler of the history of art and letters in our time may give to Sydney and Violet Schiff the place which is their due.

ACKNOWLEDGMENTS

The idea for this book began germinating four years ago. Jenny McCracken, a dear friend who shares my passion for Proust, lent me one book and gave me another. I read the one she lent me first. It was a biography of the poet and painter Isaac Rosenberg and it briefly mentioned Sydney and Violet. The book she gave me was *A Night at the Majestic* by Richard Davenport-Hines. It took its title from the 1922 dinner that the Schiffs hosted and which Proust, Joyce, Picasso, Stravinsky, and Diaghilev attended. Moreover, it had a chapter on the Schiffs. Although I knew vaguely who they were from biographies of Proust, it would not have occurred to me to write this book had Jenny not brought the Rosenberg biography and Davenport-Hines's work to my attention. I cannot thank her enough.

After several months of preliminary research, and in recognition of the fact that only a small number of scholars and aficionados of the modernist period had ever heard of the Schiffs, I wrote an unusually lengthy proposal. My loyal and editorially gifted agent, Chuck Verrill, helped me whip it into final shape. He then developed a carefully selected submissions list of a dozen publishers and sent it to me for approval. I had no problem with his choices, but I showed the list to Kitty, my wife, confidante and collaborator in all things, before responding. She suggested adding Nan A. Talese/ Doubleday. Chuck and I agreed this was a good idea, so he sent out thirteen copies of the proposal instead of twelve. In less than a week Nan bought the book. Thanks, Chuck, for your hard work, wise advice, insightful editing, and cheerful willingness to support projects with uncertain prospects. And thanks, dear Kitty, not only for thinking of Nan, but for your help in painstakingly combing through 950 letters in the British Library, most of which were handwritten and many of which were virtually indecipherable, and reading and re-reading the manuscript.

Nan's enthusiasm for the book added fuel to my own, and her literary knowledge, exquisite taste, and refined editorial judgment made a contribution to the final product that cannot be overestimated. I have long been a believer in the less-is-more school of writing, but as all writers know, it is awfully hard not to fall in love with your own words. When this happens, as it inevitably will, you need a great editor to save you from yourself. Thank you, Nan, for doing this for me and for so much more. I also want to thank Ronit Feldman, a knowledgeable and accommodating editor on Nan's staff, who was especially helpful in my search for pictures and permissions, and Dan Meyer, Nan's thoughtful and intelligent assistant, who shepherded the book through the production process. Both made my task easier and *Sydney and Violet* better. Thanks also to Nora Reichard, the senior production editor, and Rosalie Wieder, the copy editor, each of whom, in her own way, contributed significantly to the successful completion of this project.

There are many others who helped bring this work to fruition. First among them are the Beddington family members, who graciously spent time with me and searched their files and picture albums. Each of them was kind enough to answer my intrusive, sometimes repetitive, and perhaps tedious questions, to provide photographs and documents, to introduce me to other family members, and to dredge up memories that have enriched my book.

The first family member I met was Charles Beddington, and it happened serendipitously. I came across his name in an article in the *Washington Post* about the sale of an unsigned School of Canaletto painting at a small Chevy Chase auction gallery. The work sold for $687,125. The pre-auction estimated sale price was $6,000 to

$8,000. Charles, a dealer in eighteenth-century art, was mentioned because he was an adviser to an anonymous buyer and speculated that the artist was Michele Marieschi. I sent him an e-mail telling him that I was writing a book about Sydney and Violet and asking if he was related to Violet. He responded almost instantly saying that he was her great-nephew and that he was in a small way the family historian. And to my delight he also said he would be in Washington the next day. A day after that we met at the National Gallery and looked at pictures while talking about Sydney and Violet. Over the next two years we established a warm relationship over dinners in London and Washington. He supplied invaluable information and family pictures, without which the book would lack many of the vivid details and illuminating images that breathe life into its subjects. His sister, Charlotte Wallis, and his ninety-five-year-old mother, Debbie Beddington, also contributed to my understanding of Violet and Sydney.

My contacts with two other family members, Stephen Kane and Serge Beddington-Behrens, were conducted entirely by e-mail and telephone. Both were consistently cordial and willing to respond to my questions, and Dr. Kane provided original materials. He also was kind enough to research and copy letters for me at the Imperial War Museum in London and to have a drawing of Sydney by William Rothenstein at the Merton College Library at Oxford professionally photographed so that it could be used in the book. And he passed on his mother's written account of a visit to Sydney and Violet's house at 18 Cambridge Square in London and introduced me to his sister, Evelyn Richardson, and to Nadia Lasserson, both of whom shared with me their memories of Violet when they were young girls and she was an old woman. Although his recollections were more painful than pleasant, Dr. Beddington-Behrens also shared his childhood memories of Violet with me. I thank all of them for their extremely useful contributions. I also want to thank Fleur Wadley, her brother, Edward Rossdale, and their mother, Lucie Marcelle Louise Rossdale, who invited Kitty and me to their home in London, told me what they knew about Sydney and Violet, and provided a copy of Samuel Beddington's will.

I want to give special thanks to Gillian Fane, the widow of Julian Fane, the young English writer who became Violet's close friend after Sydney died. Mrs. Fane clarified a number of issues for me and was unfailingly responsive to my requests for information. The same was true of Diana Crook, the curator of the Julian Fane archive, who provided copies of original materials that helped me understand Violet's contribution to Sydney's literary output.

I am indebted to Christophe Wall-Romana, an old and dear friend who is a poet and an associate professor and director of graduate studies in the Department of French and Italian at the University of Minnesota. He helped me out when my French faltered while translating the correspondence between the Schiffs and Marcel Proust. If there are mistakes in those translations, they are of course mine. And Kitty and I are both grateful to two more old and dear friends, Marion and Irving Yass, who put us up during two of our trips to London, fed us, and made our stays incomparably more pleasant than they would otherwise have been.

I also want to thank Deborah Bull, a highly professional photo researcher who was a pleasure to work with and without whose expertise the eight pages of pictures in the book would not have been nearly as good.

And finally, I thank the librarians who guided me through collections at the following institutions: the British Library, Department of Manuscripts; the Charles E. Young Research Library, Department of Special Collections, UCLA; the Cornell University Library, Division of Rare and Manuscript Collections; the Merton College Library, University of Oxford; the Imperial War Museum; Georgetown University's Lauinger Library; the Gardner Library, University of California, Berkeley; and the Library of Congress. All of the librarians at these institutions were helpful, but two were especially so: Ana Guimaraes at Cornell and Julia Walworth at Merton College, Oxford.

NOTES

A NOTE TO READERS

xi **The cause, as in the similar cases:** Didion said she had no letters from Dunne, but says nothing about whether she had written to him. The information about Didion and Dunne and Oates and Smith is taken from "For Sorrow There Is No Remedy," a review by Julian Barnes of *A Widow's Story: A Memoir*, by Joyce Carol Oates, *New York Review of Books*, April 7, 2001, 10.

xi **Sydney wrote to his friend:** Schiff to Beerbohm, letter no. 24, Max Beerbohm Collection, Merton College Library, University of Oxford (hereafter cited as Beerbohm Collection).

xii **The Schiffs' nephew:** Edward Beddington-Behrens, *Look Back Look Forward* (London: Macmillan, 1963), 58.

PROLOGUE

2 **"On the one side":** *Taken Care Of: The Autobiography of Edith Sitwell* (New York: Atheneum, 1965), 87–88.

3 **Many years after the heyday:** John Maynard Keynes, *My Early Beliefs in Two Memoirs*, in *The Collected Writings of John Maynard Keynes*, Vol. 10 (London: Macmillan, St. Martin's Press, for the Royal Economic Society, 1972), 447.

5 **Another wondered if there was a human face:** Miranda Seymour, *Ottoline Morrell: Life on the Grand Scale* (New York: Farrar, Straus and Giroux, 1993), 354.

5 **In her memoir, Lady Ottoline:** *Ottoline at Garsington: Memoirs of Lady Ottoline Morrell, 1915–1918*, ed. Robert Gathorne-Hardy (London: Faber and Faber, 1974), 129.

6 **But according to Miranda:** Seymour, *Ottoline Morrell*, 2.

CHAPTER 1: SYDNEY'S TRAVELS

8 **In any event, he packed up:** By what means and over exactly what period of time he traveled is unknown.

11 **She had been diagnosed:** Sydney's sister Rose Morley said in a letter to Theophi-

lus E. M. Boll that it was valve disease, but there is no other confirmation. All cited source material from Rose Morley is in the Theophilus E. M. Boll Papers (Collection 2088), Department of Special Collections, Charles E. Young Research Library, University of California, Los Angeles (hereafter cited as Boll Papers).

12　**Alfred and Carrie, as all who knew her:** Ibid.

14　**They then lived in it:** Since the only detailed accounts of their life on the lake are in *Richard Kurt* and *Elinor Colhouse*, two volumes of *A True Story*, silence might seem the prudent choice at this point. But precisely because the fictionalized but loosely autobiographical version of this sad stretch of Sydney's life is almost all there is, drawing on it here, with corrections where the few known facts vary from the fictional text, seems to me a risk worth taking.

20　**Marion later became:** Rose Morley provided this information in a letter to Boll. Boll Papers.

CHAPTER 2: FAMILIES

22　**He also sensed:** Stephen Hudson, *Myrtle* (New York: Alfred A. Knopf, 1925), 189.

23　**Their son, Leopold:** All of the biographical information on Leopold Schiff comes from the Boll Papers and Boll's biographical note in *Richard, Myrtle and I* (Philadelphia: University of Pennsylvania Press, 1962).

26　**But Sydney and his brother:** This was the story told to Boll by Rose Morley.

27　**Sydney's childhood is vividly described:** Mann to Schiff, February 11, 1926, Boll Papers. Mann wrote that *Prince Hempseed* "is without doubt one of the best, truest and freshest boy stories in all English literature, and that means a great deal because England is the classical land of the Boy, and has the best Boys' stories of the World. The history of young Richard Kurt claims kinship with everything that has been achieved in this sphere by the masters of the past in England, and it renews what they have done with every modern means—a thoroughly progressive and understanding psychology."

31　**It seems likely they left Spain:** All of the information on Orobio de Castro comes from Yosef Kaplan, *From Christianity to Judaism* (Oxford: Oxford University Press, 1989).

32　**Orobio's biographer, Yosef Kaplan:** Ibid., 105.

32　**John Locke attended the debate:** John Marshall, *John Locke, Toleration and Early Enlightenment Culture* (Cambridge: Cambridge University Press, 2006).

32　**John Simon was born:** Biographical information on John Simon comes from the *Oxford Dictionary of National Biography* (Oxford: Oxford University Press, 2004) and the *Jewish Encyclopedia*, www.jewishencyclopedia.com, 1906/2002.

33　**He was also active in Reform Judaism:** Information about Charles Salaman is from the *Encyclopaedia Judaica*, 2008, available at www.jewishvirtuallibrary.org.

33　**In 1858, the same year:** Simon served as an assistant to county court judges, sometimes filling in for them.

35　**At Paderewski's request:** Frederick Beddington, *The Rest of the Family* (private edition, 1963), 10.

35　**The only physical description:** The details of life at 21 Hyde Park Square and the description of the house are taken from Beddington, *Rest of the Family*.

37 **For twenty years she was:** Violet was the best source for Sybil's relationship with Puccini.

38 **Her first marriage to a cousin:** This at least is how Stephen Hudson says it ended on page 70 of *Myrtle*.

CHAPTER 3: THE MODERNIST WORLD

44 **In a letter to Proust:** Philip Kolb, *Correspondance générale de Marcel Proust*, Vol. 19 (Paris: Plon, 1930–1936), 613.

44 **Violet's twenty-three-year-old cousin:** Based on an account provided by Dr. Stephen Kane, written by his mother, Irene, many years after these events. It is the youthful memory of a mature woman, but it is sensitive and detailed and provides a general sense of what the Schiffs' home and lifestyle must have been like. It also epitomizes Sydney's rather quaint notion of "simple tastes" and "objects without value."

48 **According to the *Times*:** This account of Marinetti's London tour is adapted from Lawrence Rainey's excellent book *Institutions of Modernism: Literary Elites and Public Culture* (New Haven: Yale University Press, 1998), 28.

51 **He used characteristics:** Somerset Maugham to Sydney Schiff, February 24, 1937, Boll Papers.

53 **He told Edward:** Edward Beddington-Behrens, *Look Back Look Forward* (London: Macmillan, 1963), 60.

CHAPTER 4: THE WAR YEARS

57 **"The Love Song of J. Alfred Prufrock":** Eliot had been working on "Prufrock" since 1910. It became his best-known poem after *The Waste Land*. Pound persuaded Harriet Monroe, editor of *Poetry* magazine, to publish it.

58 **On the strength of "Prufrock":** Vorticism is a subdivision of modernism that glorified the dynamism of the machine age. In this it was similar to futurism, but it differed in its mode of expression, which foreshadowed abstract expressionism. It began at the Rebel Art Centre, of which Lewis was a founder. Pound gave it its name.

58 **"Yor old Uncle Ezz":** Jeffrey Meyers, *The Enemy: A Biography of Wyndham Lewis* (London: Routledge & Kegan Paul, 1980), 76.

58 **Years later Lewis described:** Wyndham Lewis, *Blasting and Bombardiering* (Berkeley: University of California Press, 1967), 282.

58 **Lewis thought democracy:** Ibid., 27.

59 **Without them, he wrote:** Ibid., 273.

59 **He also accused:** Wyndham Lewis, *Rude Assignment* (London: Hutchinson & Co., 1950), 195–96.

60 **Ernest Hemingway once dismissed:** Paul O'Keefe, *Some Sort of Genius: A Life of Wyndham Lewis* (London: Jonathan Cape, 2001), 242.

60 **And Lewis was the only:** Others they knew, including Isaac Rosenberg, the artist Henri Gaudier-Brzska, and T. E. Hulme, who wrote about the aesthetics of modernism, were killed in the war.

61   **"the 'Bloomsburies' were all doing war work":** Lewis, *Blasting and Bombardiering*, 184.

61   **Sydney—once characterized:** Mina Curtiss, *Other People's Letters: In Search of Proust* (New York: Helen Marx Books/Books and Co., 2005), 26–27.

61   **Bloomsbury princeling-by-marriage:** David Garnett was the son of Constance Garnett, translator of the great nineteenth-century Russian novels and the husband of Angelica Bell, whose mother, Vanessa Bell—Virginia Woolf's sister—was married to the art critic Clive Bell. Angelica's biological father was the painter Duncan Grant.

61   **"It is the only way to get an idea":** Schiff to Beddington-Behrens, July 16, 1916, Beddington-Behrens Collection, Imperial War Museum.

62   **Although they both attended:** All of the letters in the following account are found in the Schiff Collection, Additional MSS. 52916–23, Department of Manuscripts, British Library, London (hereafter cited as the Schiff Collection). All citations to the collection refer to these volumes.

64   **"He was enthusiastic about my poems":** Quoted by Valerie Eliot from "a private paper, written in the sixties," in the introduction to *The Letters of T. S. Eliot, Volume I: 1898–1922*, ed. Valerie Eliot (New York: Harcourt Brace Jovanovich, 1988), xvii.

65   **There is a sense of ease:** Lyndall Gordon, *T. S. Eliot: An Imperfect Life* (New York: Norton, 1988), 141. Gordon attributes this in large part to the fact that both had wives who suffered from chronic illness, which might or might not have been responsible for the closeness of the two couples.

65   **It is also likely that Sydney:** Vivienne Haigh-Wood, who became Vivienne Eliot, liked friends to spell her name "Vivien." I use the legal spelling of her given name throughout except in quoted text.

65   **Accounts vary from one night:** *Ottoline at Garsington: Memoirs of Lady Ottoline Morrell, 1915–1918*, ed. Robert Gathorne-Hardy (London: Faber and Faber, 1974), 96.

66   **And in a letter to his mother:** Eliot, *Letters*, Vol. 1, 400.

67   **"One result is that everyone":** Ibid., 411.

68   **He wrote that the game:** Philip Kolb, *Correspondance générale de Marcel Proust*, Vol. 19 (Paris: Plon, 1930–1936), 478.

68   **During one of those evenings:** Frederick Beddington, *The Rest of the Family* (private edition, 1963), 21–22.

70   **His only criticism:** Eliot, *Letters*, Vol. 1, 319.

70   **"I see in R.K. a process":** Eliot to Schiff, July 25, 1919, Schiff Collection, 52918.

70   **But by then Sydney and Violet:** The first letters were exchanged in April 1919.

71   **"For the artist, who does not deal in surfaces":** Samuel Beckett, *Proust* (New York: Grove Press, 1931), 46.

75   **In Eliot's letter expressing his appreciation:** Eliot to Schiff, July 25, 1919, Schiff Collection, 52918.

75   **"My house is a decayed house":** *Estaminet* is French for a bistro or small café.

77   **"Art and Letters," Read wrote:** Herbert Read, *Annals of Innocence and Experience* (London: Faber & Faber, 1946), 178, quoted in *The Oxford Critical and Cultural History of Modernist Magazines*, Vol. 1, ed. Peter Brooker and Andrew Thacker (New York: Oxford University Press, 2009), 503.

77   **"A cultured aristocracy":** T. S. Eliot, "Notes: The Function of a Literary Review," *Criterion*, July 1923 (1), 421. The quote appears in *The Oxford Critical and Cultural History of Modernist Magazines*, Vol. 1.

CHAPTER 5: A VOLATILE RELATIONSHIP

80 **She had written caustically:** *The Collected Letters of Katherine Mansfield, Volume 3: 1919–1920,* ed. Vincent O'Sullivan and Margaret Scott (Oxford: Clarendon Press, 1993), 268n.

80 **But just before being picked up:** Ibid., 274.

80 **"The door opened softly":** Stephen Hudson, "First Meetings with Katherine Mansfield," *Cornhill,* Autumn 1958, 202–4.

81 **To which Sydney responded:** Hudson, "First Meetings with Katherine," 208.

82 **As soon as Mansfield got home:** Mansfield, *Collected Letters,* Vol. 3, 278.

82 **About the Schiffs she said:** Ibid., 281. In a letter to Murry on April 14, 1920, Mansfield wrote that Sydney had her disease "so he exaggerates the care one ought to take." There is no indication elsewhere that he had tuberculosis.

82 **And finally, in a letter to her husband:** Ibid., 291.

83 **She also wrote to Murry:** Katherine Mansfield to John Middleton Murry, October 24, 1920, Katherine Mansfield Society website, www.katherinemansfieldsociety.org/24-october/.

83 **"I have an old servant":** *The Letters of Katherine Mansfield,* Vol. 2, ed. John Middleton Murry (New York: Alfred A Knopf, 1929), 355.

83 **In an entry in her scrapbook:** *The Scrapbook of Katherine Mansfield,* ed. John Middleton Murry (New York: Alfred A. Knopf, 1940), 244.

83 **"It shocks me," she wrote:** Mansfield, *Letters,* Vol. 2, 432.

83 **Despite Mansfield's reservations:** letter from James Joyce to Wyndham Lewis, April 4, 1922, box 138, Wyndham Lewis Collection, Division of Rare and Manuscript Collections, Cornell University.

84 **Nevertheless, Mansfield never really:** John Middleton Murry to Sydney Schiff, January 15, 1922, 434. The ellipses in this paragraph are Mansfield's.

84 **In December 1921:** Mansfield, *Letters,* Vol. 2, 424.

86 **Although Lewis's respected biographer:** Jeffrey Meyers, *The Enemy: A Biography of Wyndham Lewis* (London: Routledge & Kegan Paul, 1980), 128.

87 **After the lunch at the Schiffs':** Mansfield's note to Lewis and his response, if there was one, have been lost.

87 **"I don't see how":** Lewis to Sydney Schiff, September 7, 1922, Wyndham Lewis Collection, Cornell University. (Copy transcribed from holograph; original in the Schiff Collection.)

CHAPTER 6: ANNUS MIRABILIS

91 **During this period he wrote to Sydney:** Eliot to Schiff, April 20, 1922, Schiff Collection, 52918. Also, Eliot, *Letters,* Vol. 1, 522.

92 **He then added rather obscurely:** Pound to Eliot, March 14, 1922, in Humphrey Carpenter, *A Serious Character* (New York: Houghton Mifflin, 1988), 408.

92 **The template said in part:** *The Letters of T. S. Eliot, Volume 1: 1898–1922,* ed. Valerie Eliot (New York: Harcourt Brace Jovanovich, 1988), 514.

92 **It sought thirty contributors:** Carpenter, *Serious Character,* 409.

92 **Two weeks later he wrote:** Eliot, *Letters,* Vol. 1, 555.

93 **"If it is stated so positively":** Ibid., 553.

95 **Vivienne was so moved:** Carole Seymour Jones, *Painted Shadow: The Life of Vivienne Eliot, First Wife of T. S. Eliot* (New York: Anchor Books, 2003), 346.

95 **Eliot wrote the same day:** Eliot, *Letters*, Vol. 1, 582–84.

96 **He also told him:** Ibid., 590.

96 **He responded to Pound:** Ibid., 592.

97 **In at least one instance:** The sketch was about adultery as practiced in three different cultures, American, English, and French, a subject about which Mansfield and her crowd had intimate knowledge. The English version is characterized by absurd digressions, including one about Fat Peggy (pronounced Piggy) Trevelyan, "the fattest damn woman in London," a description repeated over and over again in ever more extravagant language.

99 **Years later Lewis recounted:** Wyndham Lewis, *Blasting and Bombardiering* (Berkeley: University of California Press, 1967), 237–38.

99 **Four years later Sydney:** Paul O'Keefe, *Some Sort of Genius: A Life of Wyndham Lewis* (London: Jonathan Cape, 2001), 237–67.

102 **But having given the matter further thought:** Wyndham Lewis, *Rude Assignment* (London: Hutchinson & Co., 1950), 163.

CHAPTER 7: A FRIENDSHIP IN LETTERS I

106 **Here were two people:** Excerpts from Proust's letters in chapters 7 and 8 are all from Philip Kolb, *Correspondance générale de Marcel Proust*, Vols. 18–21 (Paris: Plon, 1930–1936); all translations are mine. I provide endnotes for individual letters only when I think it is useful.

107 **Sydney went on to say Swann:** Proust based Swann mainly on his friend the elegant, Jewish, socially sought-after Charles Haas, son of a stockbroker, as was Swann, but added a touch of erudition from Charles Ephrussi, a wealthy son of Jewish grain traders from Odessa and founder of the *Gazette des Beaux-Arts*.

109 **"The strange enchantments":** Violet Schiff, "A Night with Proust," *London Magazine*, Vol. 3, No. 9, September 1956, 20–22.

109 **At daybreak Odilon:** William C. Carter, *Marcel Proust: A Life* (New Haven: Yale University Press, 2000), 725. Carter's source is Paul Morand, *Le Visiteur du soir* (Geneva: La Palatine, 1949).

110 **Swann would become a "dreyfusard":** "Dreyfusard" was the name given to supporters of Captain Alfred Dreyfus, a Jewish officer in the French army who was falsely accused of passing secrets to the Germans and sentenced to life in prison in January 1895. He was released from prison in September 1899 but not fully exonerated until July 1906.

110 **And Joseph Conrad, a godfather:** Author's note, *Under Western Eyes* (Edinburgh: John Grant, 1925).

115 **He called *Richard, Myrtle and I* "unsatisfactory":** John Gawsworth, *Ten Contemporaries: Notes Toward Their Definitive Bibliography* (London: E. Benn, 1932), 99.

116 **"Looking for an explanation":** Kolb, *Correspondance générale*, Vol. 19, 423.

118 **Proust told him rather gently:** Ibid., 435.

120 **And he added with exaggerated politeness:** Ibid., 478.

CHAPTER 8: A FRIENDSHIP IN LETTERS II

130 **When the boy came back:** Mortimer Leo Schiff was a partner in the New York investment bank Kuhn, Loeb & Company.

136 **"Thursday evening we are going":** Only three of the four were Russian: Tchaikovsky's *Nutcracker* and *Sleeping Beauty* and Borodin's *Prince Igor*. The other was Schumann's *Carnaval*.

137 **"supper at the Hotel Majestic":** With a few minor exceptions, no details of the dinner are known by anyone today because no one who attended, including perhaps the two greatest prose writers of the twentieth century, thought it interesting enough to chronicle. This would have seemed especially odd in the case of Proust, whose novel contains several fictionalized accounts of glittering social occasions, if not for the fact that he was in a race with death to finish *In Search of Lost Time*. As for Joyce, he provided different verbal accounts to different friends, in each case exercising novelistic license and Irish wit and possibly under the influence, but he wrote nothing down himself. As far as I can tell, no one else thought to re-create the Schiffs' magnum opus in prose until 2006, when Richard Davenport-Hines did it charmingly in *A Night at the Majestic*. By then, though, there were just tantalizing tidbits of reliable information to go on, which led Davenport-Hines to make educated guesses based on what he knew about Sydney's and Violet's likes and dislikes and the tastes of the times to create what had to be an impressionistic picture. And all anyone can do now to re-create the scene and the mood of the soiree of the century, even with the benefit of Davenport-Hines's valuable research, is to once again assemble the minimal facts and memory fragments, some of which are ambiguous and others contradictory, and to make judicious suppositions. But in an effort not to further blur the boundary between fact and fiction, I've tried to capture the spirit of that extraordinary gathering while pointing out some of the semi-apocryphal tales that have distorted its memory.

138 **He also remembered meeting Proust:** Igor Stravinsky and Robert Craft, *Memories and Commentaries* (London: Faber and Faber, 2002), 77.

139 **Stravinsky learned afterwards:** Ibid., 77.

139 **Joyce actually had read:** In a letter to Frank Budgen, Joyce wrote, "I have read some pages of his. I cannot see any special talent but I am a bad critic." Cited in William C. Carter, *Marcel Proust: A Life* (New Haven: Yale University Press, 2000), 777. And in his notebook, he wrote, "Proust shows life as analytical and immobile. The reader finishes his sentences before he does." Cited in Jean-Yves Tadie, *Marcel Proust: A Life* (New York: Viking, 2000), 765.

140 **In the absence of any written comments:** Clive Bell, *Proust* (New York: Harcourt Brace, 1929), 13.

140 **secondhand accounts of the Joyce-Proust meeting:** Mary and Padraic Colum, *Our Friend James Joyce* (London: Victor Gollancz, 1959), 151–52; Ford Madox Ford, *It Was the Nightingale* (New York: Octagon Books, 1975), 293–94.

141 **"Two stiff chairs were obtained":** In the original some of Proust's remarks were in French. The translations are mine.

143 **apparently a guarded reference:** Carter, *Marcel Proust*, 780.

149 **She said Proust was violently opposed:** Claude Francis, Fernande Gontier, and

Suzy Mante-Proust, *Marcel Proust et les siens: Suivi des souvenirs de Suzy Mante Proust* (Paris: Plon, 1981), 164.

151 **"My letter would no longer be":** The translation of the Proust paragraph and the explanation of why Proust cited the Mallarmé poem are the work of Christophe Wall-Romana, a poet and associate professor in the Department of French and Italian at the University of Minnesota.

152 **Here Proust misquotes:** The poem, "Futile Petition" in English, has been set to music by both Maurice Ravel and Claude Debussy.

154 **second line of Shakespeare's sonnet number 30:** "When to the sessions of sweet silent thought / I summon up remembrance of things past."

154 **And if Beerbohm shared:** Schiff to Beerbohm, letter no. 3, Beerbohm Collection.

154 **He told Sydney he was ill:** Céleste Albaret, *Monsieur Proust* (New York: McGraw-Hill, 1976), 341.

155 **"Read the praise":** *L'Action Française* was the publication of the royalist, anti-Semitic organization of the same name. Charles Maurras, who was admired by Eliot and Lewis, among others in England, was its chief ideologist. Léon Daudet, son of the novelist Alphonse Daudet, was a writer/journalist who shared Maurras's views on Jews and government.

CHAPTER 9: A FALLING-OUT

158 **"Ever since I saw you last":** *The Letters of T. S. Eliot, Volume 2: 1923–25*, ed. Valerie Eliot and Hugh Haughton (London: Faber and Faber, 2009), 68.

159 **"liked very much to meet Beerbohm":** Ibid., 98–99.

163 **Eliot then not too subtly:** Ibid., 329.

164 **"As you know, I have read":** Ibid., 355.

164 **"In Proust," he wrote:** Wyndham Lewis, *Time and Western Man* (London: Chatto & Windus, 1927), 265.

165 **Years later he described:** Edwin Muir, *An Autobiography* (London: Hogarth Press, 1954), 137.

166 **Without explaining why:** Schiff to Muir, April 2, 1924, Schiff Collection, 52920.

166 **"The most striking thing":** Muir to Schiff, April 15, 1924, Schiff Collection, 52920.

168 **"This armed and menacing meeting":** Eliot, *Letters*, Vol. 2, 411.

168 **She added with a trace of glee:** Ibid., 392.

168 **Although "*Apes* ID":** Ibid., 412n4.

169 **He made the egregious mistake:** Ibid., 535.

169 **Things had come to a head:** Paul O'Keefe, *Some Sort of Genius: A Life of Wyndham Lewis* (London: Jonathan Cape, 2001), 255–57.

170 **Eliot noted that he had received:** Eliot, *Letters*, Vol. 2, 619.

170 **less-than-flattering review of *Myrtle*:** *Criterion* 3, no. 11 (April 1925): 475–76.

172 **Eliot asked, more as a wish:** Eliot, *Letters*, Vol. 2, 633.

172 **"My dear Violet," Eliot wrote:** Ibid., 680.

172 **Violet wrote to Eliot sometime between:** Ibid., 740–41.

173 **Eliot addressed his own career:** Ibid.

173 **"I was often with Mr. Eliot":** Wyndham Lewis, *Blasting and Bombardiering* (Berkeley: University of California Press, 1967), 287.

174 **Finally she wrote to Sydney and Violet:** Eliot, *Letters*, Vol. 2, 800.

174 **Sydney and Violet responded promptly:** For this account of Vivienne Eliot's stay at the Stansborough Park Sanitarium through her death, I have relied on various sources that sometimes were in conflict. These included the Schiff letters in the British Library, Lyndall Gordon's biography of Eliot, *T. S. Eliot: An Imperfect Life* (New York: Norton, 1999), *T. S. Eliot: A Life* by Peter Ackroyd (London: Penguin, 1984), and Carole Seymour Jones's *Painted Shadow: The Life of Vivienne Eliot, First Wife of T. S. Eliot* (New York: Anchor Books, 2003). Of the three books, *Painted Shadow* provided the most comprehensive and best-documented account.

CHAPTER 10: NEW FRIENDS

176 **He told his friend:** Schiff to Muir, November 2, 1926, Schiff Collection, 52920.

177 **Sydney, however, was no more enlightening:** Ibid.

178 **Sydney was afraid:** Schiff to Waterlow, October 8, 1925, Schiff Collection, 52922.

178 **"In reviewing in my mind":** The last book he referred to was *Richard, Myrtle and I.*

181 **Willa was particularly pleased:** Willa Muir, *Belonging: A Memoir* (London: Hogarth Press, 1968), 112–13.

181 **After the Muirs left:** Ibid.

182 **Willa was described:** J. B. Pick in his introduction to *Imagined Corners*, a novel by Willa Muir (Edinburgh: Cannongate Classics, 1987), vii.

183 **"In a State where men are dominant":** She relies for this claim on *The Dominant Sex* by Mathilde and Mathias Vaerting, trans. Eden and Cedar Paul (London: Geo. Allen & Unwin, 1923).

185 **Muir wrote to Sydney:** Muir had read the 1918 version of *Tarr*, which Lewis later acknowledged was flawed. He revised the book in 1928.

185 **Sometime in mid-1925:** Muir, *Belonging*, 120–21.

185 **"About Lewis I have never":** Muir to Schiff, May 8, 1925, Schiff Collection, 52920.

186 **He softened the blow:** Muir to Schiff, June 23, 1926, Schiff Collection, 52920.

186 **hotel had a dancing instructor:** Schiff to Muir, November 11, 1926, Schiff Collection, 52920.

186 **"a brilliant and decisive piece of work":** Muir to Schiff, April 19, 1927, Schiff Collection, 52920.

187 **Edith Sitwell, with whom the Schiffs:** *Taken Care Of: The Autobiography of Edith Sitwell* (New York: Atheneum, 1965).

188 **"The cruelties," he wrote:** Ellipsis in original.

189 **Huxley had visited the Schiffs:** Huxley to Schiff, May 6, 1930, in Aldous Huxley, *Exhumations: Correspondance inédite avec Sydney Schiff (1925–1937)*, ed. Clémentine Robert (Paris: Didier, 1976), 64–67. The letters cited below are from the same source.

190 **Sydney and Violet studied:** Ibid., June 19, 1930, 67–69.

191 **Huxley wrote again in December:** Ibid., January 5, 1931, 71.

191 **a novel about the future:** Ibid., May 7, 1931, 72.

192 **He said he hoped Sydney's shingles:** Ibid., June 21, 1931, 73.

192 **One interesting if minor:** Ibid., November 3, 1932, 75.

192 **"Our voyage was pleasant":** Ibid., February 19, 1933, 36.

193 **The last letter from Huxley:** Ibid., March 17, 1937, 78.

CHAPTER II: *THE APES OF GOD* AND MODERNIST SATIRE

195 **What's more, Lewis, whose forte:** Wyndham Lewis, *The Apes of God* (New York: Robert M. McBride, 1932), 450.

195 **The easy answer is:** Edith and her brothers, Osbert and Sacheverell, all of whom were rich and all of whom wrote, were satirized in *The Apes of God*.

196 **Edith Sitwell responded:** Edith Sitwell, *I Live Under a Black Sun* (Westport, CT: Greenwood Press, 1973), 183–4.

197 **After reading it Wilde wrote:** Julie Speedie, *Wonderful Sphinx* (London: Virago Press, 1993), 66–7.

198 **Robbie Ross and Reggie Turner:** There are many accounts of the Wilde trials, but the one to which I am most indebted was written by Douglas O. Linder and posted on the Web under the title "The Trials of Oscar Wilde: An Account," papers.ssrn.com/sol3/papers.cfm?abstract_id=1023971.

199 **"America, Germany, all the Continent":** This account of Wilde's stay with the Leversons and his relationship with Ada is taken from "Reminiscences" by Ada Leverson, which originally appeared in *Letters to the Sphinx from Oscar Wilde*, published in a limited edition by Duckworth. It was reprinted in Violet Wyndham, *The Sphinx and Her Circle* (New York: Vanguard Press, 1963), 115–18.

201 **These books have more in common:** They often referred to Leverson as "a woman of the nineties," indicating that they considered her more Victorian than modern.

202 *The Apes of God* **broke sharply:** Others outside the Bloomsbury and Bayswater circles who indulged in skewering their friends included Hemingway, Scott Fitzgerald, and Sherwood Anderson.

202 **the transparently false claim:** Richard Aldington to Sydney Schiff, June 8, 1931, Schiff Collection, 52916.

204 **A year later, however:** Ibid.

205 **Lewis was so angered:** Wyndham Lewis, *Satire and Fiction: Enemy Pamphlets No. 1* (London: Arthur Press, 1930), 28–29. In an undated letter Wells wrote that "*The Apes of God* amused me greatly in places." Yeats, in a letter that was also undated, appeared to compare Lewis favorably to Pirandello and Swift, but in each case on close reading it is not clear that he is really doing so. Here are the quotations: "Your work, like that of Pirandello, who alone of living dramatists has unexhausted, important material, portrays the transition from individualism to universal plasticity, though your theme is not, like his, plasticity itself, but the attempted substitution for it of ghastly homunculi in bottles"; "When I read [Edith Sitwell's] *Gold Coast Customs* a year ago, I felt, as on the first reading of *The Apes of God*, that something absent from all literature for a generation was back again, and in a form rare in the literature of all generations, passion ennobled by intensity, by endurance, by wisdom. We had it in one man once. He lies in St. Patrick's now under the greatest epitaph in history." (The man referred to is Jonathan Swift.)

205 **Although the scholar Robert T. Chapman:** "Satire and Aesthetics in Wyndham Lewis' *The Apes of God*," *Contemporary Literature* 12, no. 2 (Spring 1971): 133–45.

206 **The critic John Gawsworth:** *Apes, Japes and Hitlerism* (London: Unicorn Press, 1932), 30.

207 **Most people when looking:** Lewis objected to the overall conception of Proust's novel but respected his gift for characterization.

214 **"Is it really":** Wyndham Lewis to Sydney Schiff, May 21, 1933, Schiff Collection, 52919.

CHAPTER 12: VIOLET ALONE

216 **On a summer's day:** Edward Beddington-Behrens, *Look Back Look Forward* (London: Macmillan, 1963), 123.

217 **He added, rather too self-deprecatingly:** Sydney Schiff to Beerbohm, August 8, 1939, letter no. 21, Beerbohm Collection.

218 **noted with just a soupçon of irony:** Beerbohm to Sydney Schiff, March 13, 1939, letter no. 16, Beerbohm Collection.

218 **Sydney, who had no gift:** Sydney Schiff to Beerbohm, May 15, 1939, letter no. 17, Beerbohm Collection.

219 **One written by Max:** Beerbohm to Violet Schiff, Nov. 14, 1939, letter no. 10, Beerbohm Collection.

219 **There is no record:** Beerbohm to Violet Schiff, undated, letter no. 56, Beerbohm Collection (probably written in 1951).

219 **"We do so hope Stella":** Beerbohm to Violet Schiff, June 22, 1945, letter no. 36, Beerbohm Collection.

219 **Although they were not in touch:** Violet Schiff to Jack Isaacs, Schiff Collection, 52918.

220 **Beddington-Behrens quickly arranged:** Hove is a coastal town administratively unified with Brighton.

220 **Violet wrote to Richard Aldington:** Violet Schiff to Richard Aldington, February 1, 1949, Schiff Collection, 52916.

221 **Her last words:** Violet Schiff to Max Beerbohm, Nov. 1, 1944, letter no. 30, Beerbohm Collection.

221 **In December, although they had been:** T. S. Eliot to Violet Schiff, Dec. 10, 1944, Schiff Collection, 52918.

222 **Violet told Mosco Carner:** Mosco Carner, *Puccini: A Critical Biography* (London: Gerald Duckworth, 1958), 140.

223 **Three days after his death:** Julian Fane, *Memoir in the Middle of the Journey* (London: Hamish Hamilton & St. George's Press, 1971), 52.

223 **a ten- or eleven-year period:** Ibid., 53.

224 **She told him she really couldn't:** Frederick Beddington, *The Rest of the Family* (private edition, 1963), 20.

224 **In December 1953:** Violet Schiff to Max Beerbohm, Dec. 23, 1953, letter no. 87, Beerbohm Collection.

225 **Young Fane saw himself:** Fane, *Memoir*, 22.

225 **Violet was reclining:** Ibid., 49.

225 **She always found her:** Telephone interview with Evelyn Richardson, stepdaughter of Edward Beddington-Behrens, June 11, 2012.

226 **Fane, who couldn't take his eyes:** Fane, *Memoir*, 49.

226 **"a ghastly old heartless bag":** Serge Beddington-Behrens, e-mail to author, April 2012.

226 **Violet would have been:** Stephen Kane shared this recollection with me in a telephone conversation.

227 **"The front door was fitted":** Fane, *Memoir*, 52–53.

228 **She missed Sydney terribly:** Ibid.

229 **In his letter of thanks:** Eliot to Violet, Jan. 14, 1948, Schiff Collection, 52918.

230 **Despite her bad back:** The books were *Marie Donadieu* by Charles-Louis Philippe (with Esme Cook), *Le Bal du Comte d'Orgel* by Raymond Radiguet, and *L'Échelle de soie* by Jean-Louis Curtis (with Edward Beddington-Behrens).

230 **a not-unrelated summing up:** Fane, *Memoir*, 57.

231 **"I found 'Aunt Violet'":** Serge Beddington-Behrens, e-mail to author, March 8, 2012.

232 **Reflecting the not entirely:** Serge Beddington-Behrens, e-mail to author, April 2012.

233 **The best remaining evidence:** The Julian Fane Archive, East Sussex County Record Office, East Sussex.

234 **"she was impressed by erudition":** This first appeared in the *Cornhill*, Winter 1970, 255, and later in Fane's *Memoir in the Middle of the Journey*, 50.

PERMISSIONS ACKNOWLEDGMENTS

TEXT CREDITS

Grateful acknowledgment is made to the following for their permission to reprint previously published material:

Harold Ober Associates Incorporated: Excerpt from *It Was the Nightingale* by Ford Madox Ford, copyright © 1933 by Ford Madox Ford, copyright renewed 1960, 1961. Reprinted by permission of Harold Ober Associates Incorporated.

Plon-Perrin: Excerpts of the Proust-Schiff correspondence from *La Correspondance Generale de Marcel Proust* edited by Philip Kolb and translated by Stephen Klaidman (Paris: Plon, 1930–1936). Reprinted by permission of Plon-Perrin.

The Sussex Heart Charity: Excerpts from *Memoir in the Middle of the Journey* by Julian Fane (London: Hamish Hamilton and St. George's Press, 1971). Reprinted by permission of the Sussex Heart Charity—www.sussexheartcharity.org.

Wyndham Lewis Memorial Trust: Excerpt from *The Apes of God* by Wyndham Lewis (New York: Robert M. McBride & Company, 1932). Reprinted by permission of the Wyndham Lewis Memorial Trust (a registered charity).

ILLUSTRATION CREDITS

Page 1, bottom:	Courtesy of Charles Beddington
Page 3, top:	© Tate London, 2013. Courtesy of the Wyndham Lewis Estate/The Bridgeman Art Library
Page 3, bottom:	1930s drawing of Sydney Schiff by Sir William Rothenstein, courtesy of Dr. Stephen Kane
Page 4, top:	Hayward Bequest/Archive Centre, King's College, Cambridge
Page 4, center:	Hayward Bequest/Archive Centre, King's College, Cambridge
Page 4, bottom:	© National Portrait Gallery, London
Page 5, top:	Baron Adolph de Meyer Archive. © 2013 G. Ray Hawkins Gallery, Beverly Hills, CA
Page 5, bottom:	© National Portrait Gallery, London
Page 6, top:	© National Portrait Gallery, London
Page 6, center:	Marcel Proust, English school (20th century). Private Collection/© Look and Learn/The Bridgeman Art Library
Page 7, top:	Katherine Mansfield and John Middleton Murry at the Villa Isola Bella, Menton, France. Ida Baker: Photographs of Katherine Mansfield, ref:1/2-01 1908-F. Alexander Turnbull Library, Wellington, New Zealand
Page 7, bottom:	John Quinn Papers, Manuscripts and Archives Division, The New York Public Library, Astor, Lenox and Tilden Foundations
Page 8, top:	Orkney Archive

INDEX

Page numbers beginning with 241 refer to end notes.

A NOTE ABOUT THE AUTHOR

Stephen Klaidman was an editor and reporter for
twenty-three years at *The New York Times*, *The Washington
Post*, and the *International Herald Tribune*. He has taught
at Georgetown University's Law Center and its School
of Foreign Service, Johns Hopkins University's School of
Public Health, and Pennsylvania State University. For ten
years he also worked at Georgetown University's Kennedy
Institute of Ethics and Institute for Health Policy Analysis.

A NOTE ABOUT THE TYPE

This book was set in Legacy Serif. Ronald Arnholm (b. 1939) designed the Legacy family after being inspired by the 1470 edition of *Eusebius* set in the roman type of Nicolas Jenson. This revival type maintains much of the character of the original. Its serifs, stroke weights, and varying curves give Legacy Serif its distinct appearance. It was released by the International Typeface Corporation in 1992.